# We Shall Never Speak of This Again

## The Plight of the Irish in the 19th Century

James Dan Casey

James Dan Casey

Paperback: 978-1-7375716-0-5
E-Book: 978-1-7375716-1-2

Printed in the United States of America.

Cover by 100 Covers
Editor: Dr. Vonda, First Editing
Interior Design by FormattedBooks.com

# CONTENTS

## Part Two: Out of Ireland

# ACKNOWLEDGMENTS

First and foremost, I thank God for His guidance in writing this book and for His presence on the many late nights it took to complete it.

I treasure the encouragement and support I received from all my family. They gave me the confidence and motivation to finish writing the book.

A special thanks to grandsons Jacob and Caleb. Jacob's assistance with graphic design and Caleb's technical support facilitated the completion of the project.

A special thanks to Mary Skelly, Curator of the County Roscommon Heritage and Genealogy Company of Roscommon, Ireland for her work in locating baptismal records for our Irish family. This breakthrough led to the location of their Catholic parish and the locale of the Casey farm in County Roscommon.

Also, my gratitude to the extended Casey family for maintaining the tradition of gathering together to celebrate our Irish heritage and sustain a family connection through the generations.

Finally, a heartfelt thanks to our original family from Ireland who immigrated to the United States to live in a free country, a desire held by many Irish of the 19th century. They made it possible for all of us, as their descendants, to live with that same freedom. Father John, and sons Patrick, James and Michael made it to America. Mother Ellen and daughter Mary did not. May they all rest in peace.

# PREFACE

My purpose for telling this story was to inform and hopefully inspire the younger generations of my family as well as all people of Irish descent to learn more about our Irish ancestors. As generations pass, we grow further and further from our forebears and eventually their story may be forgotten altogether.

It's important for our younger generations to realize that our Irish ancestors are responsible for giving us the opportunity for a prolific life in a land of freedom and opportunity. Without our forebears' vision of a better life, our families would not live in the country we do. In that regard, we should think of our Irish ancestors as an integral part of our family. They not only lived their lives, but they largely determined ours.

However, we must not forget Ireland, their homeland. In the 19th century, as now, there was a great sense of pride in being Irish. That Irish pride prevailed amid the tragic history of that century and a culmination of hundreds of years of England's oppressive rule. Many who emigrated never released that sense of grief they felt for leaving their native land.

I did not intend to write a book. I started to write a brief history and the story took on a life of its own. This book is a contemporary perspective of the struggles and misfortune experienced by the Irish in the 19th century. It is an informative account for anyone. Many are unaware of this heart rending Irish story. I urge you to take the time to hear their version, especially if you are of Irish descent.

This is not a genealogy book or a scholarly writing, but merely an overview of the history of that time, tracking one family within its framework. Through this history, we have a chance to imagine their trials, joys, burdens and likely their sufferings. This is the key to perceiving them as real people and as truly a part of our families.

# INTRODUCTION

*This is not the land of my birth, but it is the land for which I hold the greatest affection.*[1]
—John F. Kennedy, speaking of Ireland

Seventy million people in the world are said to have Irish ancestry. If you are reading this, you may be one of them. However, many of these millions are unaware of the relentless and prolonged racial and religious persecution perpetrated on the Irish and Irish Catholics in a period of history when Irish Catholics could not vote, own land, bear arms, hold public office or even worship together unless it was in hiding. Centuries of English domination and authoritarianism crippled Irish resolve and left a beleaguered people unable to respond to the oppression.

A million Irish died of starvation and disease in the Potato Famine, a famine that could have been largely mitigated by England, Ireland's supposed sister country. Millions also emigrated throughout the 19th and into the 20th century. More than a million left during the Famine, literally driven out of Ireland by England's dogged attempt to depopulate the island. A country of more than 8 million at the mid-19th century shriveled to nearly half that by 1900. This book will tell the story of that dark time in Irish history. Volumes have been written about Ireland's history in the 19th century. This is a concise but informative version of that sad tale.

With family, most of us have very little tolerance of abuse from others. It should be the same for our ancestors. This book about your family and mine was written with the purpose of identifying those responsible for the maltreatment of the Irish and determining their accountability. The Catholic Irish were subjected to centuries of human rights violations. The draconian Penal Laws of the 18th century literally stripped Irish Catholics of their basic human rights. The farce titled the Act of Union removed Ireland's right to govern itself and put all power in London. The English government dispossessed Irish Catholics of their land. This story will describe a token Catholic Emancipation in the 19th Century that did not live up to its name. You will read of an English Parliament that was totally indifferent to and bore no sympathy for the Irish during the Potato Famine. Furthermore, their actions and omissions seemed to fulfill their desire to eliminate one quarter of the Irish population for their self-serving needs. Was anyone called to account for these egregious acts? This book will identify those responsible and their centuries of human rights violations. This happened to your family.

Read this book. You will experience outrage, frustration, sadness and finally a glimmer of hope. It should instill in you a new Irish pride. If it does not, then I haven't accomplished my goal.

The Irish family included in this history is named Casey, my family. Imagine your family in this history because they would have received the same abuse as mine. Many Irish did not survive it; likely some of my family as well as yours died. Their descendants are missing from the Irish diaspora of today.

My family became part of the millions who emigrated, the millions who had hopes and dreams for a better life in a New World. I sincerely hope this book causes you to take a new look at your heritage and to be cognizant of your ancestors at your next family gathering or reunion. They are there with you and within you.

# PROLOGUE

The family depicted in this book is real. John Casey was my Great-Great-Grandfather. He and his family immigrated to America circa 1862. He and his sons Patrick and Michael are buried in Braidwood, Illinois. John's son James moved from Illinois to Kansas and acquired Federal land through the provisions of the Homestead Act of 1862. He became a landowner, an advantage that he likely would never have had in Ireland.

John and Ellen Casey of County Roscommon, Ireland had five children, one of which we believe died as an infant. The Caseys were small tenant farmers in the townland of Carrowgarve in the northwest part of the county. They were Irish Catholic and lived in the Catholic parish of Fairymount. Their church, St. Baoithin, was only a one-or two-mile walk from the farm. All the children were baptized in Fairymount parish. A new St. Baoithin Church was built in 1858,[1] possibly with assistance from the Casey family. They would have attended Mass in the new Church until they emigrated.

County Roscommon lies in the western part of the province of Connaught. The county is landlocked, bordered on the east side by the River Shannon.[2] The geographic center of Ireland lies within the county. Roscommon is reliant on agriculture, with about three fourths of the county in farmland and pasture.[3] The remaining one fourth is comprised of water and peat bog. Peat bog is a form of wetland with a covering of sometimes several feet of decaying vegetation. The peat, called turf, was cut into bricks, dried and burned as the heat source for cabins in the past.[4] The four seasons are somewhat similar to parts of the United States. Throughout the year, temperatures vary from 36 to 66 degrees, with extremes of 27 and 74 degrees. The climate is wet, with cloudy days the norm, and an annual precipitation of 39.8 inches.[5]

My family experienced, as perhaps yours did, the constricting grip of the English government first hand, and lived through the dreadful times of the Famine. We have no written account or even anecdotes about their life in Ireland. Our elders believed that our Irish family did not want to talk of it. It may have been too uncomfortable. John's wife Ellen and daughter Mary did not make it to Illinois. They likely died in Ireland.

Our ancestors were courageous and tenacious people. They left their homeland and assimilated in a new country. John Casey was 64 years old when he immigrated to America. He proved that it is never too late to start a new life.

***Note: Genealogy is not a perfect science. Evidence is not always complete, and incorrect assumptions can be made. For the purpose of writing this historical account, I am accepting the assumption of the identified John Casey family as my family, and their home location as fact.***

# Part One

CHAPTER 1

# ORIGINS OF OPPRESSION

*Many suffer so that some day all Irish people may know justice and peace.*[1]
—Wolfe Tone, United Irishmen, 1798 Rebellion

John Casey was a Catholic tenant farmer in County Roscommon, Ireland. Why didn't he own the land? Why did he and his family leave Ireland? Why didn't he talk of Ireland to his descendants? These questions can be answered in large part through events in Irish history. In order to understand the calamity that was the Irish land scheme in the 19th century, one must look at Ireland's history and the crippling effects that English rule had upon Irish Catholics and their land ownership.

England exercised control over Ireland as early as the 12th century.[2] However, it wasn't until Henry VIII became King of England in the 16th century that England attempted to assert total dominance and rule over Ireland. Henry VIII was Catholic and had even been named Defender of the Faith by the Pope. However, his wife, Katherine of Aragon, had not given birth to a male heir to the throne. Henry became impatient and wanted to divorce her and marry one of the maidens in his wife's court. His efforts at convincing the Pope to approve the divorce failed and Henry left the Catholic Church to form the Protestant Church of England. With that, England became part of Europe's Protestant Reformation.[3]

The origins of Catholicism in Ireland began when St. Patrick brought Christianity to the island in the 5th century.[4] While in Ireland, he founded the church of St. Baoithin a couple of miles from what was later to be the Casey farm. This Church served the area from the 5th century to the 17th century, when it was sacked and burned by English soldiers. A temporary church was used in Carrowgarve, a small townland, (small unit of rural land) of less than a mile square where the John Casey family eventually lived. Mass was said there until a new St. Baoithin Church could be built.[5] In time, Ireland became a Catholic nation.

Henry VIII arranged through the Irish Parliament to be titled King of Ireland in 1541.[6] He believed that the Irish would fall in line with the Protestant religion, but a nation of Catholics refused, resulting in centuries of English religious persecution and conflict. Atrocities were committed on both sides, but in the end, Ireland would remain a Catholic nation. This conflict led to the Irish Catholics' disdain for the English. For many Irish, this hatred lasted a lifetime, and passed through the generations without relenting.

Land became one of the focal points in this conflict. In 1600, 90% of Irish land was Catholic-owned.[7] The English then began a methodical process of dispossessing Catholics from their land until by 1775, Irish Catholics owned a mere 5% of Ireland. England accomplished this massive land transfer from Catholic to Protestant ownership through land confiscation and a practice called "planting." Irish who were perceived by the English as disloyal would be expelled from their land and replaced with subjects loyal to the Crown in what the English called "plantations."[8] It began in Ireland's northern province of Ulster in 1609. Forty thousand Scottish and English Protestants[9] were "planted" in Ulster, displacing the Irish Catholics, who were compulsorily relocated. Subsequently, in 1641, the displaced Irish rebelled and attacked the Protestant settlers to drive them off their land. This struggle lasted for just under ten years, ending with approximately 12,000 Protestants dead and 7,000 Irish killed by Protestants and the English Army.[10]

## Oliver Cromwell

England would not let this Irish rebellion stand. In July 1649, Oliver Cromwell and his New Model Army sailed to Ireland to put down the uprising and exact revenge. And in turn, he furthered the dispossession of land from Irish Catholics. Cromwell first assaulted the City of Drogheda north of Dublin. The commander of the garrison in Drogheda refused to surrender. Cromwell estimated the garrison to be about 3,000 men. He issued orders that no one who chose to bear arms would be spared. In forty-eight hours, almost all in the garrison were dead, along with an unknown number of civilians, including women and children. Among the civilians were several friars who were executed[11] on Cromwell's standing order to put all Catholic clergy to death.[12] During the melee, one hundred people had sought refuge in the steeple at St. Peter's Church. Cromwell's troops summarily torched the Church, burning alive many of those who had hidden there. In his report, Cromwell "simply acknowledged that the casualties included many civilians."[13] Irish sources would later report that about 4,000 civilians were killed at Drogheda and described it as "an unparalleled savagery and treachery beyond that of any slaughterhouse."[14]

Cromwell then marched 9,000 men on the port city of Wexford on the southeast coast. Again, he asked for surrender. During the negotiations, Cromwell became impatient and ordered his artillery to begin bombardment.[15] The scene played out much as it did in Drogheda. Cromwell wrote in this report that over 2,000 Irish soldiers and civilians died, saying they "put all to the sword who came in their way."[16] A petition by the surviving inhabitants stated that all the men, women, and children of the town "to a very few" were killed during the assault.[17] The merciless Cromwell continued his campaign, haltingly at times, as Irish resistance inflicted significant losses to the New Model Army. In the end, the Irish resistance collapsed and Cromwell prevailed. It was Cromwell's soldiers who carried off artifacts and burned St. Baoithin's church in Tibohine near Carrowgarve.[18] Cromwell summed up his duty in Ireland, saying, "England received God's blessing in persecuting just and righteous causes, whatever the cost and hazard be."[19]

Then there was the matter of the Irish land. Soldiers of the New Model Army and other Protestant Englishmen had been promised Irish land. The Act of Settlement, passed by English Parliament in August of 1652, outlined the disposition of the land. Any Irish who were contributors to or had any association with those responsible for the Rebellion of 1641 would forfeit their land.[20] In this upheaval, approximately eleven million acres, over half the land in the country, was seized from Irish Catholics.[21]

The displaced Catholic landowners, numbering about 44,000, were given until May 1, 1654 to resettle in the province of Connaught. Upon their move, they would be granted land in Connaught worth only a fraction of their original holdings. The Province of Connaught, of which County Roscommon is a part, is noted for its wet bogs and significant percentage of infertile land. To the rest of Ireland in the 19th century, Connaught was perceived as backward, poor and inferior.[22] For the displaced landowners, it was a banishment of sorts. The English edict stated that any of the subject landowners that had not relocated by the May 1, 1654 deadline would be subject to trial and execution. In the eyes of Oliver Cromwell their choice was clear: "To hell or to Connaught."[23] This plunder and coerced migration earned Cromwell a place as one of the most villainous conquerors in Irish history. The disruption left Connaught with the only significant Catholic land ownership in Ireland.[24]

## Penal Laws

Years later, in 1692, the assault on Irish Catholics continued. Two powerful political forces united to further oppress the Irish Catholics. First, the Protestant English Parliament established their supremacy over Ireland by passing a law prohibiting any Catholic from being elected to Irish Parliament. Moreover, Irish Protestants were the minority in Ireland, and they needed to take additional steps to keep the Catholics at bay and assure themselves of remaining in power. Thus, the Protestant Irish Parliament continued to perpetuate a constricting dominance over the Irish Catholics by enacting what came to be known as the Penal Laws.[25] These laws were introduced piecemeal from 1695 to 1709, and were designed to keep Catholics and Presbyterians from attaining any power positions in Ireland. In order to control the country, they needed to control the land. Hence, a law was passed that no Catholic could purchase land and their land leases could not exceed 31 years. If a Catholic landowner died, the land must be divided among all the male children. This furthered the process of squeezing the Catholics into smaller and smaller parcels of land through the generations. In addition, the Penal Laws prohibited Catholics from voting or holding any public office as well as owning firearms. Catholic schools were abolished and all Catholic church hierarchy had to leave the country. Priests had to register and were prohibited from officiating over any inter-religion marriage. The practice of worship was forbidden, driving priests to say Mass in hiding.[26]

Catholic farmers were also required to pay a tithe to the Protestant Church of Ireland. The tithe was collected from the land occupier rather than the land owner. Catholic farmers, to their chagrin, were forced to pay 10% of the value of their crops to the Protestant Church of Ireland. The Catholic Church also expected them to contribute to their own priest and parish.[27] The Penal Laws pushed the Irish Catholic tenant farmer further into poverty. Widespread Catholic resistance resulted in a moderation of the Penal Laws beginning in 1760.[28] The Tithe Act, as it was known, would finally be replaced by the Tithe Commutation Act of 1838. This law effectively relieved the tenant farmers by transferring the liability of the Church of Ireland tithe to the landowners. The landowners, however, passed it right back to the tenant farmers through increased rent.[29] The farmers' only consolation was that at least they weren't paying the Protestants directly.

All of Ireland, and Irish Catholics in particular, had been subject to a longstanding onslaught of religious persecution and authoritarian rule. There was much unrest. Consequently, another rebellion was being planned. In 1791, Theobald Wolfe Tone founded the United Irishmen, a secret society comprised of Presbyterian members in Belfast, along with Catholic and some Protestant members in Dublin. Their goals were to reform the Irish Parliament, win Catholic Emancipation, and gain freedom from England. Their cause was inspired by the recent French Revolution.[30] During the following years, it became evident to Tone that freedom from England could only be accomplished by using force.[31]

Tone sought the support of France for the cause. The French had been at war with England since 1793 and were willing to assist Tone with the insurrection. The United Irishmen had 280,000 volunteers, including peasants and women with only a pitchfork or pike to bring to the fight. The disadvantage was paramount considering they would battle against the British regular army. The French stayed true to their promise and sent an armada of forty-three ships carrying 14,000 French soldiers. Unfortunately, there was a severe storm off the coast of Ireland and they were not able to land. They eventually returned to France. Tone was devastated but vowed to continue with the plan.[32]

The results were disastrous. The Irishmen were disorganized, with poor leadership. In one battle 2,000 Irishmen, many with pitchforks or pikes, faced 30,000 British troops. The insurrection failed in short order. The captured Irishmen were executed. It is estimated that 30,000 Irish were killed during the insurrection. Tone was captured and taken to Dublin to await execution. He requested death by firing squad like a soldier, but was refused.

Tone's sentence was hanging, ordered by the British military.[33] Tone decided to deny the British their hanging and slit his own throat. Although there is no direct proof of death by suicide or murder, most historians believe he took his own life.[34] The cruel and brutal response to the insurrection only deepened the Irish people's bitterness toward the English government. This is the Ireland into which John Casey was born on January 8, 1798.

CHAPTER 2

# FIGHT FOR EQUALITY

*Gentlemen, you may soon have the alternative to live as slaves or die as freemen.*[1]
—Daniel O'Connell, the Liberator, Political Activist, from a speech in County Cork

## THE UNITED KINGDOM OF GREAT BRITAIN AND IRELAND

The uprising of 1798 was the catalyst for the English government to push forward and solve the Irish problem. The Prime Minister of England, William Pitt, introduced a bill in the Irish Parliament in 1799 to form a Union. One of Pitt's goals was Catholic Emancipation and the right for Catholics to hold office and be eligible for election to Parliament. A bill favoring Catholics did not pass in an Irish Protestant Parliament, but Pitt was tenacious. With the open and audacious bribery of Parliament members, Pitt finally secured the needed votes to pass the Union, albeit without the Catholic Emancipation. The English Parliament also passed the bill, and it became law effective

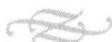

January I, 1801. The Irish Parliament was dissolved and Ireland was allowed one hundred members, an all-Protestant contingent, to represent Ireland in the English Parliament. Unfortunately, their one hundred voices were faint with a total of 650 members in the House of Commons.[2] Many Irish felt that passing the Act of Union at William Pitt's urging came with the promise of Catholic Emancipation. This was not so. King George III refused to consent to any form of Catholic Emancipation. William Pitt resigned in protest.[3] Unfortunately, this Union would not solve the Irish problem. This act of betrayal reinforced Irish contempt for the English.

With the passage of the Act of Union, John Casey, at two years old, was a subject of a new country, The United Kingdom of Great Britain and Ireland. After 1798, with the exception of one minor and failed rebellion, all was relatively quiet in Ireland—quiet, but not to be confused with lack of dissent. A young Irish Catholic lawyer, Daniel O'Connell from County Kerry, was a dissenter. He did not believe in the Union and was committed to Catholic Emancipation. Witnessing the 1798 Rebellion and its aftermath of executions and floggings of Irish rebels convinced him that violent rebellion was not the answer. He expected to effect change through persuasion, negotiation and compromise. His ultimate goal was the repeal of the Union, but Catholic Emancipation must come first.[4] O'Connell was a brilliant and inspirational speaker who used his gifts to gain supporters and bring pressure on England to repeal the remaining penal laws. Known in Ireland as the Liberator, O'Connell is a prominent figure in Irish history.

## CATHOLIC EMANCIPATION

In English Parliament, Emancipation became known as the Catholic question. O'Connell spent his time in Ireland gathering support, and in England lobbying Parliament members to introduce resolutions to further the cause of Emancipation. Henry Gratten, an Irish Protestant ally, introduced a motion for Emancipation in the House of Commons in 1817. It was defeated, but he followed with a Petition for Relief for Emancipation in 1819. It too was unsuccessful with an all-Protestant Parliament. There was no support for Emancipation that would allow Catholics the right to vote and hold a seat in Parliament. Henry Gratten died in 1820 and O'Connell aligned himself with William Plunket, an Irish Protestant lawyer. Plunket introduced a new Petition in 1821. Incredibly, he was able to gain the support needed to pass the Petition, but it was swiftly dismissed when it reached the House of Lords.[5]

In the meantime, O'Connell garnered support in Ireland by founding the Catholic Association. Its purpose was to raise money for Catholic education and support the cause of Emancipation. It was enacted in the Catholic parishes as a collection of as little as one penny per month. He got a huge response and by the end of 1823, the Association was raising £1000 per week, with half a million members contributing at least a penny per month. Parliament considered this a threat and outlawed such societies. Still, O'Connell did not propose violence. Back in London, in 1825, a new Catholic Relief Act passed the House of Commons, but again was rejected by the House of Lords.[6]

In 1828, County Clare spontaneously nominated Daniel O'Connell as a candidate for Parliament, even when, as a Catholic, he wasn't eligible. He won the election and upon hearing the news, King George IV was enraged. The King was so intensely anti-Emancipation that he forbade his Cabinet members to even raise the subject. Reverend Sydney Smith wrote an article for the Edinburgh Review stating, "The moment the very name of Ireland is mentioned, the English seem to bid adieu to common feeling, common prudence and common sense."[7]

By 1828, however, Parliament was beginning to wear down. The Catholic Question was all-consuming and there was concern about an Irish uprising, motivating them to seek a solution.[8] By late 1828, King George IV agreed to consider Emancipation. The following year, on March 5, a bill for Emancipation was introduced and passed the House of Commons and the House of Lords. After some resistance, King George signed the Emancipation into law on April 13, 1829.[9] The following day, Daniel O'Connor wrote a letter with this announcement at the top: "THE FIRST DAY OF FREEDOM!"[10] All the Penal Laws were now repealed. It was twenty-eight years since the Act of Union, but religious freedom had finally been won.

O'Connell's first attempt at taking his seat resulted in his refusal to sign the anti-Catholic oath required of Parliament members. Furthermore, a repeat election in County Clare was required for him to be sanctioned. The repeat election was swift, with O'Connell winning unopposed. O'Connell recited a revised oath of loyalty to the Crown with tolerable content for Irish Catholics. Finally, a duly elected Catholic became a member of Parliament.[11] O'Connell the Liberator and the Irish Catholics had triumphed without a shot fired.[12]

The Irish Catholics achieved a huge victory, but were the Irish really free? It appeared not. As part of the Emancipation, the members of Parliament had inserted a special requirement for the Irish to be free to vote. In order to have the right to vote, "...it was necessary for a tenant to hold a yearly lease valued at ten pounds," which was five times higher than the requirement prior to the Emancipation. The effect was to disavow the vote to all but one percent of the Irish Catholics.[13] Once again, the English continued their behavior pattern of betrayal and deceit.

In 1828, John Casey was now 31 years old. He, along with all Irish Catholics, was free of the Penal Laws but was still not allowed to vote. John was established with a small plot of three acres in Carrowgarve townland, County Roscommon. His father Patrick also occupied nine acres there. While Daniel O'Connell was fighting for the freedom of Ireland, John Casey likely married Ellen Green/Greenan. Their first son, Patrick, was born in 1834 and is believed to have died as an infant. Their second son, also named Patrick, was born in 1838, fulfilling the tradition of naming the first male child for his grandfather. He was followed by another son, James, born in 1839; Michael, born in 1843; and Mary, born in 1845. All the while, O'Connell was rallying Ireland in support for Repeal of the Union.

## O'CONNELL AND THE FIGHT FOR REPEAL

In O'Connell's mind, the Irish would not be free until the Act of Union was repealed. He believed that if he created enough agitation in Ireland without causing violence, he could coerce England to repeal the Act of Union.

His efforts at repeal culminated in 1843. Mass meetings were planned throughout Ireland to further the sentiment for repeal.

The London Times called them "monster meetings." And that they were. From April through August, four meetings took place with a combined estimated attendance of over a million Irish. The largest, with an attendance of 750,000, occurred on August 15 in County Meath. All the meetings were exceptionally peaceful. Whole families attended, had picnics, and listened to the great orator Daniel O'Connell. O'Connell's voice would carry for some distance into the crowd, but he was facilitated by stewards who further carried the message throughout the rows and rows of people that could not hear it. Witnesses said the stewards did an exceptional job.[14]

The English government took notice of the "monster meetings" and did not approve. Their fear was that O'Connell, even if promoting peaceful assembly, might provoke the masses into insurrection. The last meeting scheduled was on October 8 on the north shore of Dublin. Sir Robert Peel, the Prime Minister of England, decided he had seen enough and declared the meeting illegal. Warships were moved into the proximity of the meeting and English troops were deployed. Daniel O'Connell believed that the English would stop the event regardless of the cost of human life. In the interest of peace, he canceled the meeting.[15]

O'Connell and several others were arrested and charged with conspiracy. Trials were held with the predictable outcome of convictions. Daniel O'Connell was convicted by a jury absent of Catholics and sentenced to one year in prison. O'Connell emerged from prison a changed man. He continued to advocate repeal of the Union, but his health was failing and his fire and enthusiasm were gone.[16] His health continued to worsen and he died in 1847,[17] without seeing the repeal of the Act of Union. That would not occur for another seventy-five years, in 1922.

CHAPTER 3

# Daily Life in 19th Century Ireland

*But if the past is any indication, no hardship can really kill the unusual humor and world view of the Irish.*[1]

—Robert Sullivan, Irish Writer, Educator

## Population

In the span of the fifty years already discussed, there were other dramatic developments occurring. Ireland was experiencing a phenomenal surge in population. In 1791, the estimated population was 4,753,000. The Census of 1841 came in at 8,175,000, a 172% increase in just 50 years. This population growth rate surpassed anything recorded in all of Europe.[2] The science of demography cannot amply provide an explanation. However, there are identified contributing factors. Notably, the potato was a significant factor in life expectancy. It was the anchor staple food for rural Ireland. Coupled with milk and some occasional beef, pork or mutton, it made for a nutritious diet. Another factor was the Irish were marrying young and having large families. In order to accommodate these early marriages, the tenant farmer merely subdivided his parcel of land to accommodate a small plot of potatoes and a simple cabin. With that, the newly married couple was set.[3]

## CULTURE AND TRADITION

The Irish had their own special identity and family traditions. Regardless of their station in life, the Irish were known for their cheerfulness, hospitality and generous spirit. No one in need would be turned away.[4] Storytelling was one of their favorite pastimes, along with singing and dancing for lively family or neighborhood gatherings. Storytelling and hurling occupied many Sundays for the rural population. Hurling is a traditional Irish game played for many centuries; it may have been played as long as 3000 years ago. It is touted as "the fastest game on grass." It is played with a tennis-size leather ball and a stick called a "hurley." The game exhibits aspects of baseball and hockey and can be roughly played. The hurley is used to carry the ball, hit it like a baseball or on the ground like a hockey puck. Hurling goalposts are similar to American football goalposts, only a net is used below the crossbar. To get the ball into the net is three points and through the uprights is one point. Hurling is immensely popular in Ireland, with the women's form of the game called camogie. Modern Irish attendance is only outpaced by Gaelic football.[5]

The Irish had a tradition of work sharing they called "cooring." This occurred when a group of relatives and friends came together to help one farmer with a task. It could be planting, harvesting, building a cabin or any other undertaking he needed help with. After the day's work, the families gathered together. The host family would be responsible for the entertainment. Singing and dancing were many times part of the amusement. There would be sharing of tobacco and likely some of their homemade Irish whiskey called "poteen." The young people might gather at a "crossroads" singing and dancing, sometimes throughout the night. The crossroads fun usually included much flirting and sometimes the parish priest felt the necessity to supervise.[6]

The Irish were also known for their fierce Irish pride and love of speaking the Irish language.[7] The Irish had lived under the dominance and oppression of England for centuries. Their love of country and their language was the only thing the English could not take from them. Irish pride and their unique Irish language were their identity and comprised their last bit of self-esteem. For most, it was as vital to them as life itself.

Humor was a big part of Irish tradition. Even during the horrific times of the Famine, humor would emerge. At the workhouses, what many Irish called the poorhouses, mortality was quite high from fever during the Famine. Death carts came to the poorhouse daily and collected any corpses. The doctor would point out the beds with the deceased. On one occasion the attendant began to load a corpse on the cart when the body roused and announced he wasn't dead. The attendant quickly answered, "Do you know better than the doctor?"[8] In another instance, an undertaker had gathered bodies to inter in a burial pit. This undertaker had a reputation for choosing bodies that may not have quite breathed their last. The coffin had a hinge on the bottom that could be released and the body would fall out into the pit. One of the corpses suddenly called out to question where he was. The undertaker calmly answered, "We are going to bury you." "How'll you bury me when I'm not dead?" pleaded the man. The undertaker calmly replied, "Oh, the drop will kill you anyhow."[9]

The Irish were much more adept with humor than discussing awkward or uncomfortable subjects. On those occasions, there was likely no conversation at all. The response was silence.[10]

The 19th century Irish home was very much patriarchal. The father handled the discipline in the household and traditionally was very strict. Girls were usually not close to their fathers and rarely interacted with them. Instead, boys and girls had a close relationship with their mother. The women of the house would not sit with the father to eat. The daughters were subservient and kept quiet around their parents. The mother of the house was usually up first in the morning and in bed last at night. It was the father who arranged dowries for their daughters. The dowry could be a generous one comprised of cash, land or goods. A matchmaker was used to bring couples together, and his choice was seldom about romance, but more centered on the economics of the marriage partnership. Many times, the bride's husband might be 10 or even 20 years older.[11]

The church was the center and focal point of the community. The parish priest was given an inordinate amount of respect and was looked to as an authority figure, so much so that he was many times involved in the family decision making.[12] One of his duties was to preside over any marriages in the family. Most marriages took place in the winter, outside the summer working months. The family would make it a special day with plenty of food. The celebration would sometimes last all night and into the next day. The bride's dowry would pass from the father, not to his daughter the bride, but directly to the groom's control.[13]

Baptism was conducted very soon after a baby's birth. Infant mortality was high in the 19th century, and the family wanted the baby baptized in case there were any health problems. In Irish genealogy, the baptism date, along with the marriage date, documented in church records are considered to be more accurate than dates supplied by family members.

Marriages took place in the bride's parish. Naming children was also subject to Irish custom. There were no middle names used until late in the century and for Irish Catholics, a saint's name was required by the Church, explaining how so many Irish seem to have similar first names. In addition, if an infant died, which was common, the next child might be given the same name. This would come into play considering the Irish custom of naming the first son after his grandfather. If that first son died, then the next son would be given the same name.[14]

The priest also presided over funerals. Prior to burial there was a traditional wake where one or more family members stayed up the entire night watching over the body of their loved one. Another practice among the mourners was called "keening." One of the older women in the family would sing a sad, methodical, moaning tune continually. The practice was prevalent in the early part of the century, but had nearly disappeared by mid-century.

After the Famine, the Irish rededicated themselves to their religion. Some even felt that the Famine was a punishment from God and that called for them to draw closer to the Church. Young people entering the religious life dramatically increased and the clergy was even more revered. The emphasis on religion would continue and carry well into the 20th century.[15]

The relationship between husband and wife was many times more of a cooperative arrangement than anything else. The father and mother each had their duties to maintain the structure of the family, and that was the primary goal. The father handled the farm work, which would occupy his time between March and December. Then he had time for odd jobs on the farm, rest, and visiting with neighbors. Sometimes he would go off to visit neighbors by himself. The wife's work was year around. She was in charge of all the household duties, along with caring for the animals if they had any. She would milk the cow every day and make sure the rest of the animals were fed.[16]

The dedication of the marriage was to duty and the relationship was considered permanent. The shortcomings of a spouse, although sometimes considerable, were tolerated. Many households were troubled by the use of alcohol, a problem that was persistent throughout the century. Yet the marriage bond was not broken.[17]

The Irish Constabulary was Ireland's police force. In 1841, there were 8,000 officers, enough to man stations throughout Ireland, including the remote agricultural areas. They had a dark green military-style uniform and were mainly Catholics from the ranks of the tenant farmers. They were judged to be very helpful and were very much respected. They were poorly paid, however, and got only a few days off. Besides keeping the peace, other duties included helping with censuses, collecting agricultural statistics, and conducting other state business in their assigned area. Unfortunately, their reputation was gravely tarnished during the Famine for their required assistance with evictions.[18] There were others who chose service in the English military. Most Irish held contempt for the English and joining their military drew ire from not only them but sometimes from their own family.[19]

After the Famine, most landlords no longer allowed subdivision of the land to provide an inheritance for all the tenant's sons. Irish tradition then moved more toward inheritances granted to the oldest son. However, it was the father's decision, and he could also bypass the oldest son in favor of a younger one. The inheriting son would remain subservient and faithful to his father and the land. He might be 30 years old or more before actually inheriting. Until that time he was treated as a young son who followed instructions and did not make decisions for the farm. This perspective was held not only by his family, but also prevailed in the community, many times to the detriment of the son's emotional health. He also remained unmarried until he received the land. This inheritance practice also had an effect on the remaining children. A son marrying could well mean emigration for a sibling. Many times, the family used the dowry provided by the bride's father not for the new couple, but to finance emigration for one or more of the other siblings. A daughter's choices were to marry in Ireland, enter the religious life or, for the more industrious and adventurous, to immigrate to America. Their motivation could be to marry an American or to earn money to help support her Irish family. The remission back to Ireland was called the 'American letter" and was eagerly awaited by the Irish family. The non-inheriting son's choices were similarly limited. Like his sister, he could also choose the religious life as a priest. Otherwise, without land, he could make the less desirable choice to become a landless laborer. He then placed himself among many who competed for jobs that were not always available year-round. As a laborer, he was destined to lead a very meager life at best. The more desirable choice was to emigrate, find work, and put himself in a position to send "American letters" home to help the family. This practice became so prevalent it was an expectation for the parents. However, it also created a sense of guilt for all. The parents were eager to get the "American letter," but they also gave up their child for it. The child felt guilty for abandoning family. The father resigned himself to this practice, but it usually was a heavy emotional burden for the mother. The Irish Catholics had a great respect for the land, even when they did not own it. It was just as much of an inheritance as anything that was owned. The land provided security and food and was to be protected and passed to the next generation.[20]

The Irish language was prominent in the west and south of Ireland. Sadly, the Famine took a terrible toll in those regions, and much of the Irish-speaking population died in the Famine or emigrated. In 1835, there were four million Irish speakers in Ireland and after the Famine, in 1851, only two million remained.[21] Death and emigration had decimated the language, and it would never recover. By 1900, there were only a few small pockets of traditional Irish speakers left in Ireland.[22] Today, the Irish language is taught across the grade levels in Irish schools. Students leave school at varying degrees of proficiency and many say they do not use it daily. The clear majority of families speak English in the home. However, there remain small regions of the country where the Irish language still thrives. The Irish language is part of the Irish culture and refuses to be left to die.[23]

Education in 19th century Ireland was more for boys than girls. The priority for girls was to be well versed in cooking and maintaining a household, while the boys learned the three R's. Girls had to be prepared, for it was common for them to marry as young as sixteen, until tradition changed after the Famine. Early in the century, there was no organized school system, and children did not go to school or attended "hedge" schools. The name was derived to indicate that a school might be anywhere, including under the shade of a hedge tree. School might be in a barn or outbuilding or any other shelter that would serve as a classroom.[24] Hedge schools remained common through the 1820s, with about 400,000 students attending about 9,000 hedge schools, according to *The Oxford Companion to Irish History*. Attendance was irregular, though, because by the age of ten, boys were expected to put in a full work day, especially during cultivation, planting or harvesting. Nationally funded schools became prominent in the 1830s. At first, Irish Catholics praised the national schools, but became disillusioned with them in time and finally detested them. The consensus of the Irish Catholics was that teaching in the national schools was anti-Catholic and favored England over Ireland. In addition, all classes were taught in English, with no regard for the Irish language.[25] By 1841, literacy in Ireland was only about 50%. After the Famine, schools became more organized, with better attendance, and by 1891, literacy was over 70%.[26]

Emigration became a way of life for the Irish family. The night before the family member or members left, there would be an "American Wake." It was called a wake because when the family members left for America, it was almost sure they would never see them again. To them, it was the same as a wake for the dead. It was a bittersweet party with cause for celebration and sadness. There was dancing, drinking, singing and many heartfelt moments. Families were saying goodbye forever.[27]

Finally, John White, a British traveler, found one more tradition and culture shared by the Irish. He found the Irish to be well spoken and very sensible until the subject of English and Irish relations arose. The Englishman's observance was, "Touch on that topic, and they began to literally rave."[28]

CHAPTER 4

# Prelude to Famine

*To anyone with a drop of Irish blood in them, the land they live on is like their mother. It's the only thing that lasts, that's worth working for, for fighting for...*[1]

—Alexandra Ripley, American Writer of Scarlet

Upon seeing the Irish Census of 1841, English politician Benjamin Disraeli commented that Ireland was the "most densely populated country in Europe."[2] The population boom was having serious repercussions on the Irish land scheme. More population meant smaller farms. About 93% of Irish farms were under thirty acres, and according to the Census of 1841, 45% were fewer than five acres. It was estimated that it took an acre and a half to produce potatoes for a family of six for the year. Some families had less than one acre and were likely to have experienced hunger or starvation before the new crop came in. The father had to find work that paid him with potatoes. Farms became continually smaller with each generation, as each grown son needed a plot of land to start a family of his own.[3] As farms became smaller, an English government report estimated that one third of the small farmers could not support their family after paying the rent.[4]

Many farmers did not need extra labor other than their children. John Casey had three boys who could provide plenty of help when old enough. Some farms would require help when potatoes and grain were planted or harvested, and by 1846, there were almost a quarter million Irish farm laborers. They might have work during planting and harvesting season for the potatoes or grain, but for the other 30 weeks of the year, there was only occasional work. Some farm laborers would travel to England or Scotland to find work,[5] but others, with no land to grow potatoes, would literally walk the rural roads looking for work, with their families suffering at home from hunger. The "possession of a piece of land was literally the difference between life and death."[6]

## PERFECT STORM

The Irish land scheme had evolved. Catholics had lost almost all their land through England's confiscations and the harsh Penal Laws. Catholic land ownership had fallen from 90% in 1600 to 5% in 1804. Ireland's population was over five million in 1804, yet the land was in the hands of eight to ten thousand Protestant landowners, of which about one third were in England. Many owners rented large parcels of land, from one hundred to a thousand or more acres, to middlemen. They in turn subdivided the land and rented it in smaller plots. Some of the middlemen were unscrupulous and charged over-market rents, desiring only increased profits. Many landlords and middlemen were not interested in making improvements to the land that would curtail their profit. Tenants did not want to make improvements because it would ultimately lead to a rent increase. The small farmer held five to fifteen acres, the cottier had five acres or less, followed by the landless farm laborer.[7] With these parameters, John Casey was a small farmer holding 16 acres by 1857. By that time, John and Ellen's boys were grown enough to help in the fields. It was likely that John and the boys might need only occasional help from farm laborers or neighbors and relatives.

As noted, the population had grown 172% in fifty years, exerting an extreme demand on land rentals. This demand drove rent prices up until they reached eighty to one hundred per cent greater than those in England. The pressure on rents was exacerbated further by landlords who advertised publicly for offers on rental land. The landlord then chose one of the highest offers.[8] The small farmers subsisted on potatoes for food and grew wheat, barley, or oats to pay the exorbitant rents. Catholic tenants paid for the support of their local parish, along with the tax for the land they held, but did not own. For the small tenant farmer, the cottier and the landless laborer, life was merely about survival. Ireland's land scheme had reached a critical mass.

County Roscommon is in the western province of Connaught and is home to the geographical center of Ireland. By 1841, its population had swelled to 253,591.[9] With a town population of only 10,052, the rural population was 243,539. Subtracting land that was not occupied, (water and bog) and the town area, the rural population was jammed into 709 square miles at an average of 344 people per square mile.[10] They attempted to raise enough potatoes to eat, and other crops to pay the rent, Church of Ireland tithe, land taxes, and the Catholic tithe. Many times there was just not enough.

By 1845, Ireland was on the brink of one of the most catastrophic events in the history of the island. With Mary's birth, the Casey family now had four children under the age of nine. They had no way of knowing that their young family was headed into one of the darkest times in Irish history. There was the Irish land scheme, the reliance on the potato, and widespread poverty. All these conditions came together to form a perfect storm. No one in the country would be left untouched, and when the fury subsided, Ireland would never be the same again.

The potato came to Ireland in the late 16th century. It was perfect for Ireland's wet weather conditions.[11] The potato comprised about 60% of Ireland's food supply.[12] The English viewed Ireland's dependence on the potato as part of their ignorance. On the contrary, the Irish did not choose the potato, they were driven to it. The potato was not a labor intensive crop and had high yields on small acreage.[13] Furthermore, the potato would grow in poor, rocky soil or on steep hillsides that weren't conducive to other crops.[14] The potato, with its high nutritional value, meant longer life spans and was responsible in a major way for the explosion of the Irish population from the late eighteenth to mid-nineteenth centuries.[15] The Irish turned to the potato because it was an inexpensive crop to grow, and it was relatively easy to feed a large family.[16] A potato patch of one and a half acres could feed a family of six for a year, whereas it would take four acres of grain. Even the farm animals were nourished with a potato diet.[17]

Between 1800 and 1845, the population was progressively growing and becoming denser in the rural areas. With inheritances and landlord manipulation, the available plots of land became smaller and smaller. Tenant farmers had to maximize their grain production as a cash crop to pay the excessive land rent and taxes. The farmer's poorest or rockiest land was used for the potato crop.[18] The cottier had only a small plot for potatoes and the landless laborer had to rely on working for others and collecting his pay in potatoes. Much of the rural economy was potato bartering rather than cash.[19]

Poverty was widespread, with many of the poor living in deplorable conditions. The 1841 Irish Census revealed that "in parts of the west of Ireland more than three-fifths of the 'houses' were one-roomed windowless mud cabins..."[20] In 1843, the British government formed a Royal Commission headed by the Earl of Devon "to inquire into the law and practice with regard to occupation of land in Ireland."[21] A portion of the evidence presented in the Commission's report stated, "The majority of the peasantry, perhaps as many as three million people, lived in conditions in which a considerate owner would not have placed a dog."[22]

Nassau Senior, an English economist, blamed the Irish landlords for the poverty in Ireland. In his view, it was not the fault of the government.[23] In actuality, the answer lay in the relationship of the landlord, tenant *and* the government. By 1870, 97% of the land was farmed by tenants rather than the actual owners.[24] Before 1845, about one third of the Irish landlords lived outside Ireland.[25] Money earned by the absentee landlords was siphoned out of Ireland, never to return. There were no improvements to or investment in the land. The landlord was at the top of the food chain in the land scheme. With land rentals auctioned to the highest bidder, he became wealthier while his tenants were mired in poverty.

The tenants ran on a treadmill they could not stop. Grain production was not for food but for the payment of rent to the landlord. One fourth of all tenants held less than five acres.[26] There was no hope for the small Catholic farmer to someday buy the expensive Irish land. The landlord's boot was firmly pressed on the neck of the tenant. Irish tenants' priority was to hang onto the land by any means. Nonpayment of rent could mean eviction or non-renewal of the lease. John Casey's lease was annual, renewed each March 25.[27] Gale days to pay rent were on May 1 and November 1.[28] Every year in March, the renewal of the family's lease was not guaranteed, but rather was granted at the behest of their landlord.

The Caseys rented their land from the Balfe family of County Roscommon. They were a dominant presence in the county since the 18th century. The Balfes owned nearly all of the 536 acres of Carrowgarve. They were one of the few Catholic landlords in Ireland. Only 5% of all Irish land was Catholic owned.

The Balfes were a classic example of the disparity between the Irish landlords and their tenants. The Balfe manor was located about two miles east of Castlerea, around 13 miles from the Casey farm. Their estate was named Southpark and was built around 1773. Southpark was elaborate. The Big House boasted three stories with 34 rooms and 365 windows—the picture of excess. The demesne (attached land for owner's use) was a sizable amount of acreage with an apple orchard of thirty-two apple varieties along with numerous other fruit trees. They raised livestock and fowl, all in the effort of making Southpark self-sufficient. The Balfe sport was fox hunting. Through the years, there were as many as fifty hunting dogs at any given time that assisted in the hunts. The Balfes were considered one of the leading families in the county.[29] Daniel O'Connell the Liberator was a frequent visitor at Southpark. His son and granddaughter married Balfes.[30]

The contrast between the lives of the Balfes and those of their tenants was stark. Many of the landless laborers and cottiers lived in crude one-room mud huts. John Casey may have had occasion to visit his landlord. He could not have helped but feeling awe at the Big House, while also perhaps harboring some resentment, knowing firsthand the living conditions of the tenants. .

There was one kind act that occurred in 1845, the first year of the Famine. Nicholas Balfe was the landlord in charge of the operation and seeing the hardships that the loss of the potato crop was having, "generously forgave every tenant on his extensive estates one-half year's rent."[31] Then again, the Famine would last five years, and it is not known whether any of these benevolent acts continued.[32] Regardless, the plight of the tenant farmers, cottiers and landless laborers continued.

The government's hand was also in the pocket of the poor. It took the tenant farmers until 1836 to get unchained from paying the tithe to the Protestant Church of Ireland.[33] Even then, the tithe was reduced somewhat and placed on the landlord, who in turn, added it right back onto the tenant rent.[34] The tenant may have had some solace that they paid rent directly to the landlord rather than directly to the Protestant Church. Then, in 1838, the tenant was saddled with a tax for poor relief. If the land occupier held land worth more than four pounds, he paid the tax. Under four pounds was the landlord's responsibility,[35] which provided an incentive for the landlord to clear the land of these small holders to avoid the tax. That would take place through eviction or emigration. There was plenty of blame to go around, but at the end of the day, the poor were still poor and vulnerable, with no change in sight.

For the small tenant farmer, there were two tasks that absolutely must be met: raise a grain crop to pay the rent to hold onto the land, and grow enough potatoes to feed the family for a year. By the mid 1840s two million acres of potatoes were being planted in Ireland, with almost three million people totally dependent on the potato for food. It was also a food staple for the rest of Ireland at various degrees of dependency.[36] The only drawback of the potato dependence was their prospect of staying fresh enough in ample quantity for the entire year. It was not uncommon in the summer months, with their potato supply gone, that landless laborers would be on the roads looking for work, and their family at home with very little or nothing to eat.[37]

Nevertheless, for the poor rural population, the potato was the perfect and seemingly the only choice as a source of food. With plenty of potatoes, the population was healthy, and the families large, but there was no escape from the fatal flaws of the Irish land scheme. Meanwhile, on the other side of the world in 1842, farmers between Novia Scotia and Boston were experiencing a strange phenomenon with their potato crops.[38]

CHAPTER 5

# FAMINE

*The voices of the ordinary people who experienced those traumatic years went unheard. Those who survived did not speak of it.*[1]
—Paul Lynch, Novelist, "On Effects of the Famine"

On September 13, 1845, The *Gardener's Chronicle* made the first report of the potato blight around Dublin.[2] It would have been in County Roscommon shortly after. John and Ellen's daughter Mary Casey was baptized on December 10, 1845. As much of a celebration as a baptism can be, it was short-lived. There would be no potatoes for the winter.

It happened quite literally overnight. A dreadful scourge rolled over Ireland. It came with a putrid smell, blackened stalks and withered leaves. Something was horribly wrong with the potato crop. The potatoes had become a black, stinking mush in the ground. Some were dug and appeared normal, but that wouldn't last. Those too would rot.[3] The same blight that had occurred in North America had struck Ireland. The invisible spores of this fungus called phytophthora infestans[4] had traveled, presumably by ship, to England and Ireland.[5] As a host, Ireland was perfect.

The spore thrived in warm, wet weather. It could spread by the wind or enter the ground with rain.[6] There was virtually nothing that could be done. When the blight attacked, the crop was gone.

When first reports of the blight reached England, Prime Minister Robert Peel did not give them much credence. After all, the Irish were prone to exaggeration.[7] He became more concerned after continued reports from the island and finally took action. He assigned two English scientists to go to Ireland, assess the situation, find potential remedies, and report back as soon as possible.[8]

In the meantime, believing Ireland would need an alternate food source, Peel called a cabinet meeting to discuss repealing the Corn Laws. Although named "Corn," the laws pertained to all grain prices, mainly wheat, barley and oats. The laws were enacted in 1815 for the purpose of propping up the grain prices in the Kingdom. Grain imports were either not allowed or assigned a high tariff, waiting until the English and Irish grain reached a highly profitable price. Essentially, it was Parliament catering to the large landowners, of whom several were Parliament members. The working class bore the brunt of the grain prices.[9] The Cabinet showed little support for a repeal, and the matter was tabled.

Many members of Parliament did not believe there was a famine in Ireland.[10] An attitude of ignoring and denying there was a crisis, justified inaction. Peel, however, realized something must be done immediately. The prior year's potato supply was gone and with the failure in 1845, the rural Irish had nothing to eat. In November of 1845, Peel, without Treasury approval,[11] ordered 100,000 British pounds of Indian corn from America and 46,000 pounds from England. Essentially, he was bypassing the Corn Laws with no support from Treasury, thus putting his career at risk.[12] His intervention would not only feed the poor, but help lower and stabilize the cost of food. If his own Cabinet couldn't support him on repeal of the Corn Laws, then Parliament certainly would not. That same month, Peel's scientists returned and reported that about one half of the Irish crop had been lost and they had no solution for the blight. When Peel's Indian corn did arrive, the Irish did not know how to cook it. Many, to their intestines' detriment, simply ate it whole kernel. They finally learned that it was edible if soaked overnight in warm water, then boiled in water the next day.[13] Peel also organized an Irish supported public works system. It gave jobs to around 140,000 people. Considering the Irish average family of five, it supported around 700,000.[14]

Daniel O'Connell, as part of a citizens' committee, realized the impact the blight could have on the rural population. He proposed ceasing all grain exports from Ireland and importing additional grain from America. He further proposed acquiring a loan and levying a substantial tax on the landlords to provide for relief for those without food.[15] O'Connell's proposal was met by stiff resistance in Parliament and went nowhere.

By June of 1846, Prime Minister Robert Peel was successful in achieving Parliament's repeal of the Corn Laws. However, his efforts and persistence had created political enemies in Parliament and he lost the support of many other members. He decided that he could no longer lead an effective government and resigned.[16] Peel had acted quickly and his programs prevented an untold number of Irish from suffering hunger. Essentially, he had sacrificed his career by championing Ireland. Much later, Peel's biographer, Douglas Herd, would state that because of Peel's efforts, no one died of starvation during his administration.[17]

Peel was a member of the Tories, a political party whose largest allies were the Irish landlords. The Whigs, their opposition, promoted the economic policy of *laissez-faire*. This ideology promotes free trade without government intervention. It is the theory that the market will always correct itself without the engagement of other forces.[18] Peel's resignation paved the way for a new Whig government to take power.

## The Whigs

Lord John Russell became Prime Minister in July of 1846. He was an exceptionally small man with a caustic personality. He was noted for his attitude of self-importance and his frequent rude treatment of others.[19] Russell would largely leave the administration of the relief effort for Ireland to Charles Trevelyan, head of the Treasury. Trevelyan was up to the task. He was known for his obsession for work, many times in his office into the wee hours of the morning. Trevelyan was also known for being very religious, but imprudent, with an inflexible attitude toward the ideas of others. His approach was direct and many times ill-mannered. But the real problem with Trevelyan directing the relief was that he detested the Irish,[20] and Irish Catholics in particular.[21] Trevelyan had this to say about the Irish:

> The judgment of God sent the calamity to teach the Irish a lesson, that calamity must not be too much mitigated...The real evil with which we have to contend is not the physical evil of the Famine, but the moral evil of the selfish, perverse and turbulent character of the people.[22]

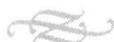

This may be seen in his actions. Sir Robert Peel, who had arranged the import of grain to feed the Irish, left office at the end of June, 1846. A few days later, on July 8, 1846, Trevelyan set the stage for his treatment of the Irish. He canceled a shipload of grain in transit to Ireland.[23] Trevelyan and John Russell were both disciples of the economic theory of *laissez-faire.* Supply and demand would correct any imbalances, not the government. They would assert this principle throughout the Famine. As Daniel O'Connell had proposed, the government should have stopped the export of food from Ireland. Charles Trevelyan and the practice of *laissez-faire* would not condone that.

Meanwhile, thinking that the blight was gone, the Irish farmers had planted a large crop of potatoes for the 1846 harvest. Unfortunately, the blight returned with a vengeance, even earlier than the year before. The 1846 potato crop would prove to be a total loss across all of Ireland.[24] Trevelyan was warned in mid-July by Routh, the chairman of the Irish relief committee, that the prognosis for the potato crop was dire. Trevelyan took this notice as a call to action. Yet his intent was not to increase relief to the poor, but to stop it. He ordered the grain depots and public works closed immediately. He had this to say to Routh: "The only way to keep the people from becoming habitually dependent on the Government is to bring the operations to a close."[25] Robert Peel's west coast grain depots providing food to the poor, along with the public works that had provided so many Irish with work and cash to buy food, were shut down in the face of an even worse failure than 1845.[26]

This move was short-lived, however. In August, many more reports of crop failure and the hungry destitute population were coming in. On August 17, 1846, John Russell presented a plan to the House of Commons. The mainstay of his plan was to start the public works again in an even greater magnitude. This effort would be paid for entirely by the Irish landowners through an additional tax rate. In addition, Russell announced that England would no longer purchase food to import to Ireland. Any imports would be at the discretion of local merchants.[27] In his mind, Peel's purchases had interfered with free market trade. Peel's grain was sold at low prices and caused a loss of revenue to grain dealers.[28]

## IRISH EXPORTS -FAMINE YEARS

In 1847, the worst year of the famine, close to 4,000 ships laden with food sailed to English port cities. England needed the inexpensive Irish food supply for the kingdom and their vast armies.[29] "An estimated 2 million people in Britain were fed with food imported from Ireland."[30] According to John Mitchel, the Irish food produced was "sufficient to feed more than twice the Irish population in excess of 8 million in 1841."[31] About 75% of Irish farm land was used for grain production and nearly all went to England. Yet ironically, Mill, the English economist said, "We must give over telling the Irish that it is not our business to find food for them. We must tell them, now and forever, that it is their business."[32]

Nevertheless, John Russell and Charles Trevelyan opted for maintaining free market trade in 1847, as grain was still being produced and exported from Ireland at a record rate. At the same time, imported food began to arrive. England persisted with the principle of *laissez faire*, and would not interfere with the high price of food. These policies were disastrous for Ireland. It is believed by many historians that the exports of food products and textiles to mainly England in 1846 were enough to feed and clothe all of Ireland. Many grain exports made by Irish landlords were for paying taxes to England. Russell and Trevelyan demanded those payments throughout the Famine, whether the landlord was able to collect his rents or not.[33] Other exports by Irish landowners were strictly for profits.[34] The merchants and grain dealers, Protestants and Catholics alike, could charge swollen commissions for selling the grain. They became very wealthy, taking advantage of the position the farmers and landlords were in.[35]

The poor, many with nothing to eat, witnessed the grain leaving the fields to be shipped out of the country. Food riots erupted in several locales, with shots fired by militia in County Waterford. The skirmish resulted in one dead and several wounded. England acted quickly. Armed guards were stationed in grain fields and British troops escorted wagons of grain to the ports. The ports were guarded, and even the ships of grain leaving Ireland had a British naval escort.[36]

The solution to prevent mass starvation in Ireland was readily at hand. It was imperative that England freeze Irish exports at the beginning of the Famine. The quantity of grain and other foodstuffs produced in Ireland would clearly have been adequate to prevent starvation on any kind of large scale. This was the English Parliament's decision to make. However, landlords and merchants had a powerful influence on Parliament. That, coupled with the doctrine of *laissez-faire,* resulted in the appropriate decision never being reached. A million or more Irish died of starvation and disease during the five years of the Famine.

The English economists of the day also had influence on Parliament and English leadership. One English economist was heard to say that "he feared the famine of 1848 would not kill more than a million people and that would be scarcely enough to do much good."[37] Thomas Malthus, another English political economist was even more graphic, saying, "The land in Ireland is infinitely more peopled than in England, and to give full effect to the natural resources of the country, a great part of the population should be swept from the soil."[38]

The exports continued and the Irish starved. According to Cormac Ograda, noted Irish historian, twenty-six million tons of grain were shipped from Ireland to England in 1845.[39] In 1847, the worst year of the Famine, about 400,000 Irish died of starvation and disease. While those people died, Ireland achieved its greatest year for exports of the Famine.[40] Along with the 4,000 ships mentioned earlier, 9,992 cattle were also shipped to English ports.[41] Overall, in the Famine years of 1846-1850, over three million animals were shipped to England.[42] John Mitchel, an Irish Nationalist of the time, put it this way: "The Almighty indeed sent the potato blight, but the English created the famine."[43]

## 1846-1847

In 1846, the crop failed for a second time. Grain crops, however, were not affected by the blight.[44] With 16 acres, John Casey likely had a crop of wheat or other grain. Thankfully, his landlord, Nicholas Balfe, had forgiven a half year's rent to all his tenants. This may very well have been enough for John Casey to keep some of his grain crop to buy food and get through 1846.

After Robert Peel resigned, John Russell presented a new plan for Famine Relief to the House of Commons on August 17, 1846. The plan had the fingerprints of Charles Trevelyan. A public works would be established that would not require additional expenditure from his Treasury, but would be supported entirely by the landlords of Ireland. The pay for the Irish workers would be eight to ten pence per day.[45] It would not be enough to support an Irish family, but just enough to keep them from starving. Five days of full pay might feed a family for three days.[46] The public works got a slow start. The biggest challenge was to find administrative staff to facilitate payment of the workers. Engineers were needed to develop work projects. When the work finally began, there were delays getting pay to the workers. By October, the pay was still delayed. Pay clerks quit rather than deal with angry workers. One pay clerk was beaten. Food prices were on the rise and even those who were receiving pay could not buy enough food to prevent their families from starving. There were even several incidents of men who had not been paid for two or three weeks dying from starvation on the job.[47]

Clothes, household goods, kitchen wares and anything else of value had been sold or traded for potatoes the first year of the famine.[48] Any farm animals, including horses, dogs, cats and even dead animals, were consumed.[49] In October, there were reports of people eating weeds in an attempt to survive. On the west coast, people had eaten all the seaweed off the beaches.[50] As the situation deteriorated, Trevelyan relented and made an attempt to buy maize. It was not available in Europe, and his order was too late in the year for a ship to sail before winter from the United States.[51] Just as it seemed that things couldn't get worse, six inches of snow fell on the island in November. This abnormal event would be the beginning of one of the worst winters in Irish history.[52]

Death hovered over Ireland. It came swooping into the mud huts and one-room cabins. It took people walking the roads, at the workhouses and even at the public works. They died of starvation or disease. Deaths occurred among those waiting on their pay, delayed by the public works.[53] By February 1847, about 700,000 Irish were on the public works, but many were just too weak to work. Some took up stealing food. Farmers had armed guards watching animals, crops and their gardens.[54] It was reported that the most suffering was taking place in the province of Connaught, of which County Roscommon and the Casey farm was a part.

Many farm families ate their seed potatoes, jeopardizing spring planting. Trevelyan had opened the food depots in the west to distribute grain, but this would only feed perhaps ten percent of the destitute. People waited in lines all night and when the distributions began, there was much fighting among the crowds. The food depots would prove to be too little too late. Then it was announced that the public works would close down. There were not enough people capable of working. They were in the throes of starvation and disease.[55] This left the Irish with no food and no means of earning money to buy it. The Director of the Irish Famine Relief, Charles Trevelyan, addressed the Irish starving population, saying, "If the Irish were starving, it must be their own fault; and God himself had sent the potato blight for the 'moral and political improvement' of the Irish people. They must take control of their lives and stop abusing British charity."[56]

In the years 1845-1846, Scotland also experienced the potato blight. They received relief promptly, and Trevelyan monitored their food depots to insure there was adequate food. There were very few deaths. Trevelyan's viewpoint was that the landlords and tenants in Scotland were far more enterprising than those in Ireland.[57] His relief efforts in both countries reflected his opinion.

CHAPTER 6

# STAGES OF STARVATION

*Humanity has but three great enemies: fever, famine, and war; of these by far the greatest, by far the most terrible is fever.*[1]
—William Osler, Canadian Doctor

In the first stages of starvation, the body prefers less activity and more sleep. As starvation progresses to about a 20% loss of body weight, physical appearance clearly shows starvation. There are mental affects at this point also. The starving person will become depressed and apathetic. They may withdraw from others and be very quiet. When the body has lost one third of its body mass, contracting disease is very likely because of a weakened immune system. Even minor infections or a virus can be fatal. With continued starvation, the pulse rate slows, blood pressure lowers and the heart muscle will begin to shrink. The person will likely be able to speak, but it will be very slowly. The brain has now become significantly affected by the starvation. A condition named "the persistent clamor for hunger" begins. In this phase, the starving person has an obsession for finding something, anything to eat. The person will sleep many hours, then upon awakening will begin the intense search for food. It is characterized by the willingness to do anything to get food. The victim may not care about the welfare of others, including their family members. Parents might take food from their children at this stage. They will have the desire to eat anything including cats, dogs, rats, bugs, weeds, grass, even sawdust. There are rare occurrences of cannibalism at this stage. Loss of tissue around the eye sockets causes the victims to look like their eyes are "bugged out." Many starving children will have an aged look. They might lose the hair on their head, while growing hair on their face and back.[2] Part of the latter stages of starvation is a condition called dropsy. Medically, the malady is named hunger edema, when the stomach and limbs swell from water accumulation to the point that they can even burst.[3] Starvation is particularly dangerous for the old and the very young. Older people may just give up, or may not have the strength to find food. Children need more protein and a severe deficiency can lead to death.[4]

The death toll rose during the winters, and especially during the agonizing winter of 1846-1847.[5] "In a famine, starvation and disease go hand in hand."[6] Deadly diseases like typhus, relapsing fever and dysentery are always present in the population, but not in epidemic proportions. At the mid to late stages of starvation a victim becomes malnourished and the immune system breaks down, making them highly susceptible to infection and disease.

The Irish in the process of starvation lost concern for hygiene. They lived in squalid conditions, sometimes with their pig kept inside the home. The clothes of the peasants were mere rags and likely never washed by the starving people. Diarrhea was prevalent, many times caused by eating unnatural or putrid foods. Dysentery was also common—contracted from a bacillus carried by flies. Flies carry the bacillus to fecal matter which in turn could be spread to the water supply. Exposure to the fecal matter or infected water produced the dysentery characterized by bloody stools. Typhus was carried by lice. Lack of hygiene and unsanitary conditions were ideal for lice. Close proximity allowed the lice to spread. Those at the public works, the workhouses and soup lines were all close enough for the transfer of lice, intensifying the epidemic. With a broken-down immune system, the fever and dysentery were many times fatal, especially in children.[7]

The year 1847 was the worst year of the famine.[8] Mortality was at least 400,000 and the year became known as "Black 47," with disease quickly outpacing starvation as a cause of death.[9] Although there were several ways for England to mitigate this disaster, Charles Trevelyan wrote, "The matter is awfully serious, but we are in the hands of Providence with no possibility of averting the catastrophe; if it is to happen, we can only await the result."[10]

Disease spread unchecked due to unsanitary conditions and lice. The vast majority of loss of life in the Famine was due to disease. The estimate is that disease killed almost ten times more than starvation.[11] But in many cases, it was a combination of starvation and disease as the fever invaded malnourished starvation victims with a compromised immune system. The most common deadly diseases were typhus, relapsing fever, dysentery, and cholera. Of those, typhus and relapsing fever were the deadliest. Both were spread by lice, hence any close contact among the Irish poor could result in a transfer. The organisms of typhus attacked the small blood vessels, hindering circulation. Along with the fever, the victim's face swelled and turned dark. Hence, the Irish dubbed it black fever.[12]

With relapsing fever, the microorganisms enter the body through the skin and in a matter of hours, the victim has a high fever and vomiting. This can go on for days, ending with death or a period of extreme sweating and exhaustion. Around a week later the victim relapses and the fever cycles through again. This process can repeat itself as many as four times, meaning likely death for a malnourished, starving victim.[13]

Many of the programs providing famine relief also facilitated the spread of typhus and relapsing fever. The grain depots and soup kitchens required standing in line and waiting. The workhouses were overcrowded, with hundreds of people in close proximity. Lice would transfer from person to person, expanding the epidemic.[14] The Irish were known for being social and very close to their relatives, but with the fever, everyone was suspect, even the dead. This led to tendencies to stay close to only immediate family and remain in their cabins unless out looking for food.[15]

Dysentery and cholera were both killing diseases mainly brought on by unsanitary conditions. Cholera was noted for its vomiting and diarrhea, while the victim with dysentery had stools with blood and mucus. The famine diseases were known for fever, vomiting and diarrhea.[16] With these symptoms, the victim needs lots of untainted water. Without it, the body becomes severely dehydrated, which can be fatal, regardless of the disease.

CHAPTER 7

# RELIEF

*The road to the workhouse became known as 'cosan na marbh' or 'pathway of the dead,' and over a quarter of those admitted died inside the workhouse.*[1]
—Derek Reed, Irish Famine Exhibition

## THE WORKHOUSE

The English Parliament enacted the Irish Poor Law in 1838 to provide relief for Ireland's destitute. The country was divided into 130 Poor Law Unions. Each union would have a workhouse. The workhouses were built to provide for 100,000 of Ireland's poorest.[2]

The English economists believed that the Irish landlords were responsible for the poverty in Ireland.[3] The English Parliament had a festering disdain for them, despite the fact that several members were powerful Irish Protestant landlords.[4] Unfortunately, many Irish landlords built huge mansions with vast demesnes. They were prone to lavish spending[5] and had no reserves for a higher tax burden. It was determined that Ireland would pay the cost of the poor law. A poor rate would be levied on the properties in each union.[6]

In Charles Trevelyan's viewpoint, the workhouses must be a most uninviting and miserable place to end up.[7] He wanted the Irish people to stay outside and fend for themselves rather than rely on the workhouse to care for them. He believed that government relief made people worse, not better.[8] In that regard, the strictest of disciplinarians were hired to manage the workhouses, with supervision to be unrelenting.[9] Upon entering, the Irish family would be split up. There were separate accommodations for men, women, boys and girls.[10] The workhouse was run like a prison, with strict rules and consequences for the miscreants.[11] Punishments could be extra work up to and including flogging for some offenses.[12] The inmates' day began at six o'clock with work beginning immediately after breakfast and continuing until six o'clock in the evening, with a short lunchbreak. Supper was at seven o'clock with absolute silence required. The inmates had nothing except their uniform, mattress and blanket. If an inmate died, his uniform was reissued, sometimes without being washed.[13] The facilities were fenced with all gates locked. Doors were also locked within the workhouse.[14] The men worked all day breaking rocks or grinding grain. Women were responsible for all household duties and chores. The food was meager and unchanging, with the menu planned for the poorest of Irish laborers.[15] Essentially, it was just enough food to prevent starvation.[16]

The workhouse system was not designed to meet the needs of the Famine. By 1847-1848, 250,000 Irish were jammed into facilities with a capacity of 100,000. The conditions were especially difficult for children. At one workhouse, 150 boys were packed into a small room with only 24 beds. There were reports of forty to as many as sixty dead children in one week. In some cases, dead and living children were discovered in the same bed.[17] One estimate places deaths at the workhouses at 200,000 during the Famine.[18] Most of the workhouses were grossly overcrowded, but others turned the poor away because financially, the workhouse was at the edge of bankruptcy.[19] The collection of the poor tax from the landlords was not going well. Even when the tax collectors were accompanied by English troops, they were still not always successful. Many paid, but others couldn't or wouldn't pay the taxes due. One Protestant landlord who refused to pay was Lord Lucan, a large landowner with thousands of tenants. "He said that he would not pay 'paupers to breed priests.'"[20]

The state of affairs was desperate during 1847-1848. Some Irish would bring their children and falsely present them as orphans to get them to a place they might get food.[21] The conditions in the workhouses, also known as poorhouses, were well known to the Irish.[22] Many families chose to die in their cabins rather than seek shelter in the poorhouse.[23] Fever was rampant, with most newcomers already infected. Overcrowded conditions were ideal for the spread of lice carrying typhus.[24] Inmates and staff alike were infected and died of fever. The conditions at the Skibbereen Workhouse in County Cork were especially grim. In April 1847, an average of twenty-five a week would die of disease. Their workhouse was built for 800, but 2,500 were housed there by 1848. It was said that some local Irish believed that getting to the workhouse would automatically get them a coffin when they died. In reality, at some workhouses, their body made it into a coffin, but one with hinges. The coffin was then taken to a mass grave where the hatch door was unhinged and the body slid into the pit.[25] It is believed that throughout the Famine, the mass grave at Skibbereen became the final resting place for between 8,000 and 12,000 Irish.[26]

The horrors of the workhouse would live on in the minds of Irish and eventually travel to America. As I grew up among Irish families, it was not uncommon to hear a phrase such as, "I don't want to end up in the poorhouse."

## Public Works

Parliament approved Robert Peel's plan for public works in Ireland in the spring of 1846. The work planned was road construction and repairs, bridges, harbors and fisheries. Landlords also hoped to get public works projects for building walls, digging ditches and draining fields and bogs. Work began in the summer with over 100,000 Irish employed. Workers typically walked several miles to and from the job site. Much of the work was building and repairing roads and was hard work. Work began at 6 AM and ended at 6 PM, six days a week. Arriving late for work was a loss of one fourth of the day's pay. Many worked all day without eating. The job site typically had an overseer with a whip to keep order. Any shirker would be fired and replaced with one of the many who were waiting for a chance to work. The substitute workers waiting were sometimes more than a hundred, all for a wage that might barely keep a family from starving. Unfortunately, most of the public works sites had pay delays, at least initially, for lack of trained administrative personnel.[27] In one case a man died and hadn't been paid for two weeks. The coroner examined him and wrote that he "died of starvation caused by the gross neglect of the Board of Works."[28]

After Robert Peel's resignation, Sir John Russell's Whigs took charge and Charles Trevelyan was placed in charge of Irish relief. He shut the works down immediately. As noted earlier, Russell decided in August that the works would be restarted on a much larger scale. Work on the uncompleted projects began in September. The works again bogged down, with applications and personnel problems causing delays. There was a lack of skilled people to design and run the projects. Consequently, there was grossly poor supervision of some of the job sites, resulting in chaos and sometimes violence. A public works official was even shot.[29] At times, the workers were literally unsupervised and did nothing.[30]

By January of 1847, 700,000 Irish were employed by the public works. Again, the program was shut down with a general admission of failure. Most were afflicted with starvation or disease and were too weak to work.[31] New roads were poorly constructed, and existing roads ineptly repaired. One road between towns was about a one and one-half hour ride. When the public works repaired it, the same road took four hours.[32] The Treasury Department sent directions to release those workers who were ill or unable to do a full day's work first, and use the able-bodied men. The response from the relief committee was that "able-bodied men had ceased to exist"[33] One member of Parliament referred to the public works as the Public Follies.[34]

As was mentioned, 1847 was a record year for food exports from Ireland.[35] Coupled with fewer imports, the food supply moved toward scarcity and caused food prices to rise dramatically. Regrettably, food was available, but with the significant price increase, people had no money to buy it.[36] One worker let go from the works who faced the reality of starvation wrote, "Nothing to do but bar the door, lie down and die."[37]

## Soup Kitchens

In early 1847, as the Soup Kitchen Act was being crafted, Parliament was certain to make the Irish landlords and landholders pay for the program. The soup kitchens were the government's best program for providing aid to the impoverished of Ireland. The Quakers, who were a major support organization during the Famine, opened the soup kitchens first in the fall of 1846. With the help of The National Relief Committee they founded, soup kitchens were set up all over Ireland.[38] In February 1847, Parliament passed the Soup Kitchens Act and also planned to distribute soup throughout Ireland. However, the project became bogged down in bureaucratic paperwork again and did not open until June.[39] The gap in time between the closure of the public works in January and the opening of the soup kitchens in June resulted in many lives lost to starvation.[40]

The kitchens were very successful, however, and by August, between the government soup kitchens and the Quakers' kitchens, three million Irish were being served daily.[41] Lines were long and some would wait all night for the kitchens to start serving.[42] The lines were supervised and crowding ahead of others would result in a beating with a stick. The soup was made with a small amount of meat, vegetables and water in large vats. Unfortunately, there were some deaths walking the distances to the kitchens, and even deaths at the kitchens. The sudden intake of food to malnourished bodies could create a shock to their system resulting in death.[43] Others were also affected negatively. It was said that soup "runs through them without affording any nourishment." It also aggravated the disease of dysentery, and exacerbated the condition of dropsy by adding to the "water-logging" of the body.[44]

The Poor Inquiry Commission had this to say about the volume of people served daily at the soup kitchens: "These three million persons were 'a dead unproductive weight.' What was to be done with them, what could be done with them?"[45] It would prove to be a haunting question, perhaps one answered by Charles Trevelyan.

By August, the soup kitchens had been operating about two or three months and were of great benefit. Trevelyan received word that the potato crop due for harvest in the fall was blight-free.[46] At that news, Trevelyan abruptly ordered the soup kitchens and the grain depots shut down immediately. He decided that the food crisis was over.[47] Thus, there were the poor, with no work, no soup, and no money to pay for the exorbitant price of food.

Trevelyan quickly wrapped up the shutdown of the kitchens and took his family for a two-week vacation in France.[48] Charles Trevelyan may have convinced himself that the crisis was in the past, but the troubles in Ireland were far from over.

CHAPTER 8

# EVICTIONS

*During the evictions, all business was suspended in Kilrush, the shops were closed and the window shutters put up, men left their work in the fields and the bell of the parish church tolled mournfully and unceasingly as a funeral.*[1]

—The Gael, August 1901

There were evictions throughout the Famine, but in 1847, they accelerated. It is estimated that between 1846 and 1854, half a million Irish were evicted from their land and homes.[2]

Land ownership in Ireland was a profitable enterprise for many years. Before the Famine, between 33% and 50% were absentee landlords.[3] Many of them resided in England and their affairs in Ireland were handled by a middleman or agent. The money earned in Ireland would then be spent in England. Everyone profited, except the tenant who was saddled with high rents due to the exploitation by the landlords and middlemen and the fierce competition for land. A tenant such as John Casey likely raised a cash crop of grain for the rent and had his potato patch for food.

The Famine changed everything. When the potato was taken out of the equation, the scheme fell apart. The tenant farmer had a dilemma. He could use the grain he raised for food, but if he did, he would not be able to pay the rent and therefore risked eviction. Or he could pay the rent with his grain crop and go without food. The cottier and laborer were in a worse quandary. The farmer had no potatoes or cash to pay them. Moreover, with potatoes rotted in the ground, he did not need the labor for harvest. The cottier and laborer were doomed to suffering from hunger.

The landowner may or may not have been able to collect rent from the tenant. Some landlords seized the crops of their tenants or took their animals as payment of rent.[4] Even at that, the land-owners' income from rents was vastly reduced. Furthermore, in June of 1847, the Irish Poor Law Extension Act was passed by Parliament, placing the cost of relief for the poor onto the landowner through increased taxes.[5] This additional financial burden would put many landlords on the road to bankruptcy.

The Poor Law Amendment Act of 1847 addressed the cost of relief for the Irish. Most of the workhouses were at capacity, so this Act provided for relief for those outside the workhouses who were impoverished. As the law was being developed, a member of Parliament named William Gregory suggested that in order to receive relief, the occupier should not be a landholder of more than a quarter acre. It passed with the Amendment and was named the Gregory Clause. If an Irish family needed help, they would need to turn back their land to the landlord, except that quarter acre. In this instance, the landlord paid all the taxes and the land occupier was exempt.[6]

The Poor Law Amendment with the Gregory Clause lit the fuse for evictions. Landlords determined that the most cost-effective path to take was to purge the small holders altogether and avoid the cost of relief to support them. Consequently, instead of allowing the tenant to surrender his holding down to a quarter acre, the landlord demanded he surrender the entire acreage and the cabin. In some cases, the tenant agreed and made their way to the workhouse only to find there was no room, and they were turned away.[7]

In order to legally evict a tenant, there had to be a court proceeding. At the hearing, the delinquent amount of rent was determined and the tenant given the opportunity to pay. The result was normally a foregone conclusion. The landlord's petition for approval to evict would be granted. The tenant was given notice of the date for eviction.[8] The court was not always sympathetic when offered an explanation by the tenant, as can be seen by a bailiff's comments at one hearing: "What the devil do we care about you or your black potatoes? It was not us that made them black. You will get two days to pay the rent, and if you don't you know the consequences."[9]

On the day of eviction, the sub-sheriff and constabulary,[10] along with men with crowbars[11] and sometimes British soldiers, would arrive and announce their intentions. Many of the families resisted. If the family would not come out then a battering ram was used to obliterate the door[12] and the family forcibly removed—physically dragged out if necessary. In some cases, the roof of the house would be torn off with the family inside. The family was then forced off the landlord's property and advised to stay off.[13]

Many powerful landlords ignored the courts and evicted at will. One of these evictions occurred on a Mr. Blake's land in County Galway on New Year's Eve 1848. The group arrived after dark with no notice and aroused the family with their announcement. The parents pleaded to postpone the eviction until morning, to no avail. The family was put out of the house on a cold December night with some of the children ill. The incident was heinous enough to be raised for discussion in the House of Commons. Despite some condemning the act, Mr. Blake suffered no consequences.[14] Lord Lucan, mentioned earlier, was another powerful landlord who boasted 2,200 Irish evicted.[15]

After the eviction, the family was forced onto the countryside with no food and no resources to get it. Some chose the workhouse over starvation and walked there, only to be turned away. Others built "scalps," which were crude shelters across a ditch with poles as support and a roof of sod. Still others merely dug a burrow in the ground and covered it with sod or sticks.[16] Eviction in the winter was akin to a death warrant.[17] Many of the families only had rags for clothes and many were barefoot.[18] They died of exposure, starvation or fever. Some historians liken the winter evictions to premeditated manslaughter.[19] One poor law inspector, Sir Arthur Kennedy, described the scene after one thousand evictions and destruction of cabins in County Clare: "wretched, helpless homeless" wander the countryside "scattering disease, destitution and dismay in all directions…The most awful cases of destitution and suffering ever seen. When the houses are torn down, people live in banks and ditches like animals, until starvation or weather drive them to the workhouse. Three cart loads, who could not walk, were brought in yesterday."[20]

Some of the cruel mass evictions were called to the attention of John Russell, who made an attempt with Parliament at some legal reform pertaining to evictions. Russell's own cabinet opposed it, and the reform that finally emerged from Parliament was largely ineffectual. Parliament ruled it was illegal to tear down a roof if the family was still in the house. In addition, nighttime evictions and those on Christmas Day or Good Friday were prohibited.[21] Charles Trevelyan, of course, weighed in on the matter of evictions. Trevelyan's belief was that the Famine was a "direct stroke of an all-wise and all merciful Providence." Irish historian Jim Donnelly fittingly says, "This mentality of Trevelyan's was influential in persuading the government to do nothing."[22]

Seemingly a more humane tactic used by landlords to clear the land was to pay for the tenants to emigrate. The cost of passage was about one half the cost of paying for them at the workhouse for a year.[23] In these cases the tenants were compelled to pay up, face eviction, or immigrate to North America. Some landlords found it more economical to charter ships for large groups of tenants they were otherwise evicting.[24] At first glance, this seems an adequate solution, but for the Irish family it meant leaving their home for a faraway place with no money for support. Many of the rural people had not ventured even four or five miles away from their home since birth.[25]

One particularly depressing case of evictions occurred in County Longford, adjacent to Roscommon. The court approved eviction of 1,490 people who were to be transported to Canada. The 1,490 Irish walked 100 miles to Dublin to board the ships. A bailiff walked with them to be sure they all boarded and did not try to sneak back. Unfortunately, the ships chartered were substandard without proper provisions. Fever raged on the ships and over 700 of the 1,490 died on board or succumbed to fever when they reached Canada.[26]

One of the most infamous instances of assisted emigration was the case of landowner Major Denis Mahon of Strokestown, County Roscommon. Strokestown is about 21 to 23 miles from the Casey farm in Carrowgarve. Mahon owned about 11,000 acres in County Roscommon.[27] The Mahon Estate originated in 1688 when hated Oliver Cromwell displaced the Irish Catholic owners and gave the Roscommon land to Nicholas Mahon for his service as an officer in Cromwell's Model Army.[28] Denis Mahon had recently inherited the land at the start of the Famine. In the spring of 1847, he proposed immigration to Canada for his tenants. About 800 accepted and he chartered two ships for passage. The travel was marred by unsanitary conditions on the ships and typhus broke out. More than 260 passengers on one of the ships died of fever.[29]

Meanwhile, back in County Roscommon, Mahon was not finished. He subsequently evicted 3,000 tenants who had not agreed to migration. Many elderly, widows and children were forced out onto the countryside with very little hope for assistance. This massive number of evictions and forced emigrations had very negative results. On November 2, 1847, Mahon was shot and killed riding in his carriage. Bonfires burned on the hillsides near Strokestown celebrating the death of the rogue landlord.[30] Mahon was not to be the last. A murderous spree over a period of two months left a total of five other landowners dead and a sixth seriously wounded. The violence prompted numerous other landlords to flee the country.[31]

CHAPTER 9

# SUFFERING

*Families, when all was eaten and no hope left, took their last look at the sun, built up their cottage doors that none might see them die nor hear their groans, and were found weeks afterwards, skeletons on their own hearth.*[1]

—John Mitchel, Describing Irish Famine
in "Jail Journal"

## COUNTY ROSCOMMON

John Casey and family lived in County Roscommon, Ireland. The county is part of the western Irish province of Connaught, where the Famine was especially deadly. The county is landlocked and has the site of the geographical center of Ireland. Roscommon is a rural county with only four small towns. Its pre-Famine population in the 1841 census was 253,591.[2] Before the Famine, County Roscommon was said to have the highest population of poor people in Ireland. There were 2,500 holdings of less than an acre and 7-9,000 under five acres. The county also had the dubious distinction of one of the highest eviction rates in the country during the Famine.[3]

County Roscommon was especially hard hit by the Famine. The county lost a shocking one third of its population during that decade.[4] However, the drop was not uniform in the county. Some areas on the western side of the county experienced as much as a 60% loss, while some on the east side were only 10%.[5] John Casey and family lived in Carrowgarve townland on the western side, in the midst of these substantial losses. It was in 1847 that the danger of typhus and relapsing fever became more dangerous. Close exposure to others could result in a transfer of lice. Starving people were going door to door looking for food. It was at this time that the generous spirit of the Irish was called into question at the sound of a knock on the door.

Thousands of farm workers fled to England in search of work. Several cities in England became overrun with Irish and began to send them back to Ireland.[6] There was starvation and disease throughout the county. The Roscommon Workhouse was located at Castlerea, about eleven miles from the Casey farm. The workhouse was full at the beginning of 1847 and had only a forty-bed fever hospital.[7] Fever was raging. The Master and the Matron of the workhouse both died of fever and the doctor deserted. At one point in 1847, 830 out of 990 inmates had the fever.[8] About 70% of the fever cases were ending in death. The fever was not just a disease of the poor; it was running rampant among the upper classes of the county also.[9] The danger of fever was always there among all classes.

A boy at the Roscommon workhouse named Johnny Callaghan worked with his dad in the bakery. Every day he watched the crowds of people at the gate begging and pleading for food.[10] One constabulary report stated that 7,500 people were living only on boiled cabbage leaves that they rationed for every forty-eight hours.[11] A Dublin newspaper, *The Nation*, reported in March of 1847, "In Roscommon, deaths by famine are so prevalent that whole families go to bed at night and are corpses by morning."[12]

Patrick Timon was a local historian at Tibohine, near Carrowgarve in County Roscommon. Timon researched the local history and found that Tibohine was also crippled by the Famine. He found accounts where wandering people arrived at the Catholic Church there in various stages of disease and starvation. There were burials night and day as they died.[13] John Casey's farm was one or two miles from the Church. As was the case in all rural areas, Black '47 was an awful year. Families had shared food and supported each other until the fever came. Dead animals were eaten. One mother gave the flesh of a dead child to her other children and told them their father got the meat in a "Big House." The farm animals had all been consumed.

The dead were transported to the cemetery at the Church by what might be called a "funeral train." The farmers developed a system where the deceased was placed in a crude coffin or a shroud and delivered door to door. The corpse was left at the front of a cabin and a knock on the door would call for that neighbor to take up the corpse and move on to the next neighbor until the deceased finally reached the cemetery and volunteers dug the grave. Sometimes mothers would come to the Tibohine Church carrying their dead child to bury. There were as many as thirty or forty burials on some days. The cemetery was full. As Timon told the story of the Famine in Tibohine in 1921, he noted that many foundations of cabins still remained there. The locals did not talk much about it. When asked who lived there, one resident responded, "God rest the dead. The Famine took them and some went on the ships with rotten bottoms." They would not use the names of those who were gone, nor did they seem to want to talk about it. They would say, "There are no people by that name now in this parish."[14]

## EMIGRATION

About 1.25 million Irish immigrated to mainly North America during the Famine years. In addition, there were also significant numbers to England.[15] Many chose Canada for cheaper fares.[16] The United States had more restrictions on ship safety, the headcount per ship and who was admitted to the United States. Ships with a fever outbreak onboard were many times turned away. Canada was a United Kingdom colony and did not pose those restrictions. It is estimated that thirty to forty thousand, after taking advantage of the cheap fares to Canada, walked across the border into the United States.[17]

Most passenger ships during the Famine period were sailing ships. Passage to North America depended on weather, but usually ran four to six weeks. Conditions on many of the ships were dreadful. Passengers typically were in steerage below deck. Foul-smelling air would exude from the hatches.[18] These unsanitary conditions were ripe for the spread of disease and many were claimed by fever either on the ship or shortly after arriving. The ships with high death tolls took on the name of coffin ships. Some of the coffin ships were not seaworthy at all and sank. About 100,000 Irish sailed on coffin ships to Canada in 1847. Approximately 20,000 died en route or shortly after arriving. Those dying in transit were thrown overboard.[19]

Even with the Famine, it was not an easy decision for many Irish to emigrate. They did not want to leave Ireland, but it seemed the Famine gave them no choice.[20] For nearly all, they would never be back. Leaving relatives for a trip to the unknown was difficult. American Wakes continued through the years of the Famine. Although the Wakes were normally festive, with singing and dancing, they became a solemn affair during the Famine. A priest might attend to pray a rosary and bless them for their trip.[21]

## Black '47

Many were sent off to America, but for those left behind, there were still more years of the horrors of the Famine. Black '47 was the worst year of the Famine, with the greatest loss of life.[22] Ironically, the potato crop in 1847 was blight-free, but regrettably, there was only a fraction of a crop, with two million tons of potatoes produced compared to fifteen million tons in 1844.[23] Many starving families had eaten their seed potatoes to stay alive during the winter.[24]

The year 1847 began amid one of the worst winters in Irish history.[25] Starvation and disease accelerated and evictions began in earnest. Food exports in '47 were at their highest during the Famine,[26] causing food to be in short supply and prices to increase. The Irish rural population was accustomed to using a barter system with potatoes and didn't use cash.[27] The public works shut down and there was no way to earn money to even try to buy food.

England became "famine weary" and with the June 1847 passage of the Irish Poor Law Extension Bill, support for the Irish poor effectively ended and the burden was placed on the financially strained Irish landlords. Parliament hated the Irish landlords and blamed them for the starving poor. Therefore, they decided the landlords must support them. However, Lord Mountcashel addressed the House of Lords conveying the estimate that after paying mortgages and loan payments, Irish landlords collectively had only about three million pounds remaining. Yet the taxes now being levied against the landlords amounted to fourteen million pounds.[28] It was apparent that the Irish landlords could not support the poor and Parliament knew or should have known that the suffering and death would continue unabated.

The west of Ireland was suffering immensely. Connaught province was the worst, followed by south Ulster and west Munster.[29] Cemeteries all over Ireland had long since filled and the Catholic Churches consecrated new grounds for Famine burials.[30] Thousands were being pushed into mass graves, the worst at Skibbereen, with as many as twelve thousand buried in one immense pit.[31] Fever swept across the island, taking the rich and the poor. Lord Clarendon in Ireland wrote Prime Minister Lord John Russell asking for help and received a response of, "The state of Ireland for the next few months must be one of great suffering. Unhappily the agitation for Repeal has contrived to destroy nearly all sympathy in this country."[32] Clarendon's plea for help had fallen on deaf ears. It was political. Sympathy and public opinion should not have been the yardstick for saving starving people.

Across the Irish Sea in February 1847, Daniel O'Connor, Ireland's Liberator, addressed Parliament for the final time. In ill health, he could only muster a whispering voice as he pleaded for his beloved country: "Ireland is in your hands, in your power," he whispered. "If you do not save her, she cannot save herself. I solemnly call on you to recollect that I predict with the sincerest conviction that a quarter of her population will perish unless you come to her relief."[33]

He was shown respect by most, but a heartless Benjamin Disraeli (Future Prime Minister) called his appearance "a feeble old man muttering before a table." Daniel O'Connell, a defeated Irishman, died three months later in Genoa, Italy.[34] As part of his Catholic faith, he wanted to travel to Rome, but fell short.[35] As for his appeal to Parliament for help, it died with him.[36]

The countryside of Western and Southern Ireland must have been surreal. Entire families lay dead in their cabins.[37] Other families were walking the roads like skeletons.[38] Bodies were found along the road with green foam on their mouth from eating weeds or grass trying to prolong life a little longer.[39] Others walked to the towns and cities looking for food, but carrying disease that spread like wildfire.[40] Everyone lived in fear of who might bring them fever. Relatives no longer associated. People isolated themselves.[41] The air was filled with the stench of the dead. The workhouses were full. Irish children looked like miniature old people, wrinkled and stooped, with the hair on their head gone and long hair growing on their faces.[42] The children and elderly comprised 33% of Ireland's population, but it was these groups that paid the heaviest toll. Sixty per cent of Famine deaths were among the children and elderly,[43] of which those under five and over sixty the most stricken.[44]

The Irish had a sense of pride and for many that meant dying at home instead of seeking help at the poorhouse. Even facing death, their pride prevailed. Starving and sometimes homeless, they knew they were going to die. It seemed that for them, it was not the fear of dying that weighed heavily on their mind, but their hope and prayer was just to have a coffin. For many, even that was denied.

James Mahony, an artist from County Cork, traveled the road to Skibbereen in the south of Ireland. His coach first stopped for breakfast at Clonakilty, where they were swarmed by the starving poor. One woman stood out, "carrying in her arms the corpse of a fine child," crying out for assistance in buying a coffin to bury her dead child. The villagers said it was not uncommon for mothers to bring their dead children to town.[45]

Mahony said of one stretch of road, "We either met a funeral or a coffin at every hundred yards." At Skibbereen, "I saw the dying, the living, and the dead, lying indiscriminately upon the same floor." In the parish of Aghadoe, Mahony came to the cabin of Tim Harrington "where four people had lain dead for six days… as the living cannot be prevailed to assist in the internment, for fear of taking the fever…I certainly saw from 150 to 180 funerals of victims."[46]

In another account, a shopkeeper told of a mother who arrived in his shop with an emaciated baby in her arms: "The poor little thing was gaunt and kept whining for something to eat," he said. "He gave the mother some milk, but later that day, he found her lying dead by the roadside. The baby was still alive in her arms."[47]

Kathleen Hurley spoke of her father's firsthand experience, saying, "My father said he saw people dead on the roadside, such sights, their bodies all skin and bones, with bunches of green grass in their mouths, the green juice of the grass trickling down their chins and necks."[48]

In the winter of 1845 and 1846, most had survived through the original Irish custom of sharing resources and helping others. When the fever progressed, things began to change. There was hoarding, with no more willingness to share.[49] Farmers armed themselves and guarded their gardens and livestock all night long.[50] It was common to find a cow with its throat slit and sewed back, still living. Thieves had stolen her blood during the night to use to fry and eat or for blood pudding.[51]

Some chose the path of crime, any crime, as long as it would result in jail time. Jail meant shelter and one meal a day.[52] Sadly, for others, the stages of starvation were too much for them and they did unconscionable things, like cutting off food to the elderly and children, or the rumored and likely factual eating of parts of a dead family member.[53]

Wealthy Protestant landlord Lord Palmerston's vision was coming to fruition: "Famine was long last dealing with the Irish land problem. A surplus and unwanted population was being disposed of."[54]

## 1848-1849

Across the Irish Sea, in the spring of 1848, a group was rising that called themselves the Young Irelanders. They were led by John Mitchel, a revolutionary writer for the Irish newspaper *The Nation* and Thomas Meagher among others. Groups had formed around Ireland and became known to English officials. A violent uprising was feared and ten thousand British troops were sent to Ireland to put down any unrest. Unfortunately, the Young Irelanders were doomed by poor leadership, little organization and no money. There were nearly six thousand assembled at one point to start a revolt. Woefully, many had come unarmed with the hope of getting food for participation, but disappeared when told they were responsible for their own provisions. For many weakened and starving Irish, the struggle to find food negated all other causes.[55]

The group fell from about six thousand down to fifty who were prepared to fight. The revolt culminated in a skirmish with police at Widow McCormick's cabbage patch, where two of the Irish were shot and killed. Two priests arrived and convinced the Irish to pull back, and the Young Irelanders' revolution ended. The leaders were arrested, convicted and transported as prisoners to a place called Van Diemen's Island (Tasmania) off the coast of Australia.[56] These events brought both Parliament and the English citizenry to a heightened agitation toward the Irish.

CHAPTER 10

# POLITICS AND RELIGION

*The time will come when we shall know what the amount of mortality has been; and though you may groan, and try to keep the truth down, it shall be known, and the time will come when the public and the world will be able to estimate, at its proper value, your management of the affairs of Ireland* [1].

—Lord Bentinck, House of Commons, 1847

## PUBLIC SENTIMENT

Early in the Famine, the public had been sympathetic toward the plight of the Irish. They showed this through significant contributions to the Relief Association established in England. Queen Victoria had made an appeal for Ireland, and the English people responded.[2] As the Potato Blight dragged on, however, England and Parliament had become tired of hearing of the Famine and the whole Irish problem. In England, public opinion, fueled by the Russell administration, had turned against the Irish and many reports regarding the scope of suffering were considered exaggerations. Charles Wood said as much: "There had been exaggeration last year and there was probably exaggeration now."[3] The feeling was that England had done too much already for this boisterous people. Lord John Russell, Charles Trevelyan and Charles Wood were cultivating this attitude behind the scenes with the *London Times.* Fueling the anti-Irish sentiment fit well with their liberal view of nonintervention with the Irish and the Famine.[4] Charles Wood, of the Treasury said this about the Irish: "We believe the real reason to be the total absence not merely of gratitude, not merely of respectful acknowledgments, but of the barest 'receipt' for all these favors."[5]

As with the early, generous support for the Famine, early reporting by the *London Times* was favorable. In March of 1846, following a series of Galway evictions, *The Times* condemned the landlord by writing, "How long shall the rights of property in Ireland continue to be the wrongs of poverty and the advancement of the rich be the destruction of the poor?"[6] Later, in a complete turnaround, *The Times* expressed their feelings on the Famine, saying, "For our parts, we regard the potato blight as a blessing."[7] Then, two years later, *The London Times* offered this ludicrous analogy on July 26, 1848:

> The English are very well aware that Ireland is a trouble, a vexation, and an expense to this country. We must pay to feed it and pay to keep it in order…we do not hesitate to say that every hard working man in the country (England) carries a whole Irish family on his shoulders. He does not receive what he ought to receive for his labor, and the difference goes to maintain the said Irish family, which is doing nothing but sitting idle at home, basking in the sun, telling stories, going

> to fairs, plotting, rebelling, wishing death to the Saxon, and laying everything that happens at the Saxon's feet.[8]

The radical English magazine *Punch* took the discriminatory rhetoric even further by creating a character called "Paddy" as the typical Irishman. Paddy was a monkey in a "tailcoat and derby hat."[9] Even the English historian James Anthony Froude wrote that Catholic Irishmen were "more like tribes of squalid apes than human beings."[10] Thomas Carlyle, another British historian, went further when he likened the whole of Ireland to a rat and posed the question of what an elephant would do with a rat, but "squelch" it. He later visited a workhouse and called the Irish people there "human swine."[11] This demonization of the Irish people from the English press and historians would go far in forming a negative bias among the English citizenry toward the Famine and all the Irish. Tim Pat Coogan, Irish historian and author of *The Famine Plot,* says that behind the scenes at the *Times,* John Russell was "regarded as a senior, if silent, partner in the exchange of news for influence…"[12] This type of manipulation of public opinion by Russell and the Whig government created a favorable atmosphere in which to impose their liberal policy on Ireland. Also, in the words of Coogan, "Whig policy was directed at getting the peasants off the land and if it took mass death to achieve that objective, then so be it."[13]

## THE 'OPERATION OF NATURAL CAUSES'

In 1847, Charles Trevelyan had declared the Famine concluded. But upon his return from vacation in France, the Famine was still very much alive. The years 1848 and 1849 would prove to be just as devastating as the years before. The potato crop in both years was a failure.[14] Suffering and death from starvation and disease continued. In June 1848, there was a directive that any person on relief outside the workhouse would be granted a coffin upon death.[15] This was important to the Irish, because too many had seen bodies half buried, mass graves at the workhouse[16] or corpses being devoured by packs of dogs.[17]

In 1848, Charles Trevelyan held on tightly to the Treasury's purse. He would not release his grip even when his superiors willed it. In July, 200,000 Irish children were being fed by the charitable British Relief Association. They appealed to John Russell, telling him the Association was nearly out of funds. John Russell committed in writing to the Association that the government would feed the children when the Association ran out of money. In November, Charles Trevelyan learned of the children. He issued instructions, also in writing, that the feeding of the children be stopped immediately and said "the government could do nothing."[18] He also advised the Poor Law Unions of Ireland that there would be no loans granted from public funds.[19] Ireland would be left up to the "operation of natural causes." Trevelyan explained that the plan was to do nothing.[20] Russell mused that "it is better that some should sink, than that they should drag others down to sink with them."[21] Lord Clarendon translated this to mean that masses of starving people exposed to disease would be eliminated by the "operation of natural causes."[22] Following the same theme, Charles Wood's response for guidance on what to do when the crop failed again in 1848 was "as little as conceivably possible."[23] This all came from government officials of what was then the richest country in the world—England, a country who had taken Ireland in the Act of Union of 1801 to be part of a

United Kingdom. They had abolished Irish Parliament and placed the power over both countries in London. This country, England, had left Ireland adrift in the Irish Sea with no way to save herself.

## 1848-1849

Sadly, 1849 was another year of total loss of the potato crop and more suffering and death. In 1848 and 1849, thousands escaped through emigration, which Trevelyan applauded. In his view, the more who vacated, the more land opened up for the profitable ventures of grain production or grazing.[24] In June, Trevelyan continued his assault on children. He argued that all children should be removed from the workhouses to make way for able-bodied men. Edward Twiselton, the Poor Law Commissioner in Ireland, refused and stood his ground. Trevelyan conceded.[25]

A horrid event known as the Doolough Famine Tragedy occurred on March 30, 1849 in South County Mayo, a neighbor county of Roscommon. About 600 men, women, and children in the community of Louisborough were in various stages of starvation. There was a rumor that if the people walked to Delphi Lodge for an inspection, they would receive relief from the landlord and the council guardians. It was a cold night and many did not have the clothing for the inclement weather. Some walked in bedclothes and some barefoot. They walked over twenty miles in the cold to reach the Lodge, only to be told that the officials were eating lunch and could not be disturbed. They waited. There was no relief and there was no food. They were turned away and began the twenty-mile trek back to Louisborough. Many did not survive. Corpses littered the road. It is not known how many died on the journey home, but some estimates are as high as four hundred. Regardless of the number, it was a shocking event that could have been averted with some compassionate consideration at Delphi Lodge.[26]

## QUEEN VICTORIA

In 1849, Queen Victoria visited Ireland for ten days in August. The Irish reaction in the cities was inexplicably jubilant. There was much preparation in the city of Dublin. Critics opined that too much money was being spent that could be used for the poor and that the Queen would be guided away from the areas plagued by the blight.[27] Their prediction was correct on both counts.

The royal yacht was welcomed in Cork Harbor on August 2. The Queen was cheered with much exhilaration as she stepped on Irish soil. She went on to tour the local area and travel on through Kingstown to Dublin. There were roars of approval as she rode through the streets in her carriage. The Irish were enamored and so was the Queen. In a letter to her uncle, she remarked, "You see more ragged and wretched people here than I ever saw anywhere else." But there was much worse that she didn't see. She was kept away from Dublin's slums and did not see the destitute that blanketed the countryside. The Queen bid farewell from Kingstown Harbor on August 12.[28] It was a wonderful visit that unfortunately accomplished nothing toward easing Ireland's pain. The Queen was an icon with no real political power to wield in the current government. That power rested in the hands of Trevelyan, Russell and Wood.[29]

## THE COVER-UP

The aforementioned power brokers had been warned by Lord Clarendon of the catastrophe of the Famine through George Grey, the Home Secretary. Clarendon said:

> I dread some calamity…some hundreds dying all at once of starvation, which would not only be shocking but bring disgrace on the Government." Grey responded coldly, "It may be that if numerous deaths should occur the Government would be blamed…but there is such an indisposition to spend more money on Ireland, that the Government will assuredly and severely be blamed if they advance money to pay debts.[30]

Edward Twiselton was the Poor Law Commissioner for Ireland. Through the years of the Famine, he held doubts as to the legitimacy of the Famine relief effort administered by Charles Trevelyan. You will recall that it was Twiselton who defied Trevelyan the removal of all children from the workhouses. In January of 1849, he said this about the workhouses, "Others might say that we are slowly murdering the peasantry by the scantiness of relief."[31]

By March 1849, he could no longer continue in good conscience. He gave his resignation to Lord Clarendon, who submitted his comments to John Russell: "The destitution here (Ireland) is so horrible, and the indifference of the House of Commons to it is so manifest, that he is an unfit agent of a policy which must be one of extermination....Twiselton feels that as Chief Commissioner he is placed in a position...which no man of honor and humanity can endure."[32]

Also in March 1849, Parliament was debating the Rate-in-Aid Act, which levied higher rates on the more solvent poor law unions to help pay for the distressed ones. Part of the Act was that the government would immediately distribute £50,000 to the distressed unions at the start. Charles Wood and George Grey were determined that the payment would be the minimal amount to only prevent a "scandal" and no more.[33] Nevertheless, The Poor Law Commissioners attempted to negotiate for more, but were refused by Charles Trevelyan, and offered these comments: "Trevelyan was unsympathetic, but admitted that the government was obliged to provide a minimal form of relief, or 'the deaths' would be 'an eternal blot on the nation.' He called paupers 'prodigal sons' who should not be given 'the fatted calf' but only 'the workhouse and one pound of meal per day.'"[34]

As can be seen, officials in the government had begun to experience a level of anxiety about what they were doing and what they had done. They had begun to address "keeping up an appearance" as being the primary goal rather than saving Irish lives. Twiselton described slow murder in the workhouse and Trevelyan's Famine policy as a policy of extermination. And finally, even Trevelyan searched for a way to avoid an "eternal blot" on the nation.

The years 1847-1849 were likely harrowing years for the Casey family. Hopefully, their grain crop was adequate to pay the rent. They too were ominously affected by the loss of the potato crops. Like all rural Irish, they were preoccupied with paying the rent, sustaining enough food and avoiding the fever. These were the peak years of the Famine. Landlords and tenants alike were desperate. Landlords were also in an especially precarious position, with paying the poor tax for the workhouse and trying to stay solvent with only a limited number of tenants paying rent. A desperate landlord with eviction as a recourse presented a quandary for all tenants.

Aside from the landlord, fever was all around them. The Tibohine Catholic Church, a mere one or two miles away from the Caseys, was burying dozens of victims of starvation and disease. The workhouse in Castlerea, only ten or eleven miles away, was inundated with fever. Then there were those on the roads with fever, knocking on doors with fever, and corpses, still carrying the lice of the fever. John and Ellen Casey likely had substantial distress for their four children, with the youngest only two and the oldest ten. We hope they took strength from their faith. "Cast your burden on the Lord, and He shall sustain you. He shall never permit the righteous to be moved (Psalm 55:22)."[35]

## Famine Politics

Throughout the famine, Russell and his administration embraced the doctrine of *laissez-faire* at the peril of Ireland. The export of food from Ireland would continue undisturbed. Charles Wood, Chancellor of the Exchequer, set the stage for England's Famine policy. He implied that the fault for the Famine lay with Ireland's "habit of depending on government. (The solution is) to force them on their own resources," or England risked "having the whole population of Ireland on us."[36] John Russell stated simply, "We cannot feed the people."[37] Although in early 1847, he was given a viable alternative: "...a 9 million pound colonization scheme to relocate two million Irish Catholics only, along with a proportionate number of priests to reclaim land in Canada was presented to Russell by eighty leading peers, members of Parliament, and landowners. Russell rejected that scheme, too, on the grounds that the starving masses in Ireland would emigrate without any such intervention by the English government."[38]

The colonization was a grand scheme that could have worked. It would require only voluntary participation to be humanitarian, for compulsory emigration would be further persecution of the Catholic poor. Regardless of the number of volunteers, it would have taken a great deal of pressure off feeding the people of Ireland. It was a way to colonize Canada and to go far in solving the Irish predicament, but to no avail as Russell, the Prime Minister of the wealthiest country in the world, dismissed it because it would require Treasury funds.

The House of Commons, as a whole, was indifferent and uninterested in the issues of Ireland.[39] The landlords in England and Ireland proposed that the Irish were inferior by nature. Their Catholic superstitions were a deterrent to their thinking and they were poor only because they were lazy.[40]

Charles Trevelyan's beliefs were largely economic theory sprinkled with a disdain for the Catholic Irish. He was consumed with the idea of giving the Irish what they deserved instead of what they desperately needed. His actions were political rather than humanitarian. In Parliament, both Tories and Whigs believed the Famine was necessary to right the overpopulation of Ireland. "A few even said the Famine was desirable."[41] Trevelyan and the House of Commons relied heavily on the advice of several economists, two of whom were J.S. Mill and Nassau Senior.[42] The economists were a heartless group, as can be noted by their rhetoric. Mill focused on excess population. He described "English

Parliament's feeding the starving masses as 'a stimulus to population.'"[43] He was in favor of a lowered population and preferred, as did his colleague Malthus, that the starving should be "removed from the soil." He saw the large Irish families as problematic, saying, "Little improvement can be expected in morality until the producing [of a] large family is regarded with the same feeling as drunkenness or any other physical excess."[44] Finally, Mill had this reflection after the Famine: "[England] is indebted for its deliverance to that most unexpected and surprising fact, the depopulation of Ireland, commenced by famine and continued by emigration."[45]

Charles Trevelyan was left unbridled to run the Famine relief on his own terms. He effectively answered to no one. In mid-1847, he threw the cost of the Famine totally onto Ireland and presided above it as an observer and veritable referee. Not only was he an unyielding enforcer of *laissez-faire,* but he harbored the belief that the Famine was somehow God's judgment upon the Irish. He said, "[The Famine] is a punishment from God for an idle, ungrateful, and rebellious country; an indolent and un-self-reliant people. The Irish are suffering from an affliction of God's providence."[46]

Trevelyan behaved as if he had omnipotent power and he was God's partner in the annihilation of the Irish. Finally, as the dust cleared, a million were dead and another million had fled or were forced out of the country. Trevelyan, in his infinite wisdom, said to Charles Wood that the Famine was an "effective mechanism for reducing surplus population," and was "the judgment of God."[47]

Years later, in 1868, Lord John Russell reminisced, "...Famine and emigration have accomplished a task beyond the reach of legislation or government..."[48]

In October of Black '47, Charles Trevelyan visited Ireland at the height of the suffering and death. It was his only visit during the Famine years. He *chose* not to tour the rural areas and see the devastation, but instead remained in Dublin for his entire stay.[49]

On April 27, 1848, Queen Victoria bestowed Knighthood upon Charles Trevelyan for his service to Ireland during the Famine. He was now to be addressed as SIR Charles Trevelyan. The Queen made a reprehensible decision and added insult to the injury of Ireland.

## RELIGION

Starvation and disease during the Famine were indiscriminate. Many Protestants were lost along with Catholics. Catholics were affected at a higher rate because they comprised 80% of the population,[50] and the severity of the Famine was greater in areas with a high percentage of Catholic population. For instance, the province of Connaught was devastated by the Famine and its population was near 90% Catholic.[51] All told, of the 2.15 million Irish lost to starvation, disease or emigration, approximately 91% were Catholic.[52]

Religion was also a factor during the Famine. Some Protestant groups went cabin to cabin encountering the starving Catholics, offering food in exchange for attending the Protestant church. The Protestant landlord Lord Lucan refused to pay taxes for the support of his destitute Catholic tenants at the workhouse. Another landlord, Lord Ventry of County Kerry, employed the services of the Protestant minister Thomas Thompson as his agent for his tenants. Reverend Thompson desired all tenants to be Protestant. His strategy was to charge higher rent for the Catholic tenants in an effort to drive them off the land. An alternative was the offer of reducing their rent for conversion. If those options failed, Reverend Thompson chose eviction. "Hundreds of Catholics are said to have been evicted because they did not 'turn'."[53]

Alexis de Tocqueville, a French diplomat, visited Ireland before the Famine and had these comments: "All of the Irish Protestants who I saw...speak of Catholics with extraordinary hatred and scorn. The latter, they say, are savages...and fanatics led into all sorts of disorders by their priests."[54]

A separate viewpoint was given by English economist Jevons as he said, "I must say....that whether considered as a spiritual religion or a practical system, Roman Catholicism is very disgusting and only better than irreligion."[55]

Charles Trevelyan made an attempt to exclude Catholic priests from relief committees in 1846. Lord Monteagle repressed the order, stating that they were "working like tigers for us." Many Catholic priests and nuns were lost to fever from ministering to those stricken in their homes throughout the countryside.

Although not widespread, the most notorious practice of coercing Protestant conversion was known as "souperism." Some Protestants, called "soupers" by the Catholics, would offer soup to the starving peasants with the caveat that they convert. In some cases, money and clothes were also offered. Sometimes meat was added to the soup, only on Friday, the day of the Catholic sacrifice to forego meat. A denial would mean no soup. In the pangs of hunger, there were those Catholics who decided that with the alternative being starvation, they would accept the soup and become Protestant. The Irish held contempt for those "jumpers" who took the soup,[56] and often shunned them. The shame and ridicule were lasting, sometimes even for generations. Other Irish remained steadfast. One Irish woman and her young son were approached by a souper with the offer of soup for their Protestant conversion.

The starving woman asked her son if they should take the soup or die. The little Irish boy answered, "'Tis better die, Mother."[57]

The subject of religious discrimination during the Famine raises more questions than answers. It is a fact that Charles Trevelyan, the spearhead for Famine relief, was Protestant.[58] Trevelyan's viewpoint was that priests were "rebellious" and after Mass, they would send the women and children away and then discuss politics, including treasonous activity, with the men.[59] It is a fact that the vast majority of the Irish landlords and absentee landlords in England were Protestant.[60] It is generally accepted that Protestants and Catholics of this era harbored some level of disdain toward each other. The question is how did this affect decision making during the Famine? England's leadership scorned the Irish in general and had the desire to clear the land of excess population. The excess population happened to be poor and Catholic.[61] The mainly Protestant landlords exercised their option to evict over 250,000 Irish during the Famine.[62] Was it because they were Catholic, or was it merely an attempt to become more profitable? It can't be fully known what is in the hearts of men. But what is known is that Protestants and Catholics alike were joined together in a mortal struggle to survive a horrendous five years of starvation, disease and death.

CHAPTER 11

# CHARITABLE DONATIONS

*We have a shared past as people who have experienced unwelcome intrusion, and a shared sense of injustice.*[1]
—Seamus McGrath, Mayor of County Cork,
Dedication of Sculpture to the Choctaw Nation

Charitable donations and works saved thousands of lives during the Famine. The earliest private donation came from the British citizens of Calcutta, India in 1845. In an effort to show unity and support for the Irish as British citizens, they raised £14,000 for the poor. In 1845, another early donation of $750 came from Boston from a group of supporters of Daniel O'Connell. Famine news was spread through newspapers throughout the world and a multitude of small donations poured in from around the globe.[2]

Charitable donations were stepped up after the second failure of the potato crop in 1846. One of the most generous and heroic efforts was made by the Central Relief Committee of the Society of Friends. The Quakers raised significant sums internationally, much of which was used for soup kitchens established throughout

Ireland, to sustain the poor during times of starvation. There were only about 3,000 Quakers in Ireland, but they were known not only for raising £200,000 for relief, but also for their tireless work delivering the soup to the destitute. The Quakers hold a special place in the hearts of the Irish for their selfless efforts that literally saved the lives of thousands of Irish,[3] sometimes at the expense of their own.

The British Relief Association was formed in January of 1847 and amassed donations internationally of about £400,000. Much of it was used to establish schools in the hard hit counties of Mayo and Sligo. Free food was distributed for children through the schools. Queen Victoria also made an appeal for donations from the people of England and donated £2,000 herself, the highest individual donation made.[4]

Unfortunately, politics and prejudice also entered the fray. *The London Times* wrote in 1847 that "giving money to Ireland would have the same effect as throwing money in an Irish bog." When the British Relief Association ran out of funds in 1848, Prime Minister Russell gave his personal written guarantee that the English government would continue to feed the children[5] who by that time had grown to as many as 200,000.[6] When Charles Trevelyan discovered that Treasury funds were being used to feed these children, he ordered it to cease immediately.[7]

The Sultan of Turkey advised the British consulate that he wanted to donate £10,000 for Famine relief. The British consulate urged him to reconsider so he would not overshadow Queen Victoria, who had given only £2,000. The Sultan, as requested by the British government, lowered his donation to £1,000, but it is believed he followed up on his own by sending two shiploads of food directly to Ireland.[8] A shipload of grain was also sent to Ireland from donors in Massachusetts. The English government seized it and put it in storage in accordance with their doctrine of *laissez faire.* They did not want it to interfere with free trade.[9]

Charitable works from Church organizations had a huge impact on Famine relief. The Churches of Ireland, Catholic and Protestant, united in the effort to help the poor. They assisted the overrun medical establishment by setting up church-run hospitals. Church organizations also raised money for many who wished to emigrate. The Church of Ireland was instrumental in running many soup kitchens. Pope Pius IX donated 1,000 Roman Crowns in 1847 and made a personal appeal to the world's Catholics for prayers and donations for Ireland.[10]

One of the most endearing donations to the Famine relief came from the Choctaw nation of Oklahoma. They recalled their own hardships on the "Trail of Tears," when in the early 1830s they were relocated from Mississippi to the Oklahoma territory. Of the 14,000 who left Mississippi, at least 2,500 died en route. The Choctaw, a nation without any great means, donated $174, an equivalent today of $5,000. In 1992, in a show of unity with the Choctaw, an Irish group walked the 600 mile "Trail of Tears." In 2015, a sculpture was erected in County Cork honoring the Choctaw nation.[11]

Also not to be forgotten are the donations from the Irish immigrants in the United States and Canada. Their offerings were as much as ten times that of any other charity. In just one year, Black '47, they contributed almost a million dollars.[12] The United States also sent two Navy ships loaded with food to Ireland.[13]

It was the landlords and farmers of Ireland who made the greatest contribution toward Famine relief through taxes and private donation. As has been pointed out, there were many landlords who had no empathy for the poor and evicted thousands through the years of the Famine. But there were also landlords who proved to be caring toward their tenants. Some agreed to forego rents until better times, even to the point of being bankrupted. Landlords' wives and children also played a big role. They prepared food and distributed it to the tenants. They started schools to educate the children of the poor. One landlord's child saw the rags the poor children were wearing and gave them many of her own clothes. She then bought cloth from her own savings and made clothes for them.[14]

All told, landlord and farmer support were the greatest of all, at £8,000,000 paid for taxes and donations. They were followed by Irish immigrants who sent £7,500,000 back to Ireland. The British contributed about £7,000,000,[15] mostly before the relief aid was cut off in 1847. Miserably, at £10,000,000, the British spent more on the military in Ireland than on the poor.[16] Expenses included troops guarding the grain in the fields, escorting the wagons of grain to the ports and guarding the granaries at the port—all money that could have gone to help the destitute.

Prematurely, in 1847, the British government announced that the Irish Famine had ended. From that point, donations trailed off, although there were a full two years of blight, starvation and disease ahead.[17]

In 1849, the Quakers, who had been so instrumental in Famine relief, announced their programs had to come to an end. They surmised that Ireland's needs were so momentous that government intervention was the only solution. They summed it up by saying, "When famine stares you in the face, political economy should be forgotten."[18]

The Famine cannot be understated. It was an immense tragedy that took the lives of a million people.[19] But it was also a time that brought out the best in some. There were those who gave generously to help the poor and others who gave their efforts selflessly, many times at the price of their own lives. It was also a time that brought out an underlying evil in others, who chose to ignore the poor or even profit at their expense. It was a time that brought about momentous change to Ireland and impacted the entire world.

CHAPTER 12

# AFTERMATH

*You cannot conquer Ireland. You cannot extinguish the Irish passion for freedom. If our deed has not been sufficient to win freedom, then our children will win by a better deed.*[1]
—Patrick Henry Pearse, Irish Teacher

## DID IT HAVE TO HAPPEN?

In 1846, the Whig government, headed by Lord John Russell, took power. The potato crop failed for the second year, and it created an emergency. The British government could have counteracted it in a number of ways. One major contention was the export of food from Ireland.[2] England could have stopped all food exports, as had been done successfully in other famines.[3] Instead, the exports proceeded uninterrupted. Wheat, barley, oats, pigs, cattle, sheep, and other foodstuffs, under military guard, rolled past the impoverished and hungry Irish, headed for the Irish port cities and on to England. English troops guarded the granaries at the Irish ports and ships sailing for England had a naval escort. The loaded ships would sail and tens or even hundreds of thousands of Irish would go to sleep hungry for yet another day

If the food remained in Ireland, a plan could have been developed for distribution.[4] Some of the most poverty-stricken areas were in remote locales with unsound roads. With a distribution plan and strategically placed depots, food arriving in Ireland's ports, along with grain produced by Irish farmers, could get to those who needed it most. Not only grain, as noted earlier, but three million animals were exported during the Famine which could have been a huge boost to the Irish food supply.[5]

In the summer of 1847, the soup kitchens had become very effective, feeding three million people a day.[6] England prematurely shut them down when the 1847 crop showed very little blight. Charles Trevelyan declared the Potato Blight at an end. What they failed to discern was that the potato crop was only about 15% of normal size, and was in no way going to provide the food needed.[7] More lives would have been saved if the soup kitchens had stayed open.

The public works could have continued. They provided employment, but the laborers were not paid well enough. A fair wage would have helped them buy enough food to remain able–bodied, along with adequately providing for their families.[8]

England could have been much more proactive with the workhouses.[9] Adequate food supplies and humane treatment would have made them a viable resource for the poor. Charles Trevelyan's strategy was to make them as undesirable as possible. They were a veritable prison. Families were kept separated, provisions were scarce, rules were strict and the supervision harsh. Trevelyan's goal was to keep the Irish away from the workhouse and they would not be a cost burden to the government. He succeeded, as many Irish chose to die in their cabin rather than go to the workhouse.

Finally, England could have placed stringent regulations on evictions.[10] Between the years of 1846 and 1855, around 500,000 Irish were evicted.[11] With no shelter, they lived in ditches or holes they dug in the ground. Of that half million who were evicted, the mortality rate had to be astronomical. In the latter years of the Famine, for tens of thousands, it was death in the workhouse or death on the country road. Death in the workhouse became even more likely when the fever became prominent. The close quarters would allow the diseased lice to travel from person to person, creating an epidemic of death. In many workhouses, there was no dignity even in death. There was no coffin, only a mass grave for a final resting place.

High above, looking down on the scene, were the English aristocracy and government. The richest country in the world, seemingly had no desire to halt the madness. Most Irish living in poverty had no funds to emigrate as an escape. Many more of the poor could have been saved if England had provided financial support for their emigration.[12]

To the English, God was exacting punishment on the Irish for their laziness and total reliance on the potato. Charles Trevelyan was a firm believer and thought that not much should be done to mitigate God's punishment. The belief that the Irish needed to be taught a lesson and become self-sufficient was pervasive in England. The English considered the Irish practice of Catholicism as superstitious and a hindrance to their thinking. These prejudices were expressed by the government, in the press, and finally filtered down to the people. The donations from England for Famine relief largely stopped after 1847.

The hunger, starvation and disease could have been vastly reduced. England had the solutions and the means at their disposal.

Thomas Cahill, writer and scholar, wrote it very simply for *Irish Central*: "None of this had to happen."[13]

## Population Loss

Ireland's population was decimated during the Famine, which drove as many as 1.25 million people out of Ireland through emigration. After the Famine, another million emigrated. In all, between 1845 and 1855, 2,250,000 Irish left the country.[14] In that decade, with death at a million added to emigration, 3,250,000 had disappeared, close to the equivalent of the cities of Chicago and New Orleans combined.[15]

After the Famine, the 1851 Census came in at 6,552,115.[16] It is estimated that had the Famine not occurred, the 1851 population would have been over 9,000,000. Instead, the population continued falling. The Famine triggered an avalanche of emigration that would not dissipate until well into the 20th century. The losses came mainly from the rural population.[17] Six million Irish emigrated between the decade of the Famine and 1901. This mass exodus left the population at 4,400,000 at the turn of the century. Literally half of the population from 1841 was gone in sixty years.[18]

John Casey and family's home Catholic parish of Fairymount suffered a loss of 30.5% of its population during the Famine. Almost one of every three people in their parish had disappeared—starved, died of disease, or emigrated. County Roscommon had the largest percentage Famine population loss of all counties in Ireland. The 1841 population of 253,589 compared to 1851 at 173,436, shows a loss of 32%. The county sustained further drastic losses, and by 2002, population stood at 53,803. The numbers then showed an increase to 64,544 by 2016. County Roscommon has never recovered, with a 75% loss in population by 2016.[19] Susan Campbell Bartoletti, author of *Black Potatoes*, put it most pertinently: "Exact numbers will never be known, since so many people disappeared without a trace."[20]

## POST FAMINE OUTCOMES

The vast majority of the 1850 potato crop came in blight-free.[21] The Famine was winding down, but its effects on Ireland and the world would be permanent. The effect of the Famine was so severe that emigration became natural and customary. Today, "70 million people around the world can claim Irish ancestry."[22]

After the Famine the continued decrease in population was multi-faceted. The Penal Law custom of dividing plots between all the children had changed to a custom of inheritance of the oldest son.[23] Landlords no longer wanted subdivision of their land to provide acreage for the other grown children. With no subdivision, no longer could a young couple set up with their own parcel of land and a small cabin. The practice of giving land for a dowry declined.[24] That left the remaining siblings with no land and no work. Many were compelled to choose emigration.

The Catholic population turned to the Church for comfort, many with a strict observance of Church doctrine. Instead of marrying, thousands entered the religious life as priests and nuns.[25] The Irish had a long history of marrying young and having many children.[26] This declined sharply after the Famine. The inheriting son would remain with the land and not marry until he actually inherited it. The strong desire to remain and protect the land had remained with the next generation. Some did not marry at all, because they were older by the time their parents died. There were also fewer choices of mates due to the loss of population. The single life became common and not an oddity.[27] After the Famine, the average age for women marrying was twenty-six and for men it was thirty.[28] The state of marriage changed so dramatically that by 1911, only 39% of women between the ages of 15 and 45 were married.[29] Delayed marriage resulted in fewer children and emigration outpaced the birth rate.

Emigration became a culture of its own. It was expected. Parents raised their children and lost most of them to emigration. Communication with America caused much excitement with the young people and a strong desire to emigrate. They would join friends and extended family in established Irish communities in America.[30]

The steamship for emigration became more prominent in the latter 1860s, with a faster crossing than the sailing ship. Fares for crossing were dropping in the latter part of the 19th century. Many fares were prepaid in New York by friends or family members. No longer did leaving for America mean it was forever.[31]

In addition, the years 1859-1864 brought an agricultural depression to Ireland. Extreme precipitation reached almost fifty inches. Water stood in the fields and caused crops to fail. There was little fodder produced for the farm animals including cattle, sheep and pigs. There were more animals, stemming from a trend to move land from tillage to pasture. Farmers began to sell animals, due to the lack of fodder, creating a glut in the market, and prices fell. The cash crops of grain failed. The entire rural population was affected. Laborers had no work and farmers lost their income from their cash crops. Landlords suffered from rents not being paid.

Evictions increased by 65% from 1861-1864 compared to the four years prior. Many laborers and farmers gave up and emigrated.[32]

The John Casey farm would have been affected by the agricultural depression. It could have been cause for the family to emigrate circa 1862. John Casey had three boys of age to become soldiers. Conscriptions into the Union Army in New York were beginning. The Civil War was common knowledge in Ireland. That said, the motive to emigrate must have been compelling.[33]

After the Famine the Irish shared a common bond of hatred toward England.[34] For those who experienced the Famine first-hand, the scars on their psyche would be permanent, especially in the south and west, where the death, disease and upheaval of the population was likely similar to a war zone. The rural Irish endured it for five years. What we have today termed Post Traumatic Stress Disorder was likely prevalent with many survivors. There was no help. Mental illness in the 19th century was considered shameful and victims were many times just institutionalized. Alcoholism became a huge problem in the decades after the Famine.[35] It became the vehicle for easing pain and for many, a slow path to the grave.

The Union between Ireland and England was so damaged, it was essentially over, although it took seventy years to finally end it with Irish independence. In 1997, British Prime Minister Tony Blair issued a statement to the Irish people acknowledging England's failure during the Famine:

> The Famine was a defining event in the history of Ireland and Britain. It has left deep scars. That one million people should have died in what was then part of the richest and most powerful nation in the world is something that still causes pain as

> we reflect on it today. Those who governed in London at the time failed their people, standing by while a crop failure turned into a massive human tragedy.[36]

This gesture, although long overdue, was well received in Ireland. It offered some solace to those not only in Ireland, but around the world whose ancestors had withstood the dreadful years of the Famine. We must not forget the million who died whose descendants never were. After the Famine, the Irish land scheme also changed. In 1841, before the Famine, 45 percent of Irish farms were less than five acres and only 19% were greater than fifteen acres. This trend reversed itself drastically. By 1851, farms under five acres were reduced to 15% and those over 15 acres increased to 51%.[37] Gone were most of the farms under three acres. Population loss had centered around the land laborers and the cottiers who held that size of acreage. Many of the farms were consolidated and became larger.

The Encumbered Estates Act of 1848 dictated the disposal of properties that were overburdened by debt. The Landed Estates Court auctioned the properties and paid the creditors. Between 1849 and 1857, five million acres of land changed hands. This amounted to about one fourth of all farmland in Ireland. Many of the new owners were land speculators from England who routinely raised rents. The suffering continued when many tenants were evicted by their landlord, who could turn a higher profit by converting the farms to pasture and raising livestock. This in turn displaced many farmers, which contributed to a high unemployment rate in the country.[38] The agricultural economy seemed to have gone full circle. The landowners, many from England, were building their wealth again, and there was still great poverty in Ireland.

John Casey's rented farm and all of Carrowgarve was sold by the Landed Estates Court in 1860. Prior to the sale, John and family had held sixteen acres as of 1857. This placed him at the top of the small farmer group. It is not known, however, if any of this acreage was acquired after the Famine when land consolidated due to the absence of many cottiers and emigrants. The sixteen acres would accommodate a potato plot and garden, space for farm animals and several acres for cash crops like wheat, oats or barley. Like most, it is likely that his grain crops were used to pay rent and hopefully something in reserve, remembering, however, that rents were 80 to 100 percent higher than in England. The effects on his family from the Famine, of course, are unknown, but as mentioned, the loss of population in Fairymount Parish was over 30%. Even considering deducting those who emigrated during the Famine, death was still all around them.

Did the Casey family have enough food? Were they able to help feed the hungry? Even if they had food, the fever and dysentery played no favorites. How was it for them with their extended family, neighbors and friends? The Irish were known for their hospitality and sharing with friends and neighbors. Did they still interact or did they stay isolated because of the possibility of fever? Could John and the boys have been part of the Tibohine funeral train where a knock on the door meant it was your turn to transport a body to the next farm on the way to the cemetery? Were wife and mother Ellen and daughter Mary victims of the Famine? There are many questions that can never be answered in this life. But it is likely that the Famine affected their family in a profound way, just like any other family in Tibohine.

By 1851, the Famine was over. The survivors had lost family and friends and saw the effects of starvation and fever causing death. The Irish witnessed bodies on the road, entire families dead in their cabins, shallow graves and mass graves. Those pictures in one's mind do not disappear.

The Famine changed the identity of Ireland. A majority of the poor Irish laborers and cottiers had been driven to America or to their graves. Many of the Irish were robbed of their pride and dignity, traits that they held in such high esteem.

The intent of this writing along with the attending historical background is that we, the Irish descendants, view these people not as mere names on paper, but real living and breathing persons who had real emotions like all of us. They are a part of us. They experienced happiness, sadness, grief, and fear, yet they were determined and tenacious and full of hope. Without them, we would not be who we are or where we are. If John Casey was a land owner, would he have left Ireland to come halfway across the world in search of a better life? Maybe not. These people had courage and a sense of adventure. They left family in Ireland, knowing they would never see them again. They were driven to build a better life in a place they knew very little about. They were bold enough to overcome the fear of the unknown and take that next step. It is never too late. John Casey was 64 years old when he ventured across the ocean to start a new life. For that boldness, and with hard work, they were rewarded with a life that is likely one they could never have had in Ireland.

Finally, we must restate the questions from the beginning. Why didn't the Casey family own their land? Why did they emigrate? The ultimate answer is that they were part of a group that was oppressed for centuries by the English government. By the time John Casey was born, given the Irish land scheme, there was very little hope that he would ever own any land. Why did they emigrate? Living in Ireland was at an impasse. There was not much hope that their station in life would be anything more in their future. They survived by a piece of paper, a lease that was renewable or not every year. They lived on the land only at the whim of the landlord.

For John Casey in particular, his rented land was sold at auction at the Court in Dublin on November 20, 1860. It is likely not coincidence that the family left for America not long after. The new landlord may have desired to convert the land to grazing and operate it himself. Or he might not have been a man of scruples and demanded a steep rent. Maybe it was the wet years and Irish depression of the early 1860s. Maybe John Casey's boys convinced him there was a better life in America and they took the path that two million Irish before them had taken. Whatever the reason, to leave Ireland, their kin and friends, it had to be a momentous decision. It was their homeland and only the unknown lay ahead.

Hopefully, they had an "American Wake," for one last night of Irish merriment. When they stepped on that ship, did they look back with relief or sorrow at leaving their dearest Ireland? Only John and sons Patrick, James and Michael would set off to America. Conjecture would tell us they were leaving three family members behind. Mother Ellen, eldest infant son Patrick, and daughter Mary would remain with the soil of Ireland. It would not be productive for them to dwell on the past, but rather to focus on their future life in America. Perhaps we have also answered the question why they did not talk to their descendants about their days in Ireland. They had likely seen and perhaps experienced an inordinate amount of poverty and suffering. And remember, it was an Irish trait to merely stay silent about awkward and uncomfortable subjects. All of us need to ingest this, to admire them and realize that we are capable of the same determination and resolve as our ancestors. When times are difficult, we must remember them and find the fortitude to summon the same qualities that were the fiber of their being, the courage and spirit to take on what was in front of them and persevere. This outcome is within reach of all of us.

CHAPTER 13

# WHO IS ACCOUNTABLE?

*Let justice be done tho' the heavens fall.*[1]
—Michael Davitt – Irish Activist

Charles Trevelyan was driven by his role as protector of the Treasury and czar of the economic policy of *laissez faire*. He was, by all accounts, a very intelligent man. In his role he was determined and stubbornly steadfast. His supporters and superiors were Prime Minister Lord John Russell and Sir Charles Wood, Chancellor of the Exchequer. Clearly, their actions and in-actions resulted in the deaths of hundreds of thousands of Catholic Irish. There were no International Courts to determine culpability in that era. By today's standards, we must question whether the English government or individuals within it were guilty of war crimes, genocide or crimes against humanity.

It was a long time ago. Why does it matter? It matters simply because these crimes were perpetrated on our families. We didn't know them, but they were family just the same. They were the ancestors of 70 million Irish descendants around the world. Their story must be told.

Some would argue that it is invalid to consider crimes by today's standards as the same as those of the time of Cromwell or the Famine. There were different standards of war. There was no Geneva Convention. There was no formal code of conduct. Regardless of the codes and standards of those days, there is a common thread that connects us to them. The conviction of the sanctity of life and basic human rights in God's standards must apply then as it does today. Tim Pat Coogan, the gifted Irish writer and historian, concluded the English perpetrated the crime of genocide on the Irish people.[2] He referenced the United Nations Convention on the Prevention and Punishment of the Crime of Genocide.[3] In 1998, the United Nations established the International Criminal Court to investigate and prosecute international crime. The following is another analysis using the Statutes of the International Criminal Court. (Statutes are similar to the United Nations Code)

## Rome Statute of the International Criminal Court

Done at Rome on 17 July, 1998

**Article 8 – *War Crimes***

1. The Court shall have jurisdiction in respect of war crimes in particular when committed as part of a plan or policy or as part of a large-scale commission of such crimes.
2. For the purpose of this Statute, "war crimes" means: (Only pertinent code included)

**b.** Other serious violations of the laws and customs applicable in international armed conflict, within the framework of international law, namely, any of the following acts:

**i.** Intentionally directing attacks against the civilian population as such or against individual civilians not taking part in hostilities;

**vi.** Killing or wounding a combatant who, having laid down his arms or having no longer means of defense, has surrendered at discretion;

**xii.** Declaring that no quarter will be given;[4]

*Distinctly, Oliver Cromwell was guilty of War Crimes in 1649. He killed a significant number of civilians and Catholic clergy by his own admission. He spared no prisoners of war. And, by his own admission, he declared at Drogheda and Wexford that 'no quarter' would be given. (Kill all enemies)*

## ROME STATUTE OF THE INTERNATIONAL CRIMINAL COURT

Done at Rome on 17 July, 1998

**Article 6 – *Genocide*** (Only pertinent code included)

For the Purpose of this Statute, "genocide" means any of the following acts committed with intent to destroy, in whole or in part, a national, ethnical, racial or religious group;

**b.** Causing serious bodily or mental harm to members of the group.

**c.** Deliberately inflicting on the group conditions of life calculated to bring about its physical destruction in whole or in part;[5]

**Item b**. *An offense of which Charles Trevelyan, John Russell, Charles Wood and perhaps even Queen Victoria were most likely guilty. A million Irish died and likely millions more suffered severe mental harm. For many, that harm would lead to an untimely death.*

**Item c**. *Irish Catholics certainly fall within the parameters of the group: 'national, ethnical, racial or religious group.' Furthermore, there was physical destruction of at least a million people.*

## ROME STATUTE OF THE INTERNATIONAL CRIMINAL COURT

**Done at Rome on 17 July, 1998**

**Article 7 – *Crime against Humanity*** (Only pertinent code included)

1. For the purpose of this Statute, "crime against humanity" means any of the following acts when committed as part of a widespread or systematic attack directed against any civilian population, with knowledge of the attack:
   **b.** Extermination
   **h.** Persecution against any identifiable group or collectivity on political, racial, national, ethnic, cultural, religious, gender as defined in paragraph 3, or other grounds that are universally recognized as impermissible under international law, in connection with any act referred in

this paragraph or any crime within the jurisdiction of this court;

For the purpose of paragraph 1:

b. **Extermination:** Includes the intentional infliction of conditions of life, inter alia the deprivation of access to food and medicine, calculated to bring about the destruction of part of the population;
g. **Persecution** means the intentional and severe deprivation of fundamental rights contrary to international law by reason of the identity of the group or collectivity;[6]

inter alia – Latin: "among other things"

***Was it Genocide or Crime against Humanity?***

Group – Irish Catholic – Agricultural Community

**Trevelyan: Deprivation of Food**

- Canceled shipload of grain en route to Ireland – 1846
- Ordered grain depots closed – 1846
- Ordered Public Works shut down – 1846
- Failure to suspend food exports from Ireland – 1846
- Shut down Soup Kitchens after three months – 1847
- Refused to order food from abroad –1847
- Ordered shutdown of food program for 200,000 Irish children – 1848
- Asked for children to be removed from the workhouses – 1849

**Guiding principles: Charles Trevelyan Quote**

- "…that calamity (Famine) must not be too much mitigated…"
- "…If the Irish were starving it must be their own fault… they must take control of their lives and stop abusing British charity"
- "…leave things (Famine) to the operation of natural causes…"
- "…provide minimal relief or the deaths would be an eternal blot on the nation…"
- "…an effective method (Famine) for reducing excess population…"
- "…By acting for the purpose of keeping them at home, we should be defeating our own object. We must not complain of what we really want to obtain (clearing land of excess population)."[7]

**John Russell:**

- "It is better that some should sink, than they should drag others down to sink with them."[8]
- "It must be thoroughly understood that we cannot feed the people (Irish)."[9]
- "Ireland for the next few months must be one of great suffering…agitation for repeal has contrived to destroy all sympathy in this country (England)."

- "Famine and emigration have accomplished a task beyond the reach of legislation or government (depopulation)."
- "...the starving masses in Ireland would emigrate without any such intervention by the English government (government-assisted emigration)."[10]

**Charles Wood:**

- "I am not appalled by your tenantry going (emigrating)... that seems to me to be a necessary part of the process."[11]
- "...do as little as possible (Irish relief 1848)...force them on their own resources."

They used their own words to describe their goal of clearing the land of excess population to make way for more efficient farming methods while avoiding any disruption of Treasury funds. They were fully supportive of emigration, and were essentially pleased with the job the Famine had done toward reaching their goal. Their own words are damning. They had a goal of reducing population and they took the actions necessary to make it happen. At first glance, they are guilty of genocide. Some historians profess it. A formidable argument can be made for it. Twiselton said the workhouse became a process of slowly murdering their inmates. He likened English policy toward Ireland to extermination and resigned because of it. Lord Clarendon feared a mass death of hundreds from starvation casting a black cloud over the actions of the English government. It is their policies that resulted in the deaths of one million Irish and serious mental harm to millions more.

Furthermore, the English had intentionally gone about a 425-year span of persecution of the Irish. It began with Henry VIII's reign. After King Henry's break from Catholicism, Parliament passed the Acts of Supremacy and Treason Acts of 1534. In 1541, Henry declared himself King of Ireland. The subsequent enforcement of the Acts resulted in many clergy and laypeople 'imprisoned, tortured or killed.'[12] The persecution would continue through the dispossession of Catholic land for Presbyterian plantations, the restrictive Penal Laws, Oliver Cromwell and all the way to the Famine. All through this period the Catholic Irish were routinely deprived of basic human rights.

The physical and mental harm caused was so severe and so prolonged that during World War II, although favoring the Allied cause, the Republic of Ireland remained neutral. While being subjected to immense criticism and pressure, a major reason for neutrality was that Ireland did not consider England an ally and could not bring themselves to fight alongside them. The decision was incredibly controversial, but President De Valera's Irish government considered the divisiveness it would cause in the Irish population and the fear that Ireland would not emerge from the war an independent nation, but would again be placed under British rule in its aftermath.[13]

The Potato Famine was merely a continuance of general policy already established. The Irish Catholics had been determined to be "less than human." The Protestant Irish landlords said it about their own nationals. The English newspapers said it. The historians said it. The government was fine with that assessment, because it facilitated a systematic plan of action to demoralize the Catholic Irish and leave them in a position where they had an acre of land on which to grow potatoes. And finally, they endeavored even to take that away by refusing to use Treasury money, shutting down the soup kitchens, public works and depots and forcing them onto the countryside or into the workhouse, while at the same time, denying loans requested by Ireland to bolster Irish relief. England was waging war on 3 million of the Catholic poor as a group. The English governing body viewed the Irish Catholics as lazy, unappreciative, irresponsible and violent. Many of the English believed them to be subhuman, a species of ape. They were called monkeys and swine. Russell and Trevelyan operated behind the scenes at newspapers fostering the negative message to the public.

Then the English went one step further with Providentialism. The English perception was that it was God acting against the Irish with the Famine. Charles Trevelyan said that the Famine must not be 'much mitigated' because it was an act of God. The perpetrators were pleased with the results of the Famine. They transferred their guilt to God. The affliction of the Irish was God's providence and thus, they were not responsible for their own actions and omissions. This thinking is unconscionable. When your own actions and omissions cause grievous harm and death, you simply do not get to blame God. One Catholic Irish descendant, Edward Kennedy said it best about his brother Robert in his eulogy. He "saw a wrong and tried to right it, saw a suffering and tried to heal it, saw a war and tried to stop it."[14] These same principles should have had equal bearing for the likes of Charles Trevelyan, John Russell, Charles Wood, and Oliver Cromwell.

## GENOCIDE OR CRIME AGAINST HUMANITY

There is a strong argument for genocide. It seems there was a target population. The Poor Inquiry Commission identified two and one-half to three million destitute for which there was no solution. Thomas Malthus merely called the need for "a great part of the population swept from the soil." Another economist feared that the Famine in 1848 would only take care of a million. Did Trevelyan and his cohorts form a plan to exterminate? Their actions are conflicting. At times they would refuse to help or even take away relief, and at other times they would reluctantly provide a minimal amount of relief. In most cases, it was too little too late. Trevelyan seemed to particularly victimize children. He stopped the feeding of 200,000 destitute children. He also wanted all the children out of the workhouses. By appearance there was no satisfactory alternate plan for these children. Everything seemed to hinge on the premise that the Irish population must not become accustomed to England's financial support.

With that said, proving the required specific intent in the mindset of the perpetrators given the Rome Statutes code for genocide would be problematic. It would need to be proven that representatives of the English government formed a plan to purposefully cause grievous harm and death in the target group, and then implemented the plan. In other words, did Trevelyan, Russell and Wood construct a plan to use the Famine as a guise in order to kill Irish Catholics? For the specific intent that genocide requires, they had to have the mindset desirous to destroy and kill, generate a plan, and execute it to achieve genocide. The debate regarding genocide and specific intent (dolus specialis) has been belabored for numerous years with many taking the position that proving genocide in court is unrealistic because of specific intent.

Most recently, China's appalling acts perpetrated against Muslims in the northwest region of Xinjiang are under scrutiny. The Trump and Biden administration both agreed that China's actions have risen to the level of genocide, yet the U.S. State Department believes genocide could not be proven in court and the acts were more concurrent with the legal requirements of crimes against humanity.[15] In the case of the Irish Famine, the

United Nations standard for specific intent to prove genocide may be too high a bar to clear.

The more viable choice for a conviction is crime against humanity. This crime is equally as heinous as genocide and specific intent is not necessary. Only simple intent is required to satisfy the requirement for crime against humanity. Intent can be explained legally as follows: "Intent is a mental attitude with which an individual acts, therefore it cannot ordinarily be directly proved but must be inferred from surrounding facts and circumstances. Intent refers only to the state of mind with which the act is done or omitted."[16]

Intent is the concept of taking a particular action and knowing that it will cause harm or death to part or all of a group. Note that the clarification of the intent definition says "*act is done or omitted.*" There is no doubt that it can be *"inferred from surrounding facts and circumstances"* that Trevelyan, Russell and Wood acted or failed to act, knowing that starvation or its aftermath of famine related disease would occur. This would meet the requirements of guilt for the statute of extermination for crime against humanity.

Persecution requires a discriminatory intent. The perpetrators clearly were discriminatory toward the Irish as a group and specifically poor Irish Catholics. The final requirement is that the perpetrator has knowledge of an attack against the civilian population and that he is part of the attack. According to the United Nations, 'attack' can mean simply "any mistreatment of the population." The test under all of the definition is met and would require a guilty verdict. Genocide seems a more lethal and desirous term for these atrocities, but crimes against humanity are just as grievous and deserving of severe punishment.

Were Trevelyan, Russell and Wood guilty of genocide? Many of us would answer a resounding yes, but a conviction of genocide will continue to remain elusive in the courts until the legal requirements for conviction are modified. Those who commit genocide will not admit there was a plan to kill and the plan was then executed. Blame can be shifted from one person or group to the other. Lies are told and accusations of others made. There will be no confessions. Proof beyond a reasonable doubt regarding the mental process of a murderer creating a genocidal plan is tenuous at best. This will continue to be debated until specific intent is changed to general or simple intent for a conviction of genocide. Until then, semantics are not as important as stopping the atrocities.

If John Casey's wife Ellen and daughter Mary died in the Famine, they were victims just like the million other Irish who lost their lives. They were victims, not just of a Famine, but a crime against humanity.

In the end, no one was held accountable. There were no consequences for those who presided over this travesty. Instead, there were accolades. Sir Charles Trevelyan never conveyed any remorse for his management of the Irish Relief.[17] During the height of the Famine, Trevelyan published a book, *The Irish Crisis,* in which he justified his lack of interference with Irish exports. He again put forth his Providential argument that the Famine was God's will in bringing a purposeful natural disaster to reduce the Irish population.[18] Apparently, in his view, he was God's servant in allowing the disaster to unfold.

After the Famine, Charles Trevelyan continued in government service, spending several years in India as the Governor of Madras and later as Finance Minister. In March of 1874, he was granted the title of Baronet, one level above Knighthood. Trevelyan died in London in June of 1886.[19] He was heralded as an outstanding civil servant in England, but a villain who would never be forgotten in Ireland.

John Russell was in and out of public office after the Famine. He served another stint as Prime Minister for a year beginning in 1865. He too was honored with the new title of Earl in 1861. Russell died in May of 1878.[20]

Charles Wood continued his government career in several positions and died in 1885.[21]

Queen Victoria carried on her reign and made her last visit to Ireland in 1900. On the eve of her visit, Maud Gonne, an Irish Revolutionary, dubbed her the Famine Queen. In 2017, British television aired a segment of "Victoria" depicting the devastation of the Irish Famine. Many of the British people were unaware of the magnitude of the Famine and were shocked by it, perhaps because there is little substantive instruction about the Famine in the English school system. Christine Kinealy, noted Irish historian, says, "We know that really she had no interest in Ireland and so to imagine she wanted to do more doesn't really ring true." Furthermore, the Queen had mocked Prime Minister Robert Peel's efforts during the first year of the Famine, saying he must have pleased the Catholics. The reign of the Famine Queen ended with her death in 1901.[22]

As for England's government, there was no change in policy. In 1866, the English colony of India experienced extreme heat and drought. Crops were lost, creating a famine in Orissa, Eastern India. The same English attitudes and policies prevailed. There was no interference with food exports. Cecil Beadon, England's colonial governor in India, said the famine was an act of Providence and "no government could do much to prevent or alleviate it" —the same narrative as Charles Trevelyan spewed twenty years before in Ireland. As Beadon decreed, the famine was not prevented or alleviated and another million people died in Orissa, Eastern India. Four more famines occurred before the turn of the century, killing millions more, all under the British Crown.[23]

CHAPTER 14

# LAND LEAGUE

*As long as Ireland is unfree the only honourable attitude for Irish men, women to have is an attitude of rebellion.*[1]

—Patrick Pearse, Irish Teacher and Activist

After the Famine, John Casey and sons departed Ireland amid the wet years and subsequent depression of 1859-1864. After 1864, conditions in rural Ireland improved until the late 1870s. As in the 1860s, excessive rain again resulted in poor harvests. The specter of the Famine was being raised as many realized food would again be scarce, especially in the west of Ireland. The farmers of the 1870s, in full memory of the Famine, were on guard to prevent anything from threatening their way of life. Crops had failed, prices had fallen, but rents remained the same. No longer in fearful subservience to the landlord, they began to exercise more assertive means to pressure landlords for rent reductions.[2]

James Daly, a newspaperman in County Mayo, was an activist for tenant rights. Daly campaigned for all tenants to have the option to purchase the land they farmed. In February of 1877, he wrote in his newspaper that "the soil is the property of the tiller."[3]

With the crop failures, and farmers becoming agitated with their landlords, Daly saw a crisis developing. In 1879, there were falling agricultural prices, evictions and hunger in the west of Ireland.[4] After threats of eviction began, Daly organized a meeting at Irishtown in County Mayo, on April 20, 1879. Reminiscent of O'Connell's monster meetings for Emancipation, the assembly was attended by as many as ten thousand, and by the end of the day, the landlord who had threatened evictions agreed to reduce rents by 25%. As a result, in August of 1879, the Land League of Mayo was created by Michael Davitt, a former Fenian who grew up in Mayo.[5]

The Fenian movement had begun in the United States in 1858. They promoted total independence from England, through use of violence if necessary. There were Fenian branches in the United States, Ireland, Canada and England. The Catholic Church did not support the Fenian movement because of their advocation of violence. The Fenians made an attempt at insurrection in Ireland in 1867, but it was quickly put down by English troops. The movement did not have enough support.[6]

In October 1879, with the help of Irish American funding, the Irish National Land League was formed in Dublin under the leadership of Davitt and Charles Parnell, a Home Rule Irish member of Parliament. The Home Rule party wanted Ireland to govern itself while remaining in the United Kingdom. Both organizations were founded as activist groups to pursue solutions to the land problem.[7]

Meanwhile, evictions accelerated due to unpaid rents during the land wars. From 1878 to 1886, there were 26,000 evictions, displacing 132,000 people.[8] Agricultural crimes against landlords also ramped up from 863 in 1879 to a peak of 4,439 in 1881.[9] Angry protests and interference with evictions by the National Land League evolved into a need for a heavy military presence.[10] The evictions created a huge disruption in Western Ireland and a massive displacement of its residents.[11]

Parnell traveled to the United States to raise money for the League and the famine in western Ireland. He traveled 16,000 miles carrying the message of tenant rights to sixty cities, in addition to addressing the United States Congress. From 1879-1882, five million dollars was sent for support of the Land League, evictions and famine.[12] By 1881, Parnell was back in Ireland and jailed for advocating a boycott of landlords and agents. While in jail he wrote a manifesto of sorts continuing to urge tenants to stop paying rent. In it, Parnell wrote, "…Do not be wheedled into compromise of any sort by the threat of eviction…they can no more evict a whole nation than they can imprison them."[13] In the meantime, tenants continued to disrupt evictions and harass landlords with threatening letters and intimidation.[14]

The Irish Land League had come to the attention of William Gladstone, prime minister of England. He ordered a commission organized to determine if unpaid rent in Ireland was the inability to pay or a conspiracy dredged up by the Land League. At issue in the land question were the three F's: fixity of tenure, fair rent, and free sale.[15] Fixity referred to tenants reserving the rights for improvements they made to the property. If the tenant left, he would be paid for the improvements. Free sale referred to the tenant's right to purchase the property.

Meanwhile, tenant unrest was on the rise. In 1879, 863 crimes had been reported, increasing to 2,591 in 1880 and peaking in 1881 at 4,439.[16] Much of the unrest was inspired by the Fenians. About one-half of the crimes were maiming or killing cattle, damage to property, and setting fires, and the rest were related to the aforementioned threatening letters to landlords. The crimes spurred the English Parliament to action, passing a Land Act in 1881. A supplement to an Act from 1870, The Land Act approved the three F's. This allowed for tenants to have rights to improvements they made and it called for a commission to determine a fair rent for a property that would remain in effect for fifteen years. Furthermore, tenants who were not in arrears could purchase the property, with the Treasury loaning eighty per cent of the cost for a period of thirty-five years. However, tenants with arrears were excluded.[17]

Unfortunately, most tenants did not have the twenty percent down payment or they were in arrears and were ineligible. Only 877 tenants were able to purchase their property under the Land Act.[18] Probably the most important result of the Land Act was that tenants were able to affect change that was favorable to them and not the landlord. It was progress made to improve the status of the tenant farmers. However, tenants still raged that the Act hadn't gone far enough. It excluded leaseholders from rent reductions and did nothing to help about 100,000 smallholders with unpaid rent. Consequently, in 1882, Parliament passed an amendment to the 1881 Act that canceled one half the rental debt for an approximate £2,000,000, but did not include the leaseholders. Further legislation in 1887 addressed the leaseholders and lowered rents by an additional 19%.[19] The Land League's influence and the subsequent Acts of Parliament paved the way for eventual land ownership by smallholders, something prior generations could have only dreamed about.

The waning years of the 19$^{th}$ century spelled an erosion of Irish culture. From 1881 to 1901, Irish speakers declined by 30%. Moreover, some of the old customs were disappearing. Children grew up fully aware they would go to America. It was considered a duty to the family. Irish mothers feared that with the children gone, they and their husbands would die alone. Nevertheless, children were encouraged to emigrate. It was one less person to support and there was the promise of the American Letter. Emigration created a conflict of fear and yearning with the parents of the young emigrants. These conflicts, along with continued cultural change, created an overall sense of demoralization in the rural countryside.[20]

# PART TWO

## OUT OF IRELAND

CHAPTER 15

# WHY DID THEY LEAVE?

*There were probably as many reasons for coming to America as there were people who came. It was a highly individual decision.*[1]
—John F. Kennedy, "A Nation of Immigrants"

## TYRANNY AND PERSECUTION

At the beginning of the 19th century, Ireland's population was just over 5 million. By 1841, the population had grown to over 8 million. More than a century later, in 1921, it had fallen to about 4.3 million. During that same time frame, over 8 million people had emigrated,[2] making this Irish exodus one of the most prolific in modern history. The number of emigrants is likely higher, because England and Ireland were the same Union, and no records were kept for Irish migrating to England. There were, however 400,000 Irish living in England in 1841.[3] The leading destinations for the emigrants were the United States, Canada, England, Australia and New Zealand.[4] The numbers beg the question of why this massive human movement took place. The poor Irish Catholics who lived off the land were a proud people. They were proud of their country, their religion, and their countrymen—so much so that some of the poor Irish preferred death in Ireland rather than emigration. For many more, emigration was a difficult decision. The only translation for emigration in the Irish language is *exile*.[5] By definition, to be exiled is to be forced to live away from one's native country. Then why did this massive expatriation occur?

The tyranny and persecution of the Irish by England was a compelling reason for any Irish Catholic to emigrate. Hatred can span generations. This all-consuming emotion was spawned by the evil perpetrated on the Irish by England for centuries. The Irish didn't have to rely on anecdotes from their ancestors for their hatred. England was still committing plenty of egregious acts against the Catholic Irish in the 19th century. The Irish Catholics were united in their hatred of England and their Protestant landlords. They desired to live in a country with freedom and fair treatment. They longed for a better life, free of suppression and maltreatment.

Irish emigration was fostered by English tyranny. As you remember from Part 1, England's dominance over Ireland had spanned at least three centuries. The Ulster plantation was seared into the memory of the Catholic Irish when over 500,000 acres of their land was confiscated by the English and became a plantation for transplanted Scottish Presbyterians and English. The Irish Catholic occupiers were enraged when ordered to leave no later than May 1, 1609. Although many stayed to work the land for the Scots,[6] there was an underlying anger among the displaced Irish that reached a boiling point and erupted into violence over thirty years later in 1641. The Irish Catholics mounted an attack on the Protestant plantation in Ulster to take back their land. There was much loss of life, and the uprising was eventually put down by English soldiers. After this rebellion in Ulster, the

English government was determined that the Irish must suffer consequences.

Oliver Cromwell brought his Model Army to Ireland to exact revenge. He began by slaughtering soldiers and innocent civilians in both Drogheda and Wexford before moving on to conquer other Irish cities. In the aftermath, Irish Catholics were dispossessed of two and one-half million acres of land and banished to the western province of Connaught. Those who had not vacated by May 1, 1654 would be hanged. A portion of the land was given to soldiers who had not been paid for months, to financial sponsors of the Model Army and to other English.[7] The English were well on their way to totally reversing land ownership in Ireland. Eventually, after further confiscations, Catholics fell from 95% ownership of Ireland to only 5%.

Then came the draconian Penal Laws enacted by the Protestant Irish and English beginning in 1695. This series of laws was an overt persecution of the Catholic religion and a clear violation of human rights. The Catholic hierarchy was expelled from Ireland and priests went into hiding. Priests said Mass at moving secret meeting places to avoid detection. Catholics could not vote, hold office, or own land along with other stipulations. The Penal laws would not be fully repealed until the 1830s.

One facet of the Penal Laws was that an Irish Catholic could not hold public office. All members of Ireland's Parliament were Protestant. At that time, about 80% of Ireland's population was Catholic, yet had no representation in government. At the end of the 18th century, England's Prime Minister saw benefit for England in having Ireland as part of a Union. He duped and bribed the Irish Parliament into passing a resolution to dissolve itself and become a part of a new Union with England. In turn, Ireland would receive some Irish Protestant representation in the English

Parliament at London. This representation of 100 Irish Parliament members out of 650 seats did not wield any real power. The Irish Protestant Parliament had made a huge error in judgment.

The end result was Irish crops, cattle and grain fed England and the money received for those goods paid the rent and little more to mostly Protestant landlords. Between one third and one half were absentee landlords, for the most part living in England. The food export was to England and the rent went to the absentee landlord to bolster their economy. The English had the food and the cash, and the Irish had nothing. The English savored a system that literally sucked the lifeblood from Ireland.

Centuries of oppression had taken their toll on the Irish Catholic rural population. They had essentially been beaten into submission. It is likely that they not only felt a diminished identity, but had no self-esteem. Many probably had severe depression and could not imagine that any better life could happen for them. They were victims of crimes against humanity. All of this turmoil and persecution gave the Irish ample reason to leave Ireland in search of a fair and free society.

## ECONOMICS AND RELIGION

Economics was another powerful reason to emigrate. Could the rural Catholic Irish adequately provide for a family off the land? There were higher end small farmers and middling farmers who perhaps earned enough income to have savings over time and, along with selling their animals, could pay the fares to emigrate.

At the lower end of the spectrum, however, there were those, especially during the Famine, who did not have the means to emigrate. The fortunate ones got prepaid tickets from family in America or may have received passage through a landlord. The rest had to find a way to survive the starvation and disease of the Famine. Most considered the poorhouse untenable. They were disease–ridden, with barely enough food to survive and sometimes no food. Families were split apart inside the poorhouse, and there were harsh punishments for any rules broken. Charles Trevelyan had designed the poorhouse to be as virulent and demeaning as possible so only the completely destitute were there. Many Irish chose to die in their cabins instead of the poorhouse. For Charles Trevelyan that was a cost saving measure.

Landless laborers, cottiers, and small landholders of less than eight acres were prime candidates for emigration, but most did not have the fare. They lived in abject poverty. It was estimated that a family needed from five to eight acres to merely live at a subsistence level. These three groups, totaling approximately three million poor Irish, comprised close to three fourths of the Irish rural population. A multitude of cottiers held only one to two acres and many of the laborers had no land at all. They worked for potatoes. The laborers typically had work in Ireland for about 200 days of the year. The rest of the year, they would walk the roads looking for work, while their families either begged or remained in their cabins in the throes of starvation. This was not due to crop failure, but a regular life for a laborer's family. Other laborers used a few pence to travel to England and work in the harvest or any other work they might find.[8] They would return to Ireland, hoping their family had survived their absence.

Imagine a poor laborer during the Famine, walking the roads, starving, looking for work or anything to eat. The English had shut down the public works, so there was no work. He needed food, but the English shut down the soup kitchens. His mind wandered. He had ancestors who were landowners. He could have had his own land, if not for the English. He would have been growing wheat or barley and cattle. He and his family could have survived the Famine. The English put him on that road half-starved and the Irishman knew it. The English then looked upon him and others as being the Irish problem. They believed the peasants who could not provide for themselves needed to emigrate or be evicted and let the Famine have its way with them. He knew that it was not if he died, it was when he died. He thought of his family and not being able to provide them food. He was so tired. If he could lie down on the side of the road just a short while, he could gather his strength. The ground was nice and cool. He wished they could have found a way to go to America. He thought of America and how wonderful it would have been. It felt so good to rest. He was so tired. He decided to close his eyes for a minute. He felt at peace, felt no pain, and he drifted away. The English weren't there with food, nor did they have a coffin for him. He was there on the side of the road for the starving dogs to ravage. The English government was nowhere to be found.

Thus, the plight of three fourths of rural Ireland—there was no hope or chance for life to get better. Even emigration was not an option, because there was no money for the fare. Yet somehow these extremely poor people retained their sense of humor and were content with their life as it was. Their view was that their circumstances were God's will and they must be satisfied with their station in life, even with the knowledge that it would not improve.

The destitute of rural Ireland had very few possessions. Their beds were made of straw and they perhaps had a table and a few cooking utensils. The 1841 census showed that there were 500,000 one-room cabins with dirt floors and no windows or chimney. Shoes were a luxury and most were barefoot and dressed in literal rags that may or may not have covered their body modestly. Pigs or other farm animals lived with the family in the cabin. Some landless laborers had no potato garden and relied on their pay in potatoes for their work. The cottiers and some of the laborers had small plots for a potato patch, raising the food that constituted their entire diet. In the early 19th century, their annual income was less than five pounds.[9] Many who wanted out of Ireland did not make it.

With the ever-increasing population, available land was becoming more and more scarce, resulting in exorbitant rents. Smaller holdings were the highest cost per acre. At the time of the Famine, a small acreage of conacre was as much as ten pounds per acre.[10] As can be imagined, failure of the potato crop had a devastating effect on these groups. For laborers, there was no work with the potato crop gone. Laborers and cottiers were almost immediately out of food. Failures of the potato crop occurred not only during the Famine, but crops failed in a number of years throughout the century, creating an immediate crisis for these two groups each time. These economic crises made these two groups the primary candidates for emigration. For many, it took the misery and suffering of the Famine to realize they had to flee Ireland.

For many others, religion was a major reason to leave Ireland. Not only did the Irish Catholics hate the English, they had a festering resentment toward all Protestants. The Catholic farmers in the North hated the Protestants of Ulster for taking their land. They hated a system that demanded subservience. The English were Protestant, along with their landlords and their members of Parliament. Until the 1830s the Irish Catholics were required to pay a tithe to the Protestant Church of Ireland. In addition, the Protestants were very aggressive in their efforts to convert Catholics, so much so that there were instances in the Famine where an Irish Catholic could get soup only if he denounced Catholicism and made a commitment to join the Protestant church.

## LEAVING THE LAND

Bitterness toward Protestants also spilled over to the land. By the mid-nineteenth century, 10,000 Protestant families literally owned Ireland.[11] Irish Catholics had at one time owned 95% of Ireland before the English gradually seized the land for Protestant ownership.

Some farmers rented their land directly from the landlord and others rented from a middleman. Both were inclined to take full advantage of the land scarcity and charge extortionate rent. The majority of both groups was Protestant. Many landlords were not sympathetic toward any reason for late rent. Eviction was a viable course to pursue, because it freed up land for the many who were waiting. The landlord could immediately have a new tenant at the same or even a higher rate.

The landlords, middlemen and even many of the tenants saw subdivision as a means of making even more money. A large parcel could be rented and subdivided, charging higher rents for the smaller plots. That system was not an exclusive method for the landlord and the middleman. Even the tenants would subdivide to provide a dowry for a daughter or a plot of land as an inheritance. Some rented to laborers or cottiers and the tenant became a landlord. The result was smaller and smaller subdivisions, so much so that it would reach a point that the parcels would not provide food for the family. For example, Trinity College in Dublin owned a vast estate. In 1843, there were 12,529 tenants. Only one percent of the tenants rented from Trinity College directly. Forty-five percent were subtenants and fifty-two percent were subtenants of subtenants.[12] In 1840, one half of all Irish farms were at subsistence level due to subdivision.[13]

By 1843, the land system in Ireland was breaking down. There were too many people for too few acres of land. Those with foresight saw emigration as the viable solution and left Ireland. Sadly, for many who remained, the future held much suffering, starvation, disease and death. The English were in favor of emigration. Many who died could have emigrated if the government had chosen to subsidize it.

Eviction had always been dreaded by the rural poor throughout the century. During the Famine it became a way of life. The Poor Law Act passed by Parliament in 1847 addressed relief for the destitute outside the workhouse. To qualify, they must hold less than a quarter acre of land, even if they had to give back land to the landlord. This Act also made landlords solely responsible for poor rates for all holdings valued at £4 or less. This legislation added more fuel to the already accelerated rate of evictions by providing a further incentive for landlords to evict their smallholders and avoid the poor tax. It is estimated that between 1846 and 1855, as many as half a million Irish were evicted.[14] Sympathy and compassion were not a part of the eviction process. The authorities came and demanded the tenants vacate immediately. If they did not comply, the authorities began to tear the roof off the house and ram the door. When they gained access, the family would be dragged, if necessary, out of their home. If they were wearing night clothes and it was December, so be it. They were then ordered off the property. The family was left to fend for themselves on the countryside. Many survived by building a shelter in a ditch. They would look for work that wasn't available and food, which many times was weeds and nettles. Some would find a way to emigrate, but others would die of exposure or starvation. In the meantime, follow-up visits at the cabin were made to ensure they did not sneak back into the skeleton of a house that was left.

The predominant question was whether the rural Irish could provide for a family off the land. If the land could not provide, like it or not, the option was emigration. Three million of the rural population were not adequately supported by the land. About half of all farms in Ireland were under five acres.[15] They were at a subsistence level even in the best agricultural years,[16] and the Famine loomed on the horizon.

As much as the landlord tried to avoid it, there would still be tenants from his estate for which he had to pay support. You will remember from Part One, Landlord Denis Mahon of County Roscommon was a master of eviction. He owned 11,000 acres and had evicted 3,000 Irish. He also crafted a cost savings plan for emigration. The Poor Law passed by Parliament required landlords to pay the cost for each inmate that came from his property. The annual cost for an inmate was $36, with the fare to Canada at $18.[17] He could send them off to Canada at half the cost of the poorhouse. A total of 800 of Mahon's tenants emigrated. It was a disastrous trip. Two hundred sixty died at sea and another 200 were deathly sick with fever on arrival. Mahon was subsequently shot to death while riding in his carriage. Five other landlords were shot in the days following, which led to other landlords fleeing the country.[18] The practice of emigration by paying fares for the destitute continued with additional landlords who provided passage to others who could not afford it.

## DEPRESSION AND EMIGRATION

From the early part of the century up to the Famine, between 800,000 to 1,000,000 Irish emigrated to North America.[19] This occurred in ebbs and flows based on the economic conditions in Ireland and America. Immigrants' letters to Ireland would relay the status of the economy and available jobs. Emigration from Ireland would then generally curtail until news from America was better. It was a judgment call for the Irish to decide where they would be better off.

Ireland experienced times of economic depression during the century, which essentially forced many Irish to leave the country regardless of conditions in America. Ireland's economy had experienced good times for several decades until the end of the Napoleonic War in about 1815. Napoleon of France had ventured out to expand on his territory between 1800 and 1815 and finally was defeated at Waterloo in Belgium. England was one of the allies that fought against France. The army's demand for food and clothing and other goods kept the Irish economy strong.

After 1815, the demand fell and the Irish economy slipped into a deep depression.[20] Agriculture was hard hit when the demand for food fell after the war. Between 1818 and 1833 grain prices fell 50%.[21] Farmers saw their income drastically reduced and at the same time, their rent and expenses the same or greater. This pushed many farmers from a profitable farming operation literally into poverty. Evictions jumped drastically. Then came extreme cold and wet weather that ruined the potato and grain crops of 1816-1819. The crops of 1825-1829 saw both drought and inordinate rain damage. In the early 1830s, there was an outbreak of cholera in the poor classes, followed in 1832 by famine in parts of the country. At that point, the potato crop had failed eight out of ten years either regionally or nationally. Finally, in the winter of 1838 came 'the night of the big wind.' Inclement cold and snow was so bitter it actually froze livestock in the fields. As if that were not enough, the potato crop failed again three more times between 1841 and 1844. Emigration was a way out, to put the plight of Ireland behind them. In a sense, they were forced out, becoming exiles.[22]

To further exacerbate these events, England, also in economic strain, convinced their clothing manufacturers to ship a deluge of low-priced clothing to Ireland. This crippled the Irish wool and cotton manufacturers and struck a death blow to the industry. Irish manufacture of woolen cloth fell 85%, purposely destroyed by the English. England also decimated the linen industry in Ireland with cheap-priced goods. Losses in wool and linen struck a severe blow to Ireland's economy. Motivated by lower prices, the Irish wore English clothes rather than clothes made in their own country.[23]

Another serious depression occurred between 1859 and 1864. Excessive rains were always a concern for agriculture in Ireland. On the Atlantic coast it might rain 250 days out of the year. In the western mountains, annual totals were as high as 60 to 70 inches.[24]

Fields and pastures were completely under water, ruining crops and grass. Cattle were sold en masse because there was no feed for them. The flood of livestock on the market destroyed the price, putting farmers in an ever-worsening position. *The Irish Farmer's Gazette* wrote that farmers were in a worse economic position than during the Famine. One economist estimated that agriculture lost £26 million during this depression, which was equal to about two years' rent for all the agricultural land in Ireland.[25]

Evictions soared, increasing by 65%.[26] Other farmers realized they would never recover and merely gave up. It was during this time that John Casey and family emigrated to the United States, likely victims of the depression.

The depression and the other dire events of the prior three decades spurred emigration to new record levels. Fares were high to the United States, so the majority of passage was to British Canada. However, some of the ships failed to moor in Canada and continued sailing to the United States. In 1819, some did settle in upper Canada to take advantage of the settlement program offer of 50 acres of free land. From 1823 to 1825, the English government provided land grants and paid fares for 2500 passengers to help populate upper Canada.[27]

A large number of the emigrants early in the century were Ulster Protestants. Tired of enduring ever increasing rents and other economic pressures, they desired a feeling of independence and land ownership, taking them to America. These Ulster Protestants were not poor laborers, but successful farmers, raising alarm with some landlords regarding the quality of the tenants being lost. However, Protestant emigration began to wane, and by the early 1830s, Catholic emigrants surpassed Protestants.[28]

By 1831, United States fares were coming somewhat closer to the high end of Canadian fares. A fare to Canada was £1.5 and passage was £2 to £3 to the United States. Passengers to the United States increased, as it was the preferred destination by the Irish. Protestants from Ulster continued to emigrate in the 1830s, but they were overtaken by Catholics during the decade and Catholics remained the dominant immigration group the rest of the century. In addition, between 1830 and 1835, 200,000 Irish migrated to England. Many did not have the money for America, but eventually some did immigrate after time in England to save for the fare.[29] The last years before the Famine, immigration to America continued to grow, with an increasing number of Catholics from the west and south. Emigration in Ireland was becoming a way of life.[30]

There were still concerns that Ireland's best were leaving. One Irish official remarked that "the young, the enterprising, and the industrious...leave us whilst the old, the impotent, the idle and indolent" stay. The most ambitious Irish were heeding the call of a New World for that sense of independence to own their land and escape the burden of taxes and a tyrant landlord.[31]

There were also other reasons to emigrate. As competition for land accelerated along with the population, rents for land continued a steep ascent. Tillage land was replaced with pasture for livestock, which took less labor and eliminated many tenants and laborers.[32]

## FATHER HORE'S DREAM

Land ownership and farming in America was a common interest for many. One unique story occurred in Wexford in 1850. A Catholic priest named Father Hore took over a parish about 30 miles south of Dublin. During the Famine, Father Hore's parishioners had endured so much suffering he felt their best alternative was to immigrate to America. He discussed his ideas with some parishioners, then gathered the entire congregation of 2,000 together to present his plan. Four hundred families totaling 1,200 people agreed to emigrate with him. Father Hore had served in the United States and was somewhat familiar with the land. His plan was to buy land in Arkansas and settle the community there. He told the parishioners it was fertile land in a good climate. They would sail to New Orleans and travel up the Mississippi River. The parishioners gathered £16,000 to buy land. The 1200 immigrants traveled to America on three different ships. Father Hore's ship arrived first, in forty days, and the second ship arrived seventeen days later. The third ship had blown off course and didn't arrive for another three weeks. After reaching Arkansas, they discovered the land that Father Hore had hoped for had sold. Some parishioners decided to remain in Arkansas, but Father Hore forged ahead to find other land to purchase. He arrived in Dubuque, Iowa, but traveled even farther north near the Wisconsin border. It was there he found suitable land to purchase. He bought 2,157 acres at $1.25 per acre with their remaining pool of money. Many had left the party along the way, settling in St. Louis and Arkansas. Only 18 families comprised of a hundred men, women, and children arrived with him in Iowa. They settled on the land, building their homes and even a church. They named their town Wexford, after their home in Ireland. They had traveled six thousand miles to reach their new home. The Catholic country parish still exists, with about one hundred members.[33]

## Family and Social Emigration

Many also emigrated for family and social reasons. After the Famine, subdivision of land was curtailed, largely because the landlord forbade it. With that, the Irish custom of inheritance was disrupted. No longer could heirs have their own little plot of land and a potato patch. This led to the granting of inheritance to only one son. Many routinely picked the oldest son, but not all. Some fathers bypassed the oldest in favor of a younger son.

The family could only afford one daughter to have a dowry. The other children or young adults found themselves without land or employment. Typically, the sons' choices were a landless laborer or the religious life. The girls had the options of the religious life or marry in Ireland. Most chose emigration.

Also, after the Famine, there was a redirection of the Irish to place the Church at the forefront spiritually and for their decision making. Some sons chose the priesthood and daughters entered the convent. However, emigration seemed to be the more likely choice. Some gladly emigrated while others looked on it only as an escape and becoming an exile. Some of the girls emigrated specifically to find an American husband.

Many Irish parents fully promoted emigration. Relatives in America encouraged them and sometimes sent prepaid tickets. If children emigrated, there was less expense for the family, plus they looked forward to the "American letter" stuffed with cash. Some were so brazen that the cash was their only interest. One farmer received a letter without money, but with a picture of the adult child who sent it. The father commented that he knew what they looked like and that he was more interested in some pictures of Abraham Lincoln.

Regardless, leaving for America was a sorrowful event. The young emigrants leaving were excited but also fraught with guilt for leaving family.[34] Families were breaking apart, knowing they would never see each other again. The American Wake went from dusk to dawn, with much laughing, crying, drinking and dancing, but there was that underlying sadness, knowing this was their last night together. As the Wake broke up, the family would accompany the emigrants on their way as far as was practical. They said their tearful goodbyes, and the emigrants trudged on. It seemed to many that, especially during the Famine, there was a funeral or a farewell to emigrants every day.[35]

CHAPTER 16

# PREPARATION

*When anyone asks me about the Irish character, I say look at the trees. Maimed, stark and misshapen, but ferociously tenacious.*[1]

—Edna O'Brien, Irish Writer

The emigrants got to their port of departure in a number of ways. Some walked; others had a horse cart, or sometimes a donkey. Typically, they traveled to reach a stagecoach line or a train. They were then carried to one of the Irish ports for departure. Some ships sailed to America from Irish ports such as Cork, but Liverpool, England was also popular with the Irish.[2]

The least expensive fare from Ireland across the Irish Sea to Liverpool was less than ten pence for a deck fare. A deck fare meant just that. Passengers stayed on the deck in good weather or in rain and storm. There was no shelter. Joining the deck passengers were any animals taking the trip and all the luggage. As many as 1,400 people might be packed together on the deck with literally no individual space. For the deck passengers, it could be a harrowing trip. In a storm or rough seas, passengers literally had to hold on to each other to keep from going overboard. Most of the emigrants were from rural areas and had no experience with sailing. They were barely underway when sea sickness spread. Given the crowding of the passengers, vomit might end up on anyone. If there were rough waters, not only would the sea sickness be worse, but cold sea water drenched the passengers on deck. The sea water slopped around the deck with vomit and animal excretions. Passage to Liverpool took anywhere from fourteen to thirty hours. Depending on the number of passengers, it could mean standing the entire trip. Some were so exhausted they required assistance to leave the ship.[3] The voyage across the Irish Sea foreshadowed things to come.

Tens of thousands made the voyage to Liverpool. It was inexpensive, and usually the poorest could manage the small fare. For those poor, however, the journey was ending because they did not have the means to buy tickets for America. The intention was to stay in Liverpool temporarily to earn the money it would take for fares to America. This did happen for some, but many more were, like it or not, anchored in the slums of Liverpool. Living in the city slums exposed the rural Irish to disease, as well as violence and robbery.[4] Sometimes a head of household would earn money for one fare and would then travel to America alone. He would earn enough for passage for his family and send for them. Sadly, some merely stayed in America, forgot their Irish family and remarried in the United States. Those who stayed in England faced the squalor of the Liverpool and London slums along with a barrage of prejudice and discrimination. Some of the most destitute Irish were summarily shipped back to Ireland.

The English perception of the Irish was poverty, drunkenness, and criminal. Above all, they were Catholic in a Protestant nation. Furthermore, the Irish would work for lower wages, which infuriated the English labor force. This prejudice sometimes percolated into violent incidents, usually anti-Catholic. By 1851, there were 108,548 Irish living in London alone. In addition, there were masses of Irish laborers who would seasonally migrate to England for the harvest, then return to Ireland. In 1847, at the worst of the Famine, 300,000 poor Irish migrated to England, descending mainly upon Liverpool.[5]

For those who had the means to continue to America, there were many challenges at the port city of Liverpool. The immigrants had to wait days and sometimes weeks for their ship's departure. The waiting immigrants faced a barrage of people offering their so-called "help." Liverpool was a major port of embarkation, with over nine million emigrants departing the city during the century. There were living accommodations to secure, along with ship schedules and tickets. They were probably grateful that so many were willing to "help." Compounding the problem, the rural Irish were not accustomed to traveling and were very gullible. Runners would handle baggage and arrange their lodging, for which they received commissions. Lodging sometimes meant a damp, dark and crowded cellar along with other immigrants. When the runner collected his commissions, he might disappear along with the immigrants' baggage. Robberies of cash or personal belongings were frequent. Money changers sold dollars for an outrageous exchange rate to the trusting Irish.

Probably the most villainous were the ticket agents. Immigrants were duped and overcharged. They might be booked on a ship whose departure was weeks away. This allowed the innkeeper to take yet more of the immigrants' money for lodging in the filthy and disease-ridden houses or cellars. The ship would not sail until it had enough cargo. Cargo was loaded first, followed by cabin passengers and finally steerage when ready to sail.[6] The ticket agent may have sold them onto an inferior ship that needed passengers but might not truly even be headed to their destination. Essentially, immigrants were harassed and intimidated until they had surrendered every bit of money they had. Some immigrants lost everything and had to remain in the slums of Liverpool. Others made it on the ship with their money completely exhausted. The harrowing trip across the Irish Sea along with the dreadful treatment and housing in Liverpool led to remorse. Many of those who actually boarded had so much regret that some begged to return to port so they could disembark.[7]

## TICKET TO AMERICA

Purchasing a reasonable fare to America was a daunting task. There were many unscrupulous players in the game. In the last half of the century, there were a variety of means to acquire tickets. The most desirable source for the immigrant was a relative or friend who bought a prepaid ticket in America. Otherwise, the emigrant had several other sources. After 1875, there were ticket broker offices, along with ticket agents who traveled the country in Ireland.[8] In England, it was best to buy from the shipping line directly, or their recommended agent. The peril lay in buying the ticket from a runner or any other middleman who had no connection with the shipping line. Many times, ship captains would sell a large volume of tickets to a broker.[9] The broker paid the runner commission to bring him immigrants. He was then free to charge whatever he could get an immigrant to pay. Other disreputable brokers would not only manipulate the price, but perhaps sell tickets for an undesirable ship or delayed departure time for tickets that he may have gotten at a steep discount. Runners would also arrange for lodging while the immigrants waited for their departure. He received a commission for relegating them to a damp cellar along with other immigrants, or a lodging in the slums. There was always the potential for the immigrants to be robbed of money or belongings.[10]

Financing the cost of passage was very difficult for many. For a laborer, it was prohibitive. Before 1815, some Irish chose to be an indentured servant for a free passage, but that practice gradually disappeared.[11] That aside, emigrants had to pay, and fares were about £10 to £12.[12] Years later, in 1840, about one half of all fares were paid by Americans, usually friends or relatives of the immigrant. For a small farmer it might hinge on having farm animals to sell[13] along with his regular crops. The large farmers would usually have made enough profit that they could save sufficient funds over time. Cottiers and laborers hopefully had a small savings they could bolster by selling furniture, begging or asking relatives to help.[14] One other tactic was to forego paying rent and buy a ticket.

The overall cost of passenger fares to America trended downward throughout the century. Fares to Canada were sometimes significantly lower. Passenger ship regulations were less restrictive to Canada than the United States, resulting in the lower fares.[15] Timber ships from Canada also got into the emigrant trade. Their holds were huge open, dank, reeking spaces with no berths and clearly unfit for passengers. Yet agents justified selling tickets by noting that the Irish had never slept in a bed, so a cold, hard deck would do just fine. Nevertheless, as little as ten shillings to a pound could get an emigrant aboard and sailing for Canada.[16]

Fares from Irish ports were also lower than Liverpool to New York. Cobh was the favored port in Ireland.[17] Liverpool to New York was the most popular in England. Fares varied significantly based on demand and season purchased.[18] First class fares could be as much as three times the cost of steerage.[19] Steerage, where almost all immigrants traveled, was the least expensive fare and was referred to as "tween decks." The cost of food was included in the ticket price, but many of the ships were inconsistent with providing food. This was very surprising and negligent when the cost to feed a passenger was only sixty cents a day, especially with a steamship fare of thirty dollars and 1,500 to 2,000 passengers, with total revenue at $45,000 to $60,000 for a one-way crossing.[20] That was an enormous amount of money in the 19th century, revealing that fares could have been far less. It was yet another way immigrants were taken advantage of. Even with the high ticket price, there was an inconsistent food service. It was wise for an immigrant to bring food to supplement what the ship provided.[21]

In the early part of the century, fares were expensive. In 1811, passage from Londonderry to New York was $50-$60.[22] The cost of passage to America was too expensive for many, especially because during the 1830s a common laborer's annual income was about 5 pounds or $24. Based on the table below, passage to New York would require a full year's earnings:

**Steerage Fares ***

| Date | Sail | Steam | Origin/Destination |
|---|---|---|---|
| 1811 | $50-$60 | | Londonderry-New York |
| 1831 | $25[23] | | Liverpool-New York |
| 1851 | $17.50[24] | | Liverpool-New York |
| 1852 | | $31[25] | Trans-Atlantic |
| 1856 | | $34.40[26] | Glasgow-New York |
| 1860 | $17-$24[27] | $41[28] | Shipping Advertisement |
| 1863 | | $37-$44.60[29] | Shipping Advertisement |

| Date | Sail | Steam | Origin/Destination |
|---|---|---|---|
| 1875 | | $29.30[30] | Set by Agreement |
| 1890 | | $30[31] | Trans-Atlantic |
| 1894 | | $12 Est.[32] | Liverpool-New York |
| 1896 | | $24 Est.[33] | Liverpool-New York |

***Fares varied significantly based on port of origin, season and level of demand. Pound to Dollar Fares Using Historical Dollar and British Pound Conversion Calculator[34]**

Multiple variables determined ticket prices at any given time. The above table is intended to give an overview of Trans-Atlantic fares that can lead to some general conclusions. As can be seen, the sailing ship began to phase out of immigrant passage during the American Civil War. By 1867, about 80.5% of immigrant passage was aboard steamships.[35] The fares indicate that crossing by sailing ship was significantly less expensive, especially when considering a family immigrating. In addition, there is a general trend for fares to decrease over time for both sailing ships and steamships.

Improvements were made to sailing ships in the 1840s and 50s, which became known as the Golden Age of Sail.[36] The immigrants' funds would likely determine their method of travel in the 1860s. The poor were confined to the less expensive sailing ship. As can be seen, some prices show steamship fares more than fifty percent higher than sailing ships. Although ship conditions for passengers were similar, travel time was significantly less by steamship. Sailing ships crossed in about five weeks, on average. However, the course and speed of the sailing ship was at the mercy of the wind and storms. In the 1830s, some voyages could be three months or, worst case, one voyage was four months.[37]

On the other hand, steamships in the 1870s crossed in about two weeks. The first steamship to cross the Atlantic was the *Royal William* in 1833. In that year and subsequent years, fares were high and the steamship was used exclusively for travel by the wealthy. By 1876, sailing ships were completely phased out of the immigrant trade and all voyages were by steamship.[38] The advent of the steamship changed the perception and the practice of the Irish immigrant. No longer did it seem that going to America was a one-way trip. At two weeks or less, Irish Americans could go to Ireland for a visit, or the Irish could go to America to work for a period of time and come back to Ireland.[39]

John Casey and his three sons, Patrick, James and Michael, immigrated to New York City circa 1862. It is not known if they traveled together or in a chain migration. John Casey, in 1857, was a small farmer with 16 acres. With that size of farm, and living modestly, he may have accumulated some savings. Farmers with that acreage would usually have some livestock. In order to leave Ireland, John would sell the livestock and get a cash boost needed for buying tickets. The choice would then need to be made for the departure port and sailing ship or steamship. In general, fares from Irish ports could be significantly less expensive, although availability of departures could have come into play. At that time, the transition from sailing ship to steamship was underway. Steamships surpassed sailing ships by the end of the American Civil War. In 1862, however, around 65% of New York City arrivals were by sailing ship and about 35% steamship.[40] At that time, steamships had less availability and were significantly higher priced. On the other hand, the steamship arrived two weeks ahead of the sailing ship.

The following cost analysis is based on largely Liverpool departure. With four Casey adults traveling, the fares were a significant sum. A sailing ship average fare would be about four pounds and five shillings or about $23.60,[41] times four adults would be $94.40. That sum translates to near $2,500 in today's money or about $625 per ticket.[42] The average farm of 16 acres usually had livestock worth about £22,[43] equivalent to $122 in 1862.[44] If John chose to travel by steamship and reached New York in about two weeks, the individual fare would average around seven pounds[45] or $38.90, times four adults, totaling $155.60. Presuming John's livestock value was average for his size of farm, the livestock value would fall short of the steamship fare. In today's money the total for the steamship would be $4,095. The steamship fares would cost $1595 more than the sailing fare, or a 64% increase. Available money may have made the choice a foregone conclusion. Speculation might tell us that given the Famine, depression and other tribulations Ireland brought forth, there were likely times that the Casey family had no money and did not know when they were going to get any. These experiences will promote frugality. I think John chose the sailing ship. This stretched the travel for an extra two weeks if the wind cooperated, but the less expensive fare would justify the extra travel time.

CHAPTER 17

# ON THE WATER

*The road from Liverpool to New York, as they who have traveled it know, is very long, crooked, rough and eminently disagreeable.*[1]

—Ralph Waldo Emerson,
Aboard the Packet Ship New York, 1833

## IMMIGRANT SHIPS

Throughout the century, Irish immigrants braved leaking ships, shipwrecks, fire, disease and even starvation onboard, to reach the Americas in search of a better life. Many did not survive their voyage. They embarked on a 3,300 mile journey[2] to North America when the vast majority had never been on a ship. The fear of shipwreck among the passengers was rampant, especially those who had never traveled by sea. A storm with the ship bucking and rolling would understandably exacerbate these fears to the point of hysteria for some. Unfortunately, records were not maintained for shipwrecks for 19th century emigrant ships crossing the Atlantic. Some documentation exists for random wrecks, or wrecks in snippets of time, but not the whole century.[3]

Australia, on the other hand, has records for the entire century. Between 1788 and 1900, over one million people immigrated to Australia, mainly from the British Isles which included the Irish.[4] The Irish were the largest immigrant group. According to an Australian study done by a Royal Commission of shipwrecks between 1856 and 1872, 30.5% were due to storms, 65% from navigational error, translated to drunkenness and ineptitude, and the remaining 4.5% were from overloading.[5]

Presumably, similar statistics might also apply to ships crossing the Atlantic. However, there were ship fires in the Atlantic. In 1848, the *Ocean Monarch*, en route to Boston, caught fire and 176 people were killed. In 1858, 500 died in a ship fire on the steamship *Austria*, and an additional 400 died in an onboard fire on the *William Nelson* in 1865.[6]

Another fire occurred on the *Caleb Grimshaw* that sailed out of Liverpool. During the voyage, the ship stalled for 19 days with no wind. As they got underway, a fire broke out on the ship. It spread until it became obvious to the crew that it would consume the ship. The blazing ship sailed for four days to the shipping lanes looking for help. The *Sarah* spotted the distressed ship and came to its aid. Captain Cooke of the *Sarah* took on as many passengers as he could, then sailed slowly along with the *Caleb Grimshaw*. About 100 passengers were still aboard the burning ship. Five days had passed when the ship was lost and the balance of the survivors were taken aboard the *Sarah*. Although ninety had died, it could have been far worse without the heroic rescue efforts of Captain Cooke and his crew of the *Sarah*. Captain Hoxie of the *Caleb Grinshaw* had abandoned ship on a lifeboat the second day of the fire. He promised the steerage passengers he would sail alongside the ship and direct the rescue efforts. The steerage passengers were on their own. After reaching New York, Captain Cooke received much homage and Captain Hoxie was vilified in the press, but was not held accountable, not even with a censure.[7]

Shipwrecks were an even greater danger. In 1834, there were seventeen wrecks in the Gulf of St. Lawrence alone, killing 731 immigrants.[8] During the years of the Famine, almost one million immigrants arrived in North America on 5,000 voyages.[9] Between 1847 and 1852, 43 out of 6877 ships did not complete their voyage, presumably sunk or grounded. One of many tragic events occurred on a ship sailing from Ireland to Liverpool in 1848. A violent storm with hurricane winds began to ravage the ship. Passengers were sent below deck for their safety. Unfortunately, they shared the space with cattle. The crew sealed an escape route with a tarp. The ship made it to Liverpool that night, but no one checked on the passengers until morning. They discovered 72 dead passengers from suffocation or trampling by the cattle. The captain and crew were tried for manslaughter.[10]

During the Famine, there was an increase in ships sailing out of Irish ports. One ship sailed from Westport in County Mayo. Relatives and friends waved their goodbyes and gave them their send-off. Many family members lingered to watch as the ship sailed away. Everything seemed fine until inexplicably the ship began to sink. They stood aghast as the ship sank below the surface and was gone. There were no survivors. The immigrants' goodbyes from their relatives were their last.[11]

The *Elizabeth and Sarah,* another Famine ship from County Mayo, sailed in July 1847. Her manifest listed 212 passengers onboard, but in actuality there were 276 aboard, yet there were only 32 berths on the ship. Based on the number of passengers, there would be 12,532 gallons of water needed. The ship only had 8,700 gallons aboard. The price of the ticket included seven pounds of food to be distributed each week. No food was ever served. Passengers had to rely on provisions they brought on board to supplement. It is likely there was lots of begging for food. The voyage lasted eight weeks because the captain chose the wrong course. At destination in Canada, the passengers were finally checked on and 42 people were dead, presumably of starvation or lack of water.[12]

Another hazard was icebergs. Four ships were lost after colliding with icebergs in 1849 alone. The *Hannah* went down on April 29, 1849 after striking an iceberg about four o'clock in the morning. During the chaotic events that followed, the captain and two officers took a lifeboat and abandoned ship, leaving the immigrants stranded. Many passengers were able to get onto the iceberg before the ship sank. They remained there 15 hours before they were rescued, clad only in their bedclothes. One hundred twenty-nine survived, many with severe frostbite. One hundred nine passengers were lost. The captain and two officers were also rescued and berated for their heinous act. The editor of the local newspaper called for their prosecution, but there is no record of them being brought to trial.[13] Less than a month later, late at night on May 10, the *Maria* struck an iceberg and sank in forty minutes. Only nine survived after successfully jumping onto the ice. Over one hundred lives were lost. Two other ships were lost to the ice that year, but neither carried immigrants.[14] Five years later, in 1854, the *Glasgow* sailed out of Liverpool with 480 emigrants and vanished, its fate never known.[15]

Emigrants purchased tickets for steerage, the least expensive ticket onboard. As cited earlier, steerage was called "tween-decks," accessed from the top deck down a ladder into steerage. The emigrants didn't sign up for five or more weeks of misery, but that's what their ticket bought. They had just left the repugnance of Liverpool and were welcomed to their new home in steerage. Steerage conditions on the Irish emigrant ships were likened to the days of transporting African slaves. Some said the slave ships had better conditions.[16] At the time, slaves were property and had value. Irish emigrants had paid the money for their ticket, and they no longer had any value. They were treated as such by the ship's crew.

## ABOARD A 19TH CENTURY IMMIGRANT SHIP

After cargo and luggage were loaded, there was a roll call for passengers and a doctor's medical check. The exam was merely asking the immigrants' names, whether they felt well, and to show their tongues.[17] This was required because the captain could be fined at the American port if carrying sick and incapacitated passengers. They were then hustled down into the ship to the steerage deck where they got the first glimpse of what was to be their home for the next five to eight weeks. What they didn't understand yet was it would be their hell for those weeks. Five weeks was an eternity in the bowels of a 19th century wooden sailing ship. The only power to get to America was the wind. Unfortunately, the winds are not reliable. Heavy winds might blow the ship off course and add days to the trip. The ship may lay dead in the water for days when the wind did not blow at all. Five weeks could quickly become eight weeks.

The steerage compartment was typically about seventy feet long, twenty to twenty-five feet wide and five and one half to six feet high. The sleeping berths or in reality the living berths, were ten feet wide and five or six feet long and resembled bunk beds.

These berths were on both sides and a row of berths down the middle on some ships. Aisles were intended to be five feet, but may have been reduced to three feet if a row of berths was in the middle. The berths were planned for six adults to lie and sleep in a bed ten feet wide. One steering passenger noted three adults and five children occupying a berth and eight men in another. Sleeping on the floor was probably not an option with the narrow aisles filled with luggage and personal items. Six people across 120 inches amounted to twenty inches per body.[18] If six people were stuffed into that space, there certainly wouldn't be any tossing and turning, trying to get comfortable. If eight were in the berth, it would require sleeping on your side with no movement. Furthermore, some of the immigrants had just met and were then sandwiched together in the berth to sleep. Some ships attached shelves to the walls for sleeping. Around 1862, another sleeping arrangement used by some ships was to build what appeared to be a closet. Upper and lower twenty inch shelves were then placed on each side and back of the closet. It would sleep six, but in very little space. The open space in the middle of the berths was only six feet by three feet.[19] John Casey and sons immigrated circa 1862, and could have had such a sleeping arrangement.

If the ship had no dining area, passengers were required to eat in their berths.[20] People were smaller then, but many would have had difficulty with the five feet length of the berth as well as the five and one half foot ceiling. Later, regulations required six feet height.[21] Early in the century, single women and single men were in the common area. A single woman with twenty inch width space may be sleeping right beside a man she didn't know. This led to some women staying up all night rather than sleeping in the berth.[22] One observer reported that all single women on board were sexually molested or assaulted in some way during the voyage.[23] The situation was improved somewhat in 1847 when new legislation required separate compartments for single women, single men, and families.[24]

Prior to 1820, ships carried an unlimited number of passengers. The overcrowding was inconceivable and contributed to the rapid spread of disease on board. Ticket brokers continued to sell tickets even when they knew the ship was at capacity. Many times, ticket sales would exceed the number of berths and passengers were forced to sleep on whatever space they could find on the floor. The captain was supportive of extra ticket sales, as it increased profit. He would not go down to steerage anyway. The goal was to cross the Atlantic and try to keep as many as possible alive.[25] It might be said it was the American dream; the ticket agent, the captain and crew all profited, but the Irish passengers did not. For them, there was only suffering awaiting them on the long voyage.

Overcrowding was an invariable practice on the immigrant ships. Every additional fare added to the profit of the voyage. In 1819, Congress made an attempt to limit overcrowding with legislation requiring two passengers per five tons of registered weight of the vessel. The fine for excess passengers was $150 per head and confiscation of the vessel if the headcount was twenty or more over.[26] Regardless, the ship captains found ways to circumvent the laws and continue overcrowding. The captain might pick up passengers along the coast after leaving port and unload them along the coast outside of New York City on arrival. The regulations were followed at the ports, but once at sea, they were ignored.

Passengers typically had a crate or trunk for belongings that went below steerage in cargo. They then had what might be thought of as carry-on baggage. This included extra clothes, cooking utensils, food and other items necessary during the trip. These items were in the aisles by their berth. With six in the berth on the bottom and six on top, the three to five feet aisles were cluttered and sometimes blocked. Privacy was impossible.

Overcrowding and unfathomable conditions in steerage continued throughout the century, even with the advent of the steamship.[27] Steerage was so much oversold at times there were not enough berths, and immigrants competed for space on the floor. The immigrants were not seaworthy and seasickness struck not long after leaving port. With perhaps 200 to 400 immigrants in steerage, the number of water closets (toilets), usually only two, was woefully inadequate. Envision hundreds of people with no open space vomiting randomly.[28] It became known that the lower berth had its disadvantages when someone on the top berth leaned over the edge to throw up. The result of an outbreak of seasickness could be very unsettling. Vomit could be in your berth, on your luggage, on the floor, or on your person. Furthermore, navigating through the violent waves of a storm would create such a pitching and rolling effect onboard ship that even the veteran seafarers might feel ill. The conditions of the water closets were foul, with a mixture of vomit and the fetid remains of unspeakable intestinal maladies. Couple that with hundreds of human bodies in such compact quarters—people who hadn't bathed in four or five weeks—and it became unbearable. There was not enough water ration to bathe. Some would try to wash with the limited ration of water, but they were just limiting their drinking water. Many just did not make the effort. The stench was literally overwhelming. Some described it as almost visible, like a fog. Dock workers in port would joke that they knew when an incoming ship carried immigrants because of the foul smell.[29]

The smells lingered because there was little ventilation. Hatches provided some fresh air, but they were shut during storms that sometimes could last a week or more. When they were closed, it became dead air like a reeking cloud. During the storm they would also contend with water raining through from the ship's deck, which was being pounded with the waves. Beds in the berths were soaked and water sometimes reached ankle deep. During the storm, steerage became a virtual, violent carnival ride. Various calamities could occur. Water closets overturned; buckets at some berths would tip over spilling their vile contents out to slosh about in the seawater covering the floor. Occupants of a berth could literally be ejected by a sudden violent wave, landing on the floor or on top of others in a neighboring berth. It is fair to say that almost all immigrants were in fear during a fierce storm. Some were praying, others screaming and children crying—an awful scene. Darkness seemed to worsen the fear. Steerage was always in stages of darkness because only the hatches brought in light. When they were shut, it was dark. The immigrants knew well that shipwreck was always a possibility, and never experiencing a seafaring storm made it feel imminent. Many thought they were living their last day and bemoaned ever leaving Ireland. Eventually the seas would calm allaying the doom in steerage.

Some days in steerage were mundane. It could be hot and humid in the enclosed space. Most ships left in late spring and might be sailing on summer days, making it even hotter. The Irish would pass their time as usual with playing music,[30] singing, storytelling and drinking. Some ships sold liquor on board and many times with a poor outcome. Even without alcohol, annoyances or disagreements, fueled by the overcrowding, would become arguments and escalate to fights. Add the alcohol and the fighting would proliferate. One upper class observer reported looking down into steerage and beholding sheer bedlam. Open space was limited and it was strewn with clothes and baggage. There were children running through the aisles attempting to traverse the many obstacles. Babies were crying and men shouting,[31] along with some sitting stupefied as if there was no commotion around them. On some ships, steerage passengers were not allowed on deck for the entire voyage of anywhere from five to eleven weeks.

The action did not diminish much at night. The night was literally a nightmare. Sleep was elusive with the heat of the summer and so many bodies together in close proximity, especially jam-packed in the berth. There was likely an aggravating chorus of snoring sprinkled with a refrain of flatulence, and people trying to argue quietly, but not succeeding. The stench hung in the rancid air. Sadly, there was the occasional muffled scream of a woman or girl being violated, much of the time by a crew member. There might be loud voices and commotion over an attempted robbery, again sometimes crew members. Money was a dangerous thing to possess and there was no safe place to keep it.[32] None of this was conducive to sleep. Sleep would come only when exhaustion willed it.

In the early 19th century, immigrants were responsible for bringing their own food.[33] The Passenger Act of 1842 designated the shipping line accountable for providing food and water to passengers. The law called for a bare minimum of seven pounds of food per week and three quarts of water a day for each immigrant.[34] The bread, biscuits and potatoes served were noted for their poor quality.[35] Sometimes the meat was spoiled.[36] All the food was poorly prepared. At times, there was not enough food, so when the bell rang for the meal, there was a dash for the food. Some ships had no dining area, so the immigrant stayed standing or took his food back to his berth.[37] Many ship cooks, stewards and captains enhanced their profit by providing leftovers from first class for a substantial fee to the immigrants.[38] Immigrants were always encouraged to bring a supplement of food with them.

A fireplace was provided for cooking their own food. Oatmeal, cakes, and soup were favorites. The bickering and arguing at the fireplace about turns and length of cooking time were unending until a crew member doused the fire for the night. Most ended up with only half-cooked meals.

The passenger supply of water was stored in barrels formerly used for oil, turpentine, vinegar or other substances and had not been cleaned. In 1817, Reverend William Bell, on a ship en route to Canada, wrote, "Our water has for some time past been very bad. When it was drawn out of the casks it was no cleaner than that of a dirty kennel after a shower of rain, so that its appearance alone was sufficient to sicken one. But its dirty appearance was not the worst quality. It had such a rancid smell that to be in the same neighborhood was enough to turn one's stomach."[39] Unfortunately, many times, even the rations were cut short. Some cases occurred where food was not served for several days, with water supplies running low and rations cut even lower.[40] The required three quarts was not enough to drink, wash utensils and try to wash one's body, presuming they found some privacy. The sinks used to wash dishes may have just been used for vomiting from seasickness. One immigrant's diary read that they were not served food for a two-week period and never had meat the entire voyage.[41]

The captain and crew were typically abusive toward the immigrants, cussing and shoving or knocking them down and intimidating them into submission.[42] Some immigrants believed they were treated like cattle, even going so far to think that given the abuse and conditions in steerage, even animals had a better voyage.[43] Other passengers were also disrespectful. First class passengers would stand on the deck above steerage and throw pennies or food down to the immigrants,[44] as if it were the zoo. Morale undoubtedly was very low in steerage. Some captains occasionally allowed short amounts of deck time for small rotating groups, so the Irish could get some fresh air. On deck, they might sing or play games with the refreshing break from their prison below.[45] Other captains did not allow deck time. Immigrants stayed in steerage for five weeks or more. Most captains never visited steerage and they would not entertain any complaints about its conditions.[46] There were rules to follow. The immigrants were given times to wake and times to sleep. Rations were strict and miscues on any of the ship's rules might result in a beating or scourging with a rope,[47] all at the captain's whim.

The abuse went even further. Crew members would make their way into the single women's compartment and sexually assault female passengers. Many times, it was the captain who set the example. In 1860, the New York Commissioners of Emigration discovered in an investigation that captains had a scheme where a female passenger was enticed to his quarters, perhaps with the ruse that she may get better rations. There were no better rations, only repeated sexual assault, as she was kept in the captain's quarters the rest of the voyage. She might be offered up in prostitution to the officers. Immigrant women made numerous complaints after reaching New York about sexual assaults by the captain and crew. There were so many complaints that it came to the attention of Congress and a law was passed requiring prison time for sexual offenses by the captains and officers. There is no record, however, that anyone actually went to prison for such offenses.[48]

Amid all the overcrowding, filth and vermin lay another imminent danger to the immigrant. Illness and disease were prevalent among the passengers. The immigrants simply ate whatever was available to them. As already mentioned, meat served was often rotten and food cooked by the immigrants half-raw. This led to a variety of gastrointestinal ailments. Vomiting, diarrhea and likely food poisoning were common. This kept the water closets particularly revolting, assuming a closet was available and it could be reached in time.

## DISEASE ONBOARD

The deadly diseases that appeared onboard were especially fearsome. Typhus, dysentery, and smallpox were the most common, all of which could be fatal. The squalid conditions jammed with human bodies were a bonanza for lice, ticks, cockroaches, rats and other pests.

The symptoms of dysentery are an inflamed colon and a prevalence of reeking, bloody stools. The bacteria can be spread by flies, inhaled, or by consuming feces-tainted water. One doctor likened the odor of the stools to "putrid flesh in hot weather." The diarrhea can continue until the body is reduced to a skeletal state. Dysentery along with severe dehydration will result in death.[49]

Smallpox is a virus and is communicable through airborne droplets. Its symptoms include high fever and muscle pain. Vomiting and convulsions can occur if contracted by children. In its most severe form, it can result in death very quickly from hemorrhaging in the skin, lungs and other organs. If less severe, a rash develops with pimples that eventually scab over. After several weeks the scabs fall off, leaving pock marks.[50]

The most prevalent and probably most deadly disease was typhus. The bedding and clothing of the immigrants were rife with lice. Infected lice enable the disease to enter the body through a cut on the skin, inhalation, or even through the mucus of the eye. Typhus onboard became known as ship's fever. Typhus fevers were high, accompanied by body aches and rash that might cover the entire body. The fever could rage on for as long as two weeks, resulting in death.

The health and wellbeing of the victim played a large part of the outcome with dysentery, smallpox and typhus. During the famine, when many immigrants were experiencing starvation and weakened immune systems, death was more likely.[51] A lack of water, which was inherent to many of the voyages, resulted in dehydration, which contributed to the victims dying.

These diseases could occur on any ship during the 19th century, but were most common during the Famine. Outbreaks of cholera onboard ship took place in 1832, 1848, and 1853. Cholera on emigrant ships was carried to the Americas, resulting in 4,000 deaths in Montreal and Quebec, as well as severe outbreaks in New York and Chicago. In addition, in a three month period in 1853, 1,328 people died on seventy-seven ships sailing from Liverpool to New York.[52]

Moreover, typhus claimed far more, especially during the Famine. In 1847, the worst Famine year for typhus, seven thousand immigrants died en route to the United States, with ten thousand more dying in quarantine after arrival.[53]

CHAPTER 18

# EXODUS

*The sword of famine is less sparing than the bayonet of a soldier.*[1]
—Thomas F. Meagher, Irish Nationalist, Brigadier General, Irish Brigade, U.S. Civil War

By the spring of 1847, the escape from Ireland had begun. The roads of Ireland were teeming with emigrants headed for the ports. Typhus was running rampant and emigration seemed to be the only way to evade it. Charles Trevelyan wrote, "The roads to the ports were thronged with emigrants." A Board of Works officer reported, "All who are able are leaving the country." The overcrowding of ships began in earnest. Old, decrepit ships were pressed into service and the ships failed to meet their allotted amounts of food and water. Passengers were entitled to seven pounds of food per week and three quarts of water a day. For many ships it just didn't happen, and the emigrants paid the price with inadequate water for fever patients and some literally starving onboard.[2] Passengers were crowded on with berth space already gone. Among the passengers were the lice that carried typhus. Instead of escaping the fever the emigrants were literally taking it with them. The disease would present itself onboard. The ships crossing the Atlantic with fever raging onboard were aptly named the coffin ships. Landlords were clearing their estates through emigration, targeting the most destitute. Lord Palmerston sent out 2,000 destitute Irish. Palmerston shipped out 477 tenants aboard the *Lord Ashburton*. Of that number, 174 were literally almost naked. When reaching Canada, 87 had to be clothed, including one lady who was completely naked.[3]

## COFFIN SHIPS TO CANADA

The most devastating events during transatlantic passage of the Irish occurred in 1847 with ships headed to Canada. Ireland was enduring the worst year of typhus during the Famine, aptly named Black '47. Many emigrants boarded ships already infected. During 1847, one out of fourteen passengers sailing from Liverpool died aboard before reaching America. Cork, Ireland departures were even worse with more than ten percent dead and thrown overboard.[4]

Immigrant ships sailed to Canada to arrive no earlier than May when the ice in the St. Lawrence River had melted.[5] The ships were jam-packed with immigrants. One of the worst was the *Ulster,* in 1831. The ship was 334 tons and carried 505 passengers. The regulation at the time was three passengers to four tons of ship weight. Following regulations would put the passenger maximum at 250 passengers. The *Ulster* was sailing with more than twice the legal limit. The ship had berths three high, with severely limited space between them. Still, there were not enough berths and immigrants rotated shifts of sleep so everyone could sleep in a berth.

These abuses finally resulted in Parliament changing the regulation to three passengers for every five tons.[6] Even with stricter regulations, overcrowding remained one of the biggest problems through most of the century.

The city of Quebec required all incoming vessels to first stop at Grosse Isle on the way up the St. Lawrence River. The purpose was a medical inspection and possible quarantine if there were contagious diseases on board. The first vessel of the season to arrive at Grosse Isle was *The Syria.* The ship was carrying 241 passengers, of which 84 had ship's fever. Nine passengers had died during the passage and were interred in the sea. Grosse Isle had a 150-bed hospital that could easily accommodate the 84. However, the officials at Grosse Isle anticipated more cases of ship's fever and sought funding to build a fever shed. The shed was hastily built and prepared for additional fever cases.

Less than a week later, eight ships arrived with a total of 430 fever victims altogether. About half were taken in at the hospital and the other half remained aboard. The hospital was overrun. Within a few days, seventeen more ships had headed up the St. Lawrence, arriving at Grosse Isle. Even more arrived, and by May 29, a total of 36 ships with 13,000 immigrants were waiting to offload. The 1,100 cases already on Grosse Isle were housed in the hospital, fever shed and a small church on the floor. By July, 2,500 fever patients were at Grosse Isle. Sometimes a fever patient waited days to be seen by a doctor. Every facility was jammed and new fever sheds had been built and quickly housed to capacity also. Several doctors had contracted the fever and died, leaving only two doctors to oversee 2,500 patients. An appeal went out among the well immigrants to help in the fever sheds, but to no avail. Even relatives of fever victims stayed away, fearing they might catch fever. On August 18, 88 patients died. A priest administering the Last Rites of the Catholic Church could not keep pace with the dying. The misery and suffering was catastrophic.[7]

Many of the arriving ships had run out of water and the fever victims were wailing and begging for a drink. As previously mentioned, adequate water intake by fever victims was an absolute necessity. Without it, death was almost certain. Onboard one ship, the fever patients had been relegated to the hold below steerage to get them away from well passengers. Steerage passengers were haunted by their cries for water. They were left there, dying, with no water, no care, no medicine, no ventilation and with more victims sent down every day.[8]

By this time, passengers were being unloaded at Grosse Isle who could only crawl. They crawled as far as they could and lay on the beach. One Catholic priest lamented that thirty-seven immigrants were "lying on the beach, crawling on the mud and dying like fish out of water." Some ships arrived that had lost over a third of their passengers to fever during the voyage.[9] Of course, death on the voyage meant no coffin, no priest, no service, just one more body cast into the sea.[10]

The oldest and most inferior ships were chartered by landlords to rid themselves of the burden of derelicts from their estate. The landlord was responsible for their care at the poorhouse, but could save one half the annual cost by paying to send them to Canada. The decrepit ships were a cost saving measure. The passengers aboard these ships were the most indigent of all. Many were half starved, half clothed and likely carrying fever. At Grosse Isle, "hundreds were literally flung on the beach, left amid the mud and stones to crawl on the dry land as they could."[11] The most infamous of the landlords were Denis Mahon of County Roscommon and Lord Palmerston, whose estate was in County Sligo. Palmerston's immigrants were promised money and clothes when they reached their destination in Canada. Many of them died aboard and were dumped into the ocean. Those who did reach Canada never found any Palmerston agent to fulfill the promise. That winter, the streets of St. John, Newfoundland were filled with scantily clad Irish walking barefoot in the snow and begging for help from anyone on the streets.[12]

By summer, the waiting ship line was miles long. Fever had not abated and the decision was made that healthy passengers would stay on board ship for a fifteen-day quarantine. The problems arose when it took days to remove the sick. During that delay, sick and well passengers were together, and a new outbreak occurred. The ship *Agnes* arrived with 427 passengers. Only about one third remained alive after a fifteen-day quarantine.[13] Grosse Isle, however, began to ship the so called "well" immigrants up the river to Quebec and Montreal. Montreal got the worst of it, receiving 2,304 immigrants in one twenty-four hour period. There were highs of 96 degrees in Montreal at the time, ideal for the transfer of fever. There were fever cases arriving on the barges and many sick and well immigrants were released in Montreal. The sickest stayed at the wharf. There were many only able to crawl, while others could not move and lay there on the wharf to die. A representative of the Montreal Board of Health visited the wharves and witnessed the macabre scene. Many were lying out in the open and a fever shed was completely full. The health official ordered carts to take the sickest to the hospital. Two died in the cart transfer and more during the first night at the hospital.[14] The hospital was overrun. It was built for 150 and was attempting to treat 872 patients. It is likely that an unknown number of Irish released into Montreal died of fever or exposure to the cold that winter. Those who survived could not find work. The Canadians were afraid to hire the Irish because of the danger they may have already been exposed.

Many local people succumbed to the fever who had visited the fever sheds to help. Eight Catholic priests, the vicar general of Montreal's Catholic bishop, and the Bishop of Toronto were some of the religious lost to fever. In addition, Mayor John Mills of Montreal contracted the fever after visiting the sheds and also died.[15] As the year ended, the grim numbers were totaled. Over one hundred thousand Irish left England for Canada in 1847. Seventeen thousand died at sea as the Famine ships became known as the coffin ships. An estimated 20,000 Irish died all along the St. Lawrence River and in the cities of Canada.[16] Of that total, almost 5,300 died at Grosse Isle, where a monument was eventually placed. The inscription reads:

> In this secluded spot lie the mortal remains of 5,294 persons, who flying from pestilence and famine in Ireland in the year 1847, found in America but a grave.[17]

Unlike Canada, there was no such human tragedy in the United States. Canada was British North America, and their passenger acts were less stringent and not as well enforced as the United States. The British government spent the first half of the century stiffening and easing restrictions on passenger travel. That, along with lax enforcement and the shipping lines circumventing the law, made regulations for the most part ineffective. The goal of the English government was to lower fares to Canada and make those passages more attractive than the United States—so attractive that in 1842, a man, his wife and four young children could travel from Belfast to Canada for £6. That same family would pay £21 for passage to New York.[18]

The purpose was to settle new territories in Canada. The Canadian government offered 200 acres of land with only two stipulations. The immigrant must build a 16 x 20 cabin and break out two acres of land per year. Meeting these criteria would qualify them for a land patent for the property. Reducing the cost of fares resulted in more traffic to Canada, but settling new territories for the most part was not happening. After reaching the St. Lawrence River, an immigrant would simply profess his intent to remain in Canada and receive free passage up the St. Lawrence. He then bid his farewell to Canada and continued his journey by walking across the border into the United States. As many as three-fourths of the Irish used this ploy in the first quarter of the century, but it became even more prominent by mid-century. In 1843, only 293 out of 20,892 immigrants actually remained in Canada.[19]

English Parliament in the first half of the century passed multiple passenger acts. Overcrowding was the foremost problem faced and Parliament imposed regulations that matched the number of passenger capacity as a ratio to the tonnage of the ship. For example, the first law passed in 1803 set a standard of one passenger to every two tons of ship weight. The shipping lines were accustomed to cramming immigrants into steerage like animals. This law limited the number of passengers ships could transport. This outraged the shipping lines and they retaliated with higher fares. Ship captains, not to be outdone, began the practice of getting their passenger number approved at port and then sailed to another part of the coast and loaded on more passengers. High fares defeated the purpose of drawing immigrants on less expensive fares to Canada. Consequently, the regulations were eased in 1817. The year 1835 saw the passenger law cut from four passengers for every five tons of ship weight down to three. This seesaw approach continued and culminated in a compromise that would not result in a fare increase.[20]

Meanwhile, in the United States, the general policy was to enact legislation that protected the immigrant as well as the United States citizens. Immigrants arriving were required to be healthy and possess some money. The passenger law passed in March of 1819 addressed the most serious issue of overcrowding. The law had capacity set at two passengers for every five tons of registered ship weight. Sizable fines were levied against ships exceeding capacity. Stiffer enforcement was added in 1847, calling for confiscation of a ship arriving with the passenger count exceeding the maximum by twenty passengers or more.[21]

Comparing England's capacity of three passengers per five tons essentially meant that English ships sailing to Canada could legally sail with one third more passengers than vessels headed for New York. For example, a ship bound for New York in the mid-century weighing 1000 tons[22] divided by five tons then multiplied by two passengers would equal a maximum of 400 passengers. Ships exceeding that passenger count risked steep fines or confiscation. A ship from Liverpool to Canada was under British regulation. That ship could legally carry 600 passengers. This was one reason the fare to Canada was less expensive, but the overcrowding extreme. The United States law reduced overcrowding and could very well have reduced infectious disease from spreading by not jamming the immigrants together. Of course, as in England, the ship captains found the means to bypass United States laws. Some disreputable captains would offload their overcrowded ship in New Jersey rather than risk fines or confiscation in New York.[23] The immigrants would then need to find and pay for their own transportation to New York City.[24]

CHAPTER 19

# ARRIVAL

*Remember, remember always, that all of us, and you and I especially, are descended from immigrants and revolutionists.*[1]
—Franklin D. Roosevelt, President

The day before arrival in the United States, everyone was required to clean themselves and the steerage compartment to prepare for the doctor and government inspector to come aboard. That is, they must clean as much as possible. Conditions in steerage were an accumulation of filth and the immigrants themselves had not bathed for at least four to six weeks. The anticipation and excitement had to be at a fever pitch among the immigrants. At long last, they would be leaving a living hell behind. Or would it follow them?

In the early part of the century, there were no regulations on immigrant ships arriving in the United States. By far, New York City was the preferred port of the immigrants. In the 1850s, three fourths of all immigrants landed there, and four fifths by the 1890s.[2] Passengers were cast off the ship into the streets of New York City among a plethora of runners, thugs, pickpockets, money changers, and duplicitous ticket agents selling land transportation fares that were sometimes double their value and sometimes worthless altogether. Unfortunately, many of the culprits were Irish whom the immigrants perceived they could trust. Instead, the goal of the vast majority was to help the immigrants by relieving them of whatever money they had left that the thieves of Liverpool and the voyage had missed.[3] Much like Liverpool, dishonesty reigned among those who feigned friendship to the immigrants. The Irish seemed to be the most gullible and prone to scams by the thieves who befriended them.[4] For example, a runner for a lodging house would charge five to fifteen dollars to take the immigrants' baggage to the lodging house. A ticket agent might charge double the actual ticket price for land travel. The immigrants were the innocent prey stepping on United States soil.[5] They were harassed and intimidated until their funds were exhausted. Immigrants saved from the swindling were those met by relatives who lifted them from the madness and provided them food and shelter.

Immigrant ships before 1819 were an atrocity—not only the filth of steerage, but the people were jammed on board like cattle. Finally, in 1819, the United States Congress reacted and passed legislation to limit passengers to a capacity of two for every five tons of registered weight of the ship.[6] Captains were also required to have a passenger list to present at port.

Upon arrival, a medical inspector checked the passengers for contagious diseases. Ships arriving with fever onboard were relegated to Staten Island for quarantine. The citizens of Staten Island detested the quarantine center, fearing the disease that it brought to the island. Ultimately, in 1858, the residents burned it and forced the quarantined immigrants to move onto a ship anchored in the Atlantic.[7]

It became evident that New York City badly needed an immigrant receiving center to reduce the chaos and protect the immigrants. A facility named Castle Garden was chosen. It lay on an artificial island 200 feet off the shore of Manhattan. In its early life it served as Fort Clinton, established to protect Manhattan in 1805. After the War of 1812, the fort was no longer needed and it was morphed into a resort and reception center for elite visitors to the city, and finally an amusement center named Castle Garden in 1847. The water was filled and a road was built between the Castle and Manhattan. A twenty-four acre open grassy area on the shore was named Battery Park.[8] The *New York Daily Times* railed against Castle Garden, stating that it would bring down property value, increase potential for disease and fill the air with disgusting odors.[9] The project still moved forward, however, and Castle Garden was opened on August 1, 1855.[10]

Castle Garden was a large circular building with a dome and a great hall in the center. The structure, a former fort, was heavily fortified with six foot walls of stone. With its great hall, it was ideal for processing immigrants and was lauded for its efficiency.[11]

Upon entry, immigrants passed through a corridor where they were more closely scrutinized for any ailments or disabilities. The concerns were twofold: keeping disease out of the city and identifying those who could not financially support themselves, requiring assistance from the city. The captain of the ship could be fined for bringing those who would need support from the city. After the medical inspection, the immigrants ended up at registration in the center of the great hall. There, they were questioned and registered, along with discussing their destination in order to help them to obtain transportation through legitimate ticket agents. Then it was off to the baths, where cleansing solution sat two feet deep and long water troughs were used as part of the cleansing process. If the immigrants arrived by about one o'clock PM, they were processed out by evening. For later arrivals, there were sleeping accommodations for three thousand immigrants at the center.[12] Castle Garden took the bedlam of runners, thieves and swindlers out of the process of immigrants entering the United States. However, the runners refused to accept this affront and subsequently made attempts to break into the center and even attempted to seize a ship. In the end, although very persistent, all their efforts failed and immigrant flow was not disrupted.[13]

As written by George Svejda of the National Park Service, Castle Garden was "...a great human expression which can be placed among the shining achievements of American history during the 19th century."[14] Castle Garden surely made the Irish immigrants giddy with excitement and hope for their new life in the United States. They were not accustomed to the treatment they received.[15] Many had come through the Famine years and the grueling Atlantic passage with all its horrors. At last, they were treated like human beings rather than peasants who needed removed from Ireland or cattle crowded on a ship. Maybe America would be what they had dreamed.

Castle Garden burned to the ground in July of 1876, but was rebuilt at a furious pace and reopened in November of that year.[16] In its later years, Castle Garden became inadequate for the flow of immigrants and closed its doors at the end of 1889. Immigrants were then processed at the Barge Office, also near Battery Park, until the opening of Ellis Island as the new Immigration Center in 1892.[17] During its thirty-four year run, Castle Garden processed 8,280,917 immigrants into the United States.[18] Four of them were my ancestors: John Casey and his sons Patrick, James and Michael. Castle Garden and Battery Park are maintained today by the National Park Service and are a popular stop for visitors.[19]

In January 1892, Castle Garden was replaced with Ellis Island, a new Federal center also located in New York Harbor. The center was a three-story wooden building built to process 10,000 immigrants a day. Sadly, this building also burned in 1897, disrupting the service and destroying all the records from Castle Garden. The building was replaced in 1900.[20]

As immigrant ships entered New York Harbor after 1875, their first sight was the majestic Statue of Liberty, a beacon of hope and optimism, along with its message of "Give me your tired, your poor." With a 19th century Irish immigrant ship, America was getting both the tired and the poor. Such a sight as never seen by Irish rural folk who had never journeyed more than four or five miles from home—it had to be exciting and a realization of a dream for those Irish. For some, it truly was a dream come true, but for many it was an illusion and they were on the cusp of more heartache as they reached America. Sometimes numerous ships with immigrants were waiting in line for processing. It was January 1, 1892 when Annie Moore, a fifteen-year-old Irish girl began her processing through Ellis Island. She was the first of twelve million immigrants that passed through until its closing in November of 1954. On April 7, 1907, a record 11,747 immigrants were processed.[21]

First and second class passengers were the first to leave the ship. They received a brief medical exam onboard and were released into the city, bypassing Ellis Island. Any passenger who was identified with a medical problem had to join those from steerage for further exam. Inspectors were especially looking for tuberculosis, fever, the obviously insane[22] and trachoma, a serious eye disease that could be fatal or leave the victim blind. Trachoma always ended with deportation. Children twelve or over found with any significant medical problem were deported unaccompanied.

Those under twelve were returned with a parent.[23] About twenty per cent of all immigrants were tagged for medical reasons at Ellis Island and were for the most part closely examined and released.[24] Only about two percent of all immigrants were returned to their originating port. Still, Ellis Island was nicknamed the "Island of Tears" or "Heartbreak Island."[25]

An active day of processing was 3000 to 5000 immigrants. On the whole, immigrants spent about three hours at Ellis Island.[26] There were, however dormitories available for those detained or arriving late.[27] The Registry Room was located upstairs. It was a Great Hall similar to the Castle Garden center. Just like Castle Garden, Ellis Island was known for its efficacy and humane treatment of the immigrants.[28] Again, this was treatment that was foreign to most of the Irish. Thankfully, the worst was behind them—or was it?

CHAPTER 20

# AMERICA

*If you're Irish, it doesn't matter where you go, you'll always find family.*[1]
—Victoria Smurfit, Irish Actress

Many Irish who had relatives in America had shelter and jobs waiting for them. Many others did not have support in America and, in the absence of any money, were compelled to stay in New York City. Their only choice was to swarm to the repulsive neighborhoods of places like Five Points and Hell's Kitchen. Both areas had employment within walking distance.[2]

Living conditions in the New York City slums were probably worse than Ireland. There were open sewers and rancid trash dumped on the street. Pigs, cattle and packs of dogs roamed the streets freely, depositing manure everywhere. The dog population was so out of control that the city placed a bounty on them. Groups of young boys had their fun and earned money by hunting dogs and beating them to death. The pigs foraged for food in the streets and the stench was unbearable. Tenants were crowded into tenements which also contributed to the squalor. In 1850 in New

York City, as many as 30,000 people were crammed into small, dank and dark cellars.[3] When it rained, water would drain into the cellars, making life miserable and ripe for disease. The conditions in which the Irish lived resulted in a high mortality rate. Children under five were lost at a dismal 61.5% death rate, while the average of all children who died was 13.43 years.[4] In 1842, the cellars were outlawed as rental space.

Others that were somewhat more fortunate lived in shanty towns with other Irish. The Irish fashioned these "Paddy towns" or "Little Dublins," as if they lived in Ireland. They might have a cow or pig and a small potato patch. One reason they lived together was they felt more at home and had not yet assimilated with the Americans. And, they were avoiding the discrimination they received elsewhere as Irish and as Catholics. The United States was a Protestant-based nation and many harbored a disdain for the Irish Catholics.[5]

Furthermore, natives also hated the Irish infiltrating the city's labor force with a readiness to work for lower wages. However, there were many employers who refused to hire the Irish and displayed their "No Irish Need Apply" signs. Many Americans did not welcome the Irish in general, and being Catholic made them pariahs. The hostilities toward the Catholic Irish reached a boiling point in Philadelphia in 1844. Hatred for the Catholic Irish fueled three days of riots, resulting in thirteen dead and fifty injured. A Catholic church and a seminary were burned.[6] Overall, for some, the Irish immigrant's position in life may have been worse than in Ireland. Drunkenness, fights and crime among the Irish men became a problem and further alienated them in their communities. Irish men worked on low level and dangerous jobs on the canals, docks and construction. As many as one third sustained crippling injuries at work on the railroad. Few went west for farming because they had no experience except for digging potatoes. For females, there was a huge demand for servant girls. It was said that many American girls snubbed these jobs as below their capabilities, but the Irish girls clamored for the work and usually did quite well, even with a grueling schedule of sometimes 6 AM to 11 PM.[7]

Many Irish longed for their homeland. A visit was more feasible in the latter part of the century with steamship fares decreasing, and becoming a shorter voyage. Some were disillusioned with America, especially the Irish speakers and the unskilled laborers. They had difficulty assimilating and could not get past the feeling they were exiled from Ireland. They felt Americans did not take care of their elders and the cities were immoral, with profane language spoken everywhere. Some returned to Ireland to stay. Even the Church was not the same. There were fewer priests, especially Irish priests. At mid-century the ratio was one priest to 3,000 parishioners and in the Western United States one to 7,000.[8] Nevertheless, the Irish Catholics were proud of their crown jewel, St. Patrick's Cathedral, completed in New York City in 1878. There are 21 altars in the cathedral, with 15 to 18 Masses per day. Among many others, the poor Irish immigrants played a noteworthy role in bringing St. Patrick's Cathedral to fruition.[9]

John's son James Casey, living in the Midwest, many times had Mass in his home said by a traveling priest. When a Church was formed in a town about 20 miles away, he would travel miles by wagon on Saturday to gather neighbors, and then departed hours before dawn to reach Mass the next day. For most, the Church remained the central point of Irish life. The Irish had a huge impact on the American Catholic Church. From the 1870s and well into the 20th century, there was a boom, building new churches, cathedrals, convents, schools, seminaries, and colleges. The Irish preferred Catholic schools with Irish history taught along with

American history. The Irish steadfastly maintained their Irish culture throughout the century.[10] The Irish did not discuss Ireland with anyone, not even their children.[11] This rang true with the Casey family. None of the Irish Casey family spoke about their life in Ireland.

One dark stain on the Irish in New York was the Draft Riots of 1863. They were largely held responsible for the riots that caused the death of at least 120 people. The Irish sentiment toward the Civil War was mixed. Some had gone to the American consulate attempting to get draft exemptions, but many others accepted the United States Army's $700 enlistment bonus, equivalent to about ten years' earnings for an Irish laborer.[12] For those who took advantage, they could send generous "American Letters" to their Irish family. But sadly, many died on a battlefield or in a field hospital before they could spend their bonus. The news of a combat death of an Irish soldier spread quickly through their home communities in Ireland and led to much grieving by all. They had lost their loved one and would no longer receive their "American Letter." Two hundred thousand Irishmen served[13] bravely and gained much respect from their fellow soldiers as well as the public in general.[14]

In a speech given by President Kennedy before Irish Parliament in June 1963, he told the United States Civil War story of the Fighting Irish 69th Brigade at the 1862 Battle of Fredericksburg in Virginia. The Irish brigade made attack after attack against the Confederate lines with Old Glory and their Irish colors leading the charge. General Robert E. Lee was so moved by their fierce and tenacious charges that he said, "The gallant stand which this bold brigade made on the heights of Fredericksburg is well known. Never were men so brave. They ennobled their race by their splendid gallantry on that desperate occasion. Their brilliant though hopeless assaults on our lines excited the hearty applause of our officers and soldiers."[15] Among those applauding and cheering for the Irish Brigade's valor was the Confederate 24th Georgia Regiment. The 24th Georgia flew their own green colors. They too were an Irish unit. The Irish on the field that day had traveled over 3,000 miles to America and found themselves pitted against each other in a life or death struggle at Fredericksburg, Virginia. The 24th was loathe to fire on their fellow countrymen, but reluctantly followed orders. Of the 1,200 soldiers of the Irish Brigade that took the field that day, almost 1,000 were casualties including over 500 killed.[16] General Thomas Meagher, a talented Irish leader, was the commander of the Brigade. He was mentioned in Part One, as one of the Young Irelanders in a failed 1848 revolt in Ireland.

When the American people learned of the 69th's bravery that day, it was a significant step in the challenge of the Irish becoming welcome in the United States.[17] Still, the Irish were continued subjects of discrimination by many. They experienced prejudice in employment, because they were Irish and they were Catholic. Many Irish were born, lived and died subjected to religious discrimination and persecution both in Ireland and the United States. Although Irish discrimination waned, the religious discrimination lasted well into the 20th century.[18] In 1960, John F. Kennedy was narrowly elected President under the dark cloud of his Catholicism.

Many Irish fanned out from New York City to find work in other states. They pursued jobs in railroad construction, canal building, and coal mining, among others. The Irish worked at the lowest level and the most dangerous jobs for the least pay. It was said that there was "an Irishman buried under every (railroad) tie." Many Irish remained in the cities, including strong presences in New York, Boston and Chicago. The 1890 Census showed

483,000 Irish immigrants in New York state, with 190,000 living in New York City. Boston became the city most heavily populated with Irish. Most of the 260,000 in Massachusetts lived in Boston. In addition, Illinois harbored 124,000 Irish, of which 79,000 lived in Chicago.[19] Many were unskilled laborers, but a large number of immigrant city dwellers were also policemen, firemen, union leaders, and some held political positions, along with Irish in other fields of work. Second-and third-generation Irish extended even further into a variety of professional positions.[20]

By 1900, there were about 5,000,000 Irish in America, two-thirds of whom were born in the United States. By that time, the Irish reached the levels of native white America, with 35% in white collar jobs or farming, 50% skilled labor and only 15% unskilled labor.[21] However, there were also a great many that were bound to the squalor of Five Points and Hell's Kitchen. Hell's Kitchen had the infamous claim of "the most dangerous place on the whole American continent." Fights and violence were the norm. It is said that the moniker of "Fighting Irish" was born in Hell's Kitchen. Five Points was known for its deadly gangs and held the notorious contention of a murder a day. At one point there were more Irish in New York City than in Dublin.[22]

John, Patrick, James and Michael Casey moved to several states before finally settling in Braidwood, Illinois. The Caseys worked in the coal mines, yet another dangerous field. In 1883, in Braidwood, the Diamond mine flooded and seventy-four men were trapped about eighty feet below the surface of the mine. All seventy-four perished. Braidwood received condolences from around the world for the worst coal mine disaster in history at that time. Thankfully, none of the Caseys were working in the Diamond mine that ill-fated day.[23] John Casey died in Braidwood in 1887, living a long life of eighty-seven years. Michael married

Mary McDermott in Braidwood and had nine children. Michael died in 1897 and Mary in 1893. Patrick, who remained single, took the responsibility of raising their children after Michael and Mary died. Patrick passed away in Braidwood in 1916. The other son, James, his wife Hanora Flynn and their family moved on to Kansas, where they earned Federal land through the Homestead Act of 1862. He and his family and descendants have farmed there to this day. Hanora died in 1906 and James, the last surviving member of the original Irish family, died in 1930. He and Hanora are buried in Plainville, Kansas. It is clear that these were adventurous and resilient people, true pioneers.

There had to be many stories to tell about life in Ireland, but none of the Caseys chose to share their memories. They left their descendants with a blank spot in their heritage. "Indeed, many Irish purposely avoided telling their children anything about Ireland."[24] There was much turmoil and upheaval in Ireland to try to forget. John was born in 1798, the year of the bloody Irish rebellion against the English. He was a toddler when the Protestant Irish Parliament signed away Irish freedoms to the English in the Act of Union of 1801. He was there during the struggle for the release of the Penal Laws and Catholic Emancipation. He and his family lived through the horrific times of the Irish Potato Famine. They endured the Irish depression of the late 1850s and early 60s. They survived the filth, misery and disease of steerage on the harrowing Atlantic passage to the United States. At some time during those years, the brothers lost their mother, a baby brother and a younger sister. It is not known when or how.

John was sixty-four years old when he crossed the Atlantic to start a new life. The boys were in their early twenties. One must wonder if John talked to the boys about their time in Ireland. There was plenty of idle time on the ship crossing the Atlantic.

There were good times to remember and a homesickness for their beloved, green, downtrodden homeland of Ireland. But, the bad times were very bad. They could have talked about the loss of their mother, brother and sister and the horrors of the Famine. Maybe they shared their feelings, although that was out of character for Irishmen of that time. And why didn't they tell their descendants about Ireland? It could have been too painful to remember.

Perhaps John closed the chapter on the painful memories of Ireland, and told the boys,

*"We shall never speak of this again."*

**Thank you for reading my book!**

Did you find the book thought provoking? Did it evoke any emotion?

Please leave a review at your merchant with your thoughts about the book. I would appreciate it.

To review at Amazon:

1. Amazon Book Search: *We Shall Never Speak of This Again*, to the book's detail page.
2. Click on the number of ratings beside the gold stars.
3. On the review page, click on "Write a Customer Review."

**Please Visit my Website!**

https://www.jamesdancasey.com

1. Please leave your E-mail in the Contact: Message section.
2. I will keep you informed of upcoming projects.

# NOTES

## Introduction

[1] "Ireland Quotes," *Your Dictionary*, accessed May 2, 2021, https://www.quotes.yourdictionary.com/ireland/.

## Prologue

[1] "St. Baoithin's Catholic Church," *Ireland XO.com*, accessed May 2, 2021, https://irelandxo.com/ireland-xo/visiting/st-baoithins-roman-catholic-church/.

[2] "Roscommon County Directory, 1862," *Library Ireland,* accessed May 21, 2021, https://www.libraryireland.com/Thom1862/Roscommon.php/.

[3] Editors of Encyclopedia Britannica, Updated by Amy Tikkanen, "Roscommon County, Ireland," *Britannica,* accessed May 2, 2021, https://www.britannica.com/place/Roscommon-county-Ireland/.

[4] "Peat: The Forgotten Fossil Fuel," *National Geographic*, last updated December 7, 2011, accessed May 2, 2021, https://www.nationalgeographic.org/media/peat-forgotten-fuel/.

[5] "Roscommon Climate," *Climate-Data-Org*, accessed May 3, 2021, https://en.climate-org/europe/ireland/roscommon/roscommon-11861/.

## Chapter 1

[1] "Wolfe Tone Quotes and Sayings, Page 1," *Inspiringquotes.us*, accessed May 2, 2021, https://www.inspiringquotes.us/author/5451-wolfe-tone/.

[2] Christine Kinealy, *A Death Dealing Famine, The Great Hunger in Ireland,* (Chicago, Illinois: Pluto Press, March 20, 1997,) 199, cited in *Google Books*, 19. https://books.google.com/books?id=pWELdyf54HQC&printsec=copyright#v=onepage8tq8f=false/.

[3] Ben Johnson, "Henry VIII," *Historic UK, The History and Heritage Accommodation Guide,* accessed May 2, 2021, https://www.historic-uk.com/HistoryUK/HistoryofEngland/Henry-VIII/.

4 Tarlich O'Raifeartaigh, "St. Patrick, Bishop and Patron Saint of Ireland," *Britannica,* accessed May 2, 2021, https://www.britannica.com/biography/Saint-Patrick/.

5 Patrick Timon, "My Heritage," *History of Tibohine, Roscommon Archeological and Historical Society Journal,* Volume 1, accessed May 2, 2021, https://www.myheritage.com/site-28186361/timon-family-tree#/.

6 Kinealy, *A Death-Dealing Famine,* 17.

7 "Irish Potato Famine, Before the Famine," *The History Place,* accessed May 2, 2021, https://www.historyplace.com/worldhistory/faminebefore.htm/.

8 Kinealy, *A Death-Dealing Famine,* 18.

9 "Movement of British Settlers into Ulster during the 17th Century," *Ulster Historical Foundation, Telling the Story of the People of Ulster,* accessed May 2, 2021, https://www.ancestryireland.com/understanding-plantation/movement-of-british-settlers-into-ulster-during-the-17th-century/.

10 R. Barry O'Brien, "The Rebellion of 1641," *Library of Ireland, from The Irish Ecclesiastical Record,* 4th Series, Vol. XVII, No. 449, May 1905, accessed April 25, 2020, https://www.libraryireland.com/articles/rebellion1641/index.php/.

11 Michael O. Siochru, *God's Executioner: Oliver Cromwell and the Conquest of Ireland,* (London, England: Faber and Faber, Ltd., 2008), 82, 84,85, 93.

12 Siochru, *God's Executioner,* 227.

13 Siochru, *God's Executioner,* 90.

14 Richard O'Ferrall and Robert O'Connell, *Commentarius Rinuccinianus, de Sedis Apostolicae Legatione ad Foederatos Hiberniae Catholicos per Annos,* 1645-9, 6 vols., vol. 295, (Dublin 1932-49), cited in Michael O. Siochru (London, England: Faber and Faber Ltd., 2008*), 95.*

15 Siochru, *God's Executioner,* 96-7.

16 14 October 1649, Cromwell to Lenthall, in Abbot (ed.), *Writings of Oliver Cromwell,* vol. 2, pp. 140-3, cited in Michael O. Siochru (London, England: Faber and Faber Ltd., 2008), 97.

17 O'Ferrell and O'Connell, Commentarius *Rinuccinianus,vol.* 4, pp.296-7, 'Petition of the surviving inhabitants of Wexford', National Library of Ireland, MS 9696, ff. 30-3, cited in Michael O. Siochru. *God's Executioner,* (London, England: Faber and Faber Ltd., 2008*),* 97.

18 Timon, "My Heritage*," History of Tibohine, Roscommon Archeological and Historical Society Journal,* vol. 1., accessed July 1, 2021, https://www.myheritage.com/site-28186361/timon-family-tree#/.

19 Siocru, *God's Executioner,* 117.

20 Siocru, *God's Executioner,* 226-9.

[21] Tony Rea and John Wright, *Ireland: A Divided Island, (*Oxford, New York, Oxford University Press, 1998,) accessed May 30, 2021, https://books.google.com.bo/books?id=wL5Nup6gIKUC&printsec=frontcover&source=gbs_atb#v=onepage&q&f=false/, 6.

[22] Barry Murphy, "Connacht," *Barry's Guided Tours,* 2013, accessed May 5, 2021, https:barrysguidedtours.com/Connacht/.

[23] Murphy, *Connacht,* accessed May 5,2021.

[24] Siocru, *God's Executioner,* 247.

[25] "Constitutional Differences," *UK Parliament,* accessed June 29, 2021, https://www.parliament.uk/about/living-heritage/evolutionofparliament/legislativescrutiny/parliamentandireland/overview/constitutional-differences/.

[26] Cecil-Woodham Smith, *The Great Hunger, Ireland 1845-1849,* (New York: Old Town Books, 1962), 27.

[27] "'Tithe War' in North United Catholic and Dissenter," *The Irish Times,* July 2, 2013, accessed May 5, 2021, http://www.irishnews.com/opinion/2013/07/02/news/-tithe-war-in-north-united-catholic-and-dissenter-63852/.

[28] "Religion, The Penal Laws," *Ulster Historical Foundation. Telling the Story of the People of Ulster,* accessed May 5, 2021, https://www.ancestryireland.com/history-of-the-irish-parliament/background-to-the-statutes/religion/.

[29] "'Tithe War' In North United Catholic and Dissenter," *The Irish New.*

[30] Editors, Encyclopedia Britannica, "Irish Rebellion, Irish History, 1798." *Britannica.com,* accessed May 5, 2021, https://www.britannica.com/event/Irish-Rebellion-Irish-history-1798/.

[31] Michael Green, "A Biography of Wolfe Tone," *Wolfe Tone,* accessed March 30, 2021, https://www.ireland-information.com/articles/wolfetone.htm/.

[32] Green, "A Biography of Wolfe Tone."

[33] Green, "A Biography of Wolfe Tone."

[34] Tommy Graham, Editor, "The Death of Wolfe Tone," *The Irish Times,* March 17, 2008, accessed March 30, 2021, https://www.irishtimes.com/opinion/letters/the-death-of-wolfe-tone-1.904217/.

## Chapter 2

[1] Irish Central Staff, "Daniel O'Connell-Quotes from Ireland's Liberator," *Irish Central,* May 15, 2020, accessed May 5, 2021, https://irishcentral.com/roots/history/Daniel-oconnell-quotes/.

2 Margie Bloy, Ph.D., Senior Research Fellow, "Britain, Ireland and the Disastrous 1801 Act of Union," *The Victorian Web,* last modified 1997, last added, January 14, 2002, accessed May 1, 2020, https:victorianweb.org/history/ireland1.html/.

3 Bloy, Ph.D., *The Victorian Web.*

4 Antonia Fraser, *The King and the Catholics: England, Ireland, and the Fight for Religious Freedom, 1780-1829, (*London, England: The Orion Publishing Group, Ltd., 2018), 69-70.

5 Fraser, *The King and the Catholics,* 98, 100.

6 Fraser, *The King and the Catholics,* 134-35, 141-2.

7 Fraser, *The King and the Catholics,* 215.

8 Fraser, *The King and the Catholics,* 207, 214.

9 Fraser, *The King and the Catholics,* 243, 258.

10 Fraser, *The King and the Catholics,* 259.

11 Fraser, *The King and the Catholics,* 266-7, 272.

12 Fraser, *The King and the Catholics,* 275.

13 Thomas Keneally, *The Great Shame,* (New York, Nan A. Talese, Doubleday Imprint,) 8, cited in Edward J. O'Boyle, Phd. Mayo Research Institute, *Classical Economics and the Great Irish Famine: A Study in Limits,* 33, accessed July 1, 2021, https://www.mayoresearch.org/files/GREATFAMINE.pdf/, 11.

14 Tim Pat Coogan, *The Famine Plot*, (New York: Palgrave Macmillan, 2012), 47.

15 Coogan, *The Famine Plot*, 48.

16 Woodham-Smith, *The Great Hunger,* 18.

17 Coogan, *The Famine Plot*, 48.

## CHAPTER 3

1 "100 Irish Quotes and Sayings," *Inspirational Words of Wisdom,* 90, accessed May 5, 2021, https://www.wow4u.com/irishquotessayings/.

2 Cormac O Grada, "The Population of Ireland, 1700-1900: A Survey," *Persee,* 1979, accessed May 5, 2021, https://www.persee.fr/doc/adh_0066-2062_1979_num_1979_1_1425/.

3 Woodham-Smith, *The Great Hunger,* 29-30.

4 Woodham-Smith, *The Great Hunger,* 24-5.

5 "The Biggest Traditional Irish Sports," *Gaelic Matters.com, The Home of Gaelic and Irish Culture*, accessed May 5, 2021, https://www.gaelicmatters.com/traditional-irish-sports.html/.

6 Hugh Brody, *Inishkillane: Change and Decline in the West of Ireland,* (Middlesex England and Victoria, Australia: Penguin Books, 1974,) 26-31.

7 Susan Campbell Bartoletti, *Black Potatoes: The Story of the Great Famine, 1845-1850,* (Boston: Houghton Mifflin Company, 2001,) 172.

8 Coogan, *The Famine Plot*, 125.

9 Bartoletti, *Black Potatoes*, 103.

10 Coogan, *The Famine Plot*, 125.

11 Brody, *Inishkillane*, 110-12, 116, 126, 175-6.

12 D. W. Miller, "Catholic," Hynes, Connell, 113-61; G. Birmingham, *Irishmen All* (London, 1914), 184; S. O'Faolain, *The Irish: A* Character *Study* (NY, 1949), 129-46, cited in Kerby A. Miller, *Emigrants and Exiles: Ireland and the Irish Exodus to North America,* (New York, Oxford, Oxford University Press, 1985,) 127.

13 Brody, *Inishkillane*, 175-6, 25,110.

14 Miller, *Emigrants and Exiles* 89, 116.

15 Miller, *Emigrants and Exiles* 126-127.

16 Brody, *Inishkillane*, 20, 62-3, 112.

17 Miller, *Emigrants and Exiles,* 320, 407, 499.

18 Ian Maxwell, *Everyday Life in 19th Century Ireland,* (Dublin: The History Press, 2012), 113-116.

19 Lance Daly, Director, *Black '47: Justice Comes Home*, Fastnet Films and Sansa Film, Hugo Weaving and James Frecheville, 2017.

20 Miller, *Emigrants and Exiles,* 72, 78, 404-405.

21 Dennis Walsh, "Ireland's History in Maps." *Rootsweb,* accessed on May 6, 2021, http://sites.rootsweb.com/-irkik/ihm/.

22 "The Great Irish Potato Famine, Decline of the Irish Language and Culture," *History Cooperative,* last updated October 31, 2009, accessed July 12, 2020, https://historycooperative.org/the-irish-famine/.

23 Eanna O. Caollai, "Report reveals student support for compulsory Irish," *The Irish Times*, updated March 15, 2021, accessed April 19, 2021, https://www.irishtimes.com/news/education/report-reveals-student-support-for-compulsory-irish-1.4510604/.

24 Bartoletti, *Black Potatoes, 27.*

25 "Ireland, Educational System-Overview," accessed April 8, 2021, https://education.stateuniversity.com/pages/695/Ireland-EDUCATIONAL-SYSTEM-OVERVIEW.html/.

26 Maxwell, *Everyday Life in 19th Century Ireland, 158*-9.

27 Bartoletti, *Black Potatoes*, 120-1.

28 Miller, *Emigrants and Exiles* 341.

## CHAPTER 4

1 "Irish Quotes," *Goodreads*, accessed April 4, 2021, https://www.goodreads.com/quotes/tag/irish?page=6/.

2 Woodham-Smith, *The Great Hunger,* 31.

3 Woodham-Smith, *The Great Hunger,* 32-5.

4 "The Great Irish Potato Famine," *History Cooperative,* October 31, 2009, accessed May 6, 2021, https://historycooperative.org/the-irish-famine/.

5 "The Great Irish Potato Famine," *History Cooperative.*

6 Woodham-Smith, *The Great Hunger,* 32-5, 471.

7 Terence A. M. Dooley, *Estate Ownership and Management in Nineteenth and Early Twentieth-century Ireland,* accessed May 6, 2021, http://www.aughty.org/pdf/estate_own_manage.pdf/.

8 Woodham-Smith, *The Great Hunger,* 32-5.

9 "Census 2016: Looking Back 175 years-Changes in the Western Region Population," *WDC Insights,* accessed May 6, 2021, https://wdcinsights.wordpress.com/2017/05/22/census-2016-looking-back-175-years-changes-in-the-western-region-population/.

10 Isaac Weld, "Survey of the County of Roscommon Situation-Extent-Boundaries," *Statistical Survey of the County of Roscommon,* 2, (Printed by R. Graisberry, 1832), accessed May 30, 2021, https://books.google.com/books/about/Statistical_Survey_of_the_County_of_Rosc.html?id=SMU8jh4Tj5AC/.

11 "The Irish Potato Famine, 1847," *EyeWitness to History.com*, accessed May 6, 2021, http://www.eyewitnesstohistory.com/irishfamine.htm/.

12 Jim Donnelly, "The Irish Famine," *BBC*, updated February 17, 2017, accessed July 11, 2020, http://www.bbc.co.uk/history/british/victorians/famine_01.shtml/.

13 Cynthia E. Smith, "The Land-Tenure System in Ireland: A Fatal Regime," *Marquette Law Review,* Volume 76, Issue 2, Winter, 1993, accessed May 6, 2021, https://scholarship.law.marquette.edu/cgi/viewcontent.cgi?/.

14 Smith, "The Land-Tenure System in Ireland: A Fatal Regime," *Marquette Law Review.*

15 "The Irish Potato Famine, 1847," *Eyewitness to History.com.*

16 Smith, "The Land-Tenure System in Ireland: A Fatal Regime." *Marquette Law Review.*

17 Irish Central Staff, "Ireland's Great Hunger-What Really Happened to the Food in Ireland," *Irish Central*, February 1, 2019, accessed May 6, 2021,

https://www.irishcentral.com/roots/history/facts-great-hunger-irish-famine-food-ireland-dates/.

18 Cynthia E. Smith, "The Land-Tenure System in Ireland: A Fatal Regime." *Marquette Law Review.*

19 Admin., "The Great Famine 1845-1849," *Irish Country Life History,* November 12, 2012, accessed May 21, 2020, http://countrylifehistory.ie/index.php/2012/11/the-great-famine-1845-1849/.

20 Woodham-Smith, *The Great Hunger, 20.*

21 Woodham-Smith, *The Great Hunger, 21.*

22 Evidence given to the Devon Commission, 1843-1845, by Mayo clergy, quoted by Liam Swords in *The Famine in North Connaught,* (Dublin, Columba Press, 1999), cited in Coogan, *The Famine Plot*, (New York: Palgrave Macmillan. 2012),19-20.

23 Coogan, *The Famine Plot,* 39.

24 Michael Winstanley, *Ireland and the Land Question, 1800-1922, Lancaster Pamphlets,* 2007, cited in, Dr. Marjorie Bloy, "Land holding in Ireland 1760-1880," *The Age of George III,* accessed February 29, 2020, http://www.historyhome.co.uk/c-eight/ireland/ire-land.htm/.

25 Maxwell, *Everyday Life in $19^{th}$ Century Ireland,* 41.

26 John Dorney, "The Great Irish Famine 1845-1851 – A Brief Overview," *The Irish Story*, accessed May 19, 2020, https://www.theirishstory.com/2016/10/18/the-great-irish-famine-1845-1851-a-brief-overview/#.YLRqQ8ftx9A/.

27 Michael Winstanley, *Ireland and the Land Question, 1800-1922, Lancaster Pamphlets*, 2007, cited in, Dr. Marjorie Bloy, "Land holding in Ireland 1760-1880," *The Age of George III,* accessed February 29, 2020, http://www.historyhome.co.uk/c-eight/ireland/ire-land.htm/.

28 Maxwell, *Everyday Life in $19^{th}$ Century Ireland,* 50.

29 Mary and Gordon Elmer, "Balfe History" *SCR,* accessed May 6, 2021, https://www.scribd.com/doc/106952600/Balfe-History/.

30 Mary and Gordon Elmer, "Balfe History."

31 Leslie A. Willow*, Daniel O'Connell: The British Press and the Irish Famine: Killing Remarks, Roscommon Morning Chronicles,* 10 December, 1845, 8. Accessed on May 6, 2021, https://books.google.com/books?id=zn1BDgAAQBAJ&pg=PT118&lpg=PT118&dq=nicholas+balfe+forgave+one+ha+one+lf+his+tenants'+rent+in+1845&source=bl&ots=SgJOW4L4ty&sig=ACfU3U2lC6Op-IlzZEpz5DkGi8MaR9VeIw&hl=en&sa=X&ved=2ahUKEwjZyPT0qbbwAhWQW80KHS_3DIAQ6AEwA3oECAUQAw#v=onepage&q=nicholas%20balfe%20forgave%20one%20half%20his%20tenants'%20rent%20in%201845&f=false/.

[32] Elmer, "Balfe History," *SCR*.

[33] Coogan, *The Famine Plot,* 155.

[34] Coogan, *The Famine Plot, 155.*

[35] Michael Winstanley*, Ireland and the Land Question, 1800-1922, Lancaster Pamphlets, 2007,* cited in, Dr. Marjorie Bloy, "Land holding in Ireland 1760-1880," *The Age of George III*, accessed February 29, 2020, http://www.historyhome.co.uk/c-eight/ireland/ire-land.htm/.

[36] Brendan Graham, "Historical Notes: God and England made the Irish famine," *Independent,* December 3, 1998, accessed May 6, 2021, https://www.independent.co.uk/arts-entertainment/historical-notes-god-and-england-made-the-irish-famine-1188828.html.

[37] Bartoletti, Black Potatoes, 29.

[38] Woodham-Smith, *The Great Hunger,* 94.

## CHAPTER 5

[1] Paul Lynch, "Victoria, Famine Queen, and the Silence of Survivors," *The Irish Times*, October 6, 2017, accessed May 6, 2021, https://www.irishtimes.com/culture/books/Victoria.famine-queen-and-the-silence-of-survivors-1.3246729/.

[2] Woodham-Smith, *The Great Hunger,* 40.

[3] Woodham-Smith, *The Great Hunger,* 41.

[4] Woodham-Smith, *The Great Hunger, 94.*

[5] Woodham-Smith, *The Great Hunger,* 39.

[6] Coogan, *The Famine Plot,* 51.

[7] Woodham-Smith, *The Great Hunger,* 40.

[8] Woodham-Smith, *The Great Hunger,* 44.

[9] David Ross, "The Corn Laws," *Britain Express*, accessed May 6, 2021, https://www.britainexpress.com/History/victorian/corn-laws.htm/.

[10] Coogan, *The Famine Plot,* 55.

[11] Wesley Johnston, "The Famine 3, Peel's Relief Programme to July, 1846", *Ireland's Great Famine 1845-1849,* accessed May 6, 2021, https://www.wesleyjohnston.com/users/ireland/past/famine/tory_july_1846.html/.

[12] Woodham-Smith, *The Great Hunger,* 54.

[13] Coogan, *The Famine Plot,* 79.

[14] Wesley Johnston, "The Famine 3, Peel's Relief Programme to July, 1846, *Ireland's Great Famine 1845-1849.*

[15] Woodham-Smith, *The Great Hunger, 48-9.*

[16] Bartoletti, *Black Potatoes,* 49.

[17] Coogan, *The Famine Plot,* 105.

18 "The Famine 3, Peel's Relief Programme to July, 1846, I*reland's Great Famine 1845-1849.*"

19 Woodham-Smith, *The Great Hunger, 103.*

20 Woodham-Smith, *The Great Hunger, 59.*

21 Coogan, *The Famine Plot,* 60.

22 Coogan, *The Famine Plot,* 63-4.

23 Coogan, *The Famine Plot,* 63-4.

24 Woodham-Smith, *The Great Hunger, 105.*

25 Woodham-Smith, *The Great Hunger,* 89.

26 Woodham-Smith, *The Great Hunger,* 89-90.

27 Wesley Johnston, "The Famine 4, The Winter of 1846-1847, I*reland's Great Famine 1845-1849,* accessed May 31, 2020, https://www.wesleyjohnston.com/users/ireland/past/famine/whig_1846_1847.html/.

28 Woodham-Smith, *The Great Hunger,* 106-7.

29 Christine Kinealy," Food Exports from Ireland 1846-1847," *History Ireland, Ireland's History Magazine,* published in 18th-19th-Century History, Features, Issue 1, Spring 1997, *The Famine*, Volume 5, accessed May 7, 2021, https://www.historyireland.com/18th-19th-century-history/food-export/.

30 Christine Kinealy, *The Great Calamity: The Irish Famine 1845-1852,* (Boulder: Roberts Rinehart Publishers, 1995, first published in Ireland by Gill and Macmillan, Ltd, 1994), 4.

31 John Mitchel, *An Apology for the British Government in Ireland.* (Dublin: O'Donoghue and Company, 1905), 156.

32 John Stuart Mill, "Editorials from the Morning Chronicle," in *John Stuart Mill on Ireland with an Essay by Richard Ned Lebow,* (Philadelphia: Institute for the Study of Human Issues, 1979), 35. cited in Edward J. O'Boyle, Phd. Mayo Research Institute, *Classical Economics and the Great Irish Famine: A Study in Limits,* 19, accessed May 21, 2021, https://www.mayoresearch.org/files/GREATFAMINE.pdf/,

33 The Irish Famine: Complicity in Murder," *The Washington Post,* September 27, 1997, accessed February 27, 2020, https://www.washingtonpost.com/archive/opinions/1997/09/27/the-irish-famine-complicity-in-murder/5a155118-3620-4145-951e-0dc46933b84a/.

34 Bartoletti, *Black Potatoes,* 55-6.

35 Miller, *Emigrants and Exiles,* 288.

36 Bartoletti, *Black Potatoes,* 55-6.

37 Thomas Cahill, "Why the Famine came to Ireland," *Irish Central,* 2010, accessed May 19, 2020, https://www.irishcentral.com/roots/why-famine-came-to-ireland-93283629-237694481/.

[38] Peter Gray, *Famine, Land and Politics: British Government and Irish Society, 1843-1850*, (Dublin: Irish Academic Press, 1999,) cited in Tim Pat Coogan, *The Famine Plot,* (New York: Palgrave Macmiillan, 2012), 36.

[39] Christine Kinealy, "Food Exports from Ireland 1846-1847," *History Ireland, Ireland's History Magazine,* $18^{th}$-$19^{th}$-Century History, Issue 1, Spring 1997, accessed May 21, 2021, https://www.historyireland.com/$18^{th}$-$19^{th}$-century-history/food-exports-from-ireland-1846-47/.

[40] Guest Contribution, "The Great Irish Potato Famine," *History Cooperative,* October 31, 2009, accessed May 21, 2021, https://historycooperative.org/the-irish-famine/.

[41] Irish Central Staff, "Ireland's Great Hunger-What Really Happened to the Food in Ireland," *Irish Central*, February 1, 2019, accessed on February 27, 2020, https://www.irishcentral.com/roots/history/facts-great-hunger-irish-famine-f00d-ireland-dates/.

[42] Christine Kinealy,"Food Exports from Ireland 1846-1847," *History Ireland, Ireland's History Magazine.*

[43] "Mitchel 1858," 219, *Encyclopedia.com.*, June 27, 2018, accessed June 1, 2020, https://www.encyclopedia.com/people/history/british-and-irish-history-biographies/johnmitchel/.

[44] "The Irish Potato Famine 1846-1850," *DoChara, Insider Guide to Ireland,* 2008, last updated, March 31, 2017, accessed May 19, 2020, https://www.dochara.comtheirish/food-history/the-history/the-irish-potato-famine-1845-1850/.

[45] Wesley Johnston, "The Famine 4, The Winter of 1846-1847," *Ireland's Great Famine 1845-1849.*

[46] Bartoletti, *Black Potatoes*, 63.

[47] Woodham-Smith, *The Great Hunger,* 128, 131, 141.

[48] Thomas Cahill, "Why Famine Came to Ireland," *Irish Central,* accessed June 1, 2020, https//www.irishcentral.com/roots/why-famine-came-to-ireland-93283629-237694481/.

[49] Bartoletti, *Black Potatoes,* 94.

[50] Woodham-Smith, *The Great Hunger,* 185.

[51] Woodham-Smith, *The Great Hunger,* 119.

[52] Bartoletti, *Black Potatoes,* 61.

[53] Coogan, *The Famine Plot*, 113.

[54] Miller, *Emigrants and Exiles,* 290.

[55] Woodham-Smith, *The Great Hunger,* 166, 157, 147, 186, 180.

[56] Thomas Cahill, "Why Famine came to Ireland," *Irish Central.*

57 Ruan O'Donnell, *A Short History of Ireland's Famine,* (Dublin: O'Brien's Press, Ltd., 2008), accessed May 7, 2021, https://www.scribd.com/book/353199388/A-Short-History-of-Ireland-s-Famine/.

## Chapter 6

1 "Famine Quotes," *Your Dictionary,* accessed May 7, 2021, https://quotes.yourdictionary.com/famine.

2 *W. R. Aykroyd,* "The Effects of Lack of Food," *The Conquest of Famine,* Chapter 2, Summarized by Josef Skoldeberg, accessed May 21, 2021, http://la.utexas.edu/users/hcleaver/357L/357Lsum_s4_Aykroyd_Ch2.html.

3 "A Guide to Ennistymon Union 1839-1850- Disease," Courtesy of North Clare Historical Society, *Clare County Library,* accessed June 21, 2021, https://www.clarelibrary.ie/eolas/coclare/history/etworkhouse.htm/.

4 W. R. Aykroyd, "The Effects of Lack of Food," *The Conquest of Famine,* Chapter 2.

5 Johnson "The Famine 4: The Winter of 1846 to 1847, *The Irish Famine: The Winter of 1846 to 1847.*

6 *W. R. Aykroyd,* "The Effects of Lack of Food," *The Conquest of Famine,* Chapter 2.

7 Laurence Geary, "Epidemic Diseases of the Great Famine," *History Ireland,* (Published in 18th-19th-Century History, Features. Issue 1,Spring 1996), The Famine, Volume 4, accessed May 7, 2021, https://www.historyireland.com/18th-19th-century-history/epidemic-diseases-of-the-great-famine/.

8 "The Great Irish Potato Famine," *History Cooperative,* October 31, 2009, accessed May 21, 2021, https://historycooperative.org/the-irish-famine/.

9 William G. Powderly, *M. D.* "How Infection Shaped History: Lessons from the Irish Famine," *Transactions of the Clinical and Climatological Association, PMC,* 2019, accessed May 7, 2021, https://www.ncbi.nlm.nih.gov/pmc/articles/PMC6735970.

10 Cecil Woodham, Smith, *The Great Hunger, Ireland, 1845=1849,* (New York: Old Town Books, 1962), cited in Coogan, *The Famine Plot,* (New York: Palgrave Macmillan, 2012), 182.

11 William G. Powderly, M.D., "How Infection Shaped History: Lessons From the Irish Famine."

12 "A Guide to Ennistymon Union 1839-1850-Disease," *Clare County Library.*

13 "A Guide to Ennistymon Union 1839-1850-Disease,"*Clare County Library.*

14 Coogan, *The Famine Plot,* 131.

15 Woodham-Smith, *The Great Hunger,* 221.

16 "A Guide to Ennistymon Union 1839-1850-Disease" *Clare County Library.*

## CHAPTER 7

1 Derek Reed, "The Workhouse," *Irish Famine Exhibition,* December 21, 2019, accessed May 7, 2021. https://www.theirishpotatofamine.com/blogs/blog-1/the-workhouse/.

2 Coogan, *The Famine Plot*, 39, 41.

3 Coogan, *The Famine Plot*, 39.

4 Coogan, *The Famine Plot*, 39.

5 Woodham-Smith, *The Great Hunger, 63.*

6 Bartoletti, *Black Potatoes,* 90.

7 Coogan, *The Famine Plot*, 132.

8 Coogan, *The Famine Plot*, 165.

9 Maxwell, *Everyday Life in 19th Century Ireland, 100.*

10 Coogan, *The Famine Plot*, 133.

11 Bartoletti, *Black Potatoes,* 30, 31.

12 Maxwell, *Everyday Life in 19th Century Ireland, 98*

13 Derek Reed, "The Workhouse," *Irish Famine Exhibition,* December 21, 2019, accessed April 10, 2021, https://www.theirishpotatofamine.com/blogs/blog-1/the-workhouse/.

14 Bartoletti, *Black Potatoes,* 30-1.

15 Maxwell, *Everyday Life in 19th Century Ireland,* 97.

16 Bartoletti, *Black Potatoes,* 158.

17 Coogan, *The Famine Plot*, 135.

18 Guinnane, 3, cited in Edward J. O'Boyle, Phd. Mayo Research Institute, "*Classical Economics and the Great Irish Famine: A Study in Limits,*" accessed May 7, 2021, https://www.mayoresearch.org/files/GREATFAMINE.pdf, 9/.

19 Bartoletti, *Black Potatoes,* 89.

20 Coogan, *The Famine Plot*, 112.

21 Coogan, *The Famine Plot*, 133.

22 Maxwell, *Everyday Life in 19th Century Ireland, 98.*

23 "The Workhouse - an Unworkable Solution to Irish Poverty," *Old Filibuster – Curmudgeonly Musings,* accessed May 7, 2021, http://www.oldfilibuster.com/the-workhouse-ndash-an-unworkable-solution-to-irish-poverty.html/.

24 Coogan, *The Famine Plot*, 133.

[25] Cardinale, Vogel, O"Brien, Batzer, "Sliding Coffin Cross Display Will Mark 1845-1850 Irish Famine," *The Buffalo News*, September 29, 1996, accessed May 31, 2021, https://buffalonews.com/news/sliding-coffin-cross-display-will-mark-1845-50-irish-famine/article_554d9943-5e28-5e06-99a1-92b755a46234.html/.

[26] Coogan, *The Famine Plot*, 125.

[27] Bartoletti, *Black Potatoes,* 46-7.

[28] Capt. Gordon Report, No. 9, 1846. Enclosed, Geo. Pincher, Sub-Inspector Police to Inspector-General, November 2, 1846; also copy of evidence Drs. Daniel Donovan and Patrick Due. B of W Corr. I, pp. 219-220, cited in Cecil Woodham-Smith, *The Great Hunger,* (New York: Old Town Books, 1962), 141.

[29] Woodham-Smith, *The Great Hunger,* 111, 153.

[30] Woodham-Smith, *The Great Hunger,* 111, 146, 151, 153.

[31] Dorney, "The Great Irish Famine 1845-1851 – A Brief Overview," *The Irish Story.*

[32] Woodham-Smith, *The Great Hunger,* 166, 171.

[33] Woodham-Smith, *The Great Hunger,* 186.

[34] Woodham-Smith, *The Great Hunger,* 180.

[35] "The Great Irish Potato Famine," *History Cooperative.*

[36] Woodham-Smith, *The Great Hunger,* 63, 180.

[37] Woodham-Smith, *The Great Hunger,* 187.

[38] Coogan, *The Famine Plot,* 137-9.

[39] Coogan, *The Famine Plot,* 143, 145.

[40] Coogan, *The Famine Plot*, 145..

[41] Woodham-Smith, *The Great Hunger,* 296.

[42] Woodham-Smith, *The Great Hunger,* 180.

[43] Bartoletti, *Black Potatoes,* 75-9.

[44] Aykroyd, "The Effects of Lack of Food," *The Conquest of Famine, Chapter 2.*

[45] Woodham-Smith, *The Great Hunger,* 296.

[46] Bartoletti, *Black Potatoes,* 88.

[47] Coogan, *The Famine Plot*, 165.

[48] Woodham-Smith, *The Great Hunger,* 303.

## Chapter 8

[1] "Evictions," *The Gael,* August, 1901, accessed May 8, 2021, http://www.maggieblanck.com/Mayopages/Eviction.html/.

2 Jim Donnelly, "The Irish Famine," *BBC History* February 17, 2011, accessed May 16, 2020. http:www.bbc.co.uk/history/british/victorians/famine_01.shtml.

3 Maxwell, *Everyday Life in 19th Century Ireland, 41.*

4 Coogan, *The Famine Plot*, 116, illustration 8, The London Illustrated News, 1849.

5 Bartoletti, *Black Potatoes,* 107.

6 "Poor Law Amendment Act of 1847 and the Gregory Clause," *Encyclopedia.com*, accessed May 8, 2021, https://www.encyclopedia.com/international/encyclopedias-almanacs-transcripts-and-maps/poor-law-amendment-act-1847-and-gregory-clause/.

7 Bartoletti, *Black Potatoes,* 112.

8 "Background on the Irish Famine you won't find Elsewhere," *Wordpress.com,* accessed July 21, 2020, https://theninthwavenovel.wordpress.com/the-famine/.

9 Niall O'Dowd, "Was it Genocide? What the British ruling class really said about the Irish Famine," *Irish Central,* June 16, 2019, accessed May 21, 2020, https://www.irishcentral.com/roots/genocide-what-british-ruling-class-said-irish-famine.

10 Maxwell, *Everyday Life in 19th Century Ireland, 51-2.*

11 Bartoletti, *Black Potatoes,* 107.

12 Maxwell, *Everyday Life in 19th Century Ireland, 53.*

13 Woodham-Smith, *The Great Hunger, 71-2.*

14 Coogan, *The Famine Plot,* 95-6.

15 Coogan, *The Famine Plot,* 88.

16 Coogan, *The Famine Plot,* 89.

17 Coogan, *The Famine Plot,* 90.

18 Maxwell, *Everyday Life in 19th Century Ireland, 49.*

19 Coogan, *The Famine Plot,* 90.

20 Woodham-Smith, *The Great Hunger,* 364-5.

21 Coogan, *The Famine Plot,* 99-100.

22 Donnelly, *The Irish Famine, An Act of Providence,* February 17, 2011, *BBC History.*

23 Woodham-Smith, *The Great Hunger, 213, 227.*

24 Coogan, *The Famine Plot,* 191.

25 Maxwell, *Everyday Life in 19th Century Ireland, 93.*

26 Dr. Christine Kinealy, Contributor, "Roscommon Part III: The Hungry Years," *Irish America,* December/January 2018, accessed May 31, 2021, https://irishamerica.com/2017/12/roscommon-part-iii-the-hungry-years.

[27] "The Execution of Landlord Denis Mahon," *Background on the Irish Famine You Won't Find Elsewhere,* February 16, 2016, accessed May 31, 2021, https://theninthwavenovel.wordpress.com/2011/02/16/the=execution-of-denis-mahon/.

[28] Stephen A. Brighton, *Historical Archaeology of the Irish Diaspora: A Transnational Approach, The Social History and Archaeology,* 54, accessed June 21, 2021, https://books.google.com/books/about/Historical_Archaeology_of_the_Irish_Dias.html?id=4p07hjxezAcC/.

[29] Coogan, *The Famine Plot,* 180.

[30] Coogan, *The Famine Plot,* 178-81.

[31] Cecil Woodham-Smith, The Great Hunger, 324, 327.

## CHAPTER 9

[1] John Mitchel, *Describing Irish Famine in Jail Journal,* accessed May 9, 2021, https://irishfreedom.net/Famous%20Qoutations/Famous%20Quotations.htm/.

[2] "Census 2016: Looking Back 175 Years-Changes in the Western Region Population," *WDC Insights,* May 22, 2017, accessed June 22, 2021, https://wdcinsights.wordpress.com/2017/05/22/census-2016-looking-back-175-years-changes-in-the-western-region-population/.

[3] Scally, 1995, 224, cited in Stephen A. Brighton*, Historical Archaeology of the Irish Diaspora: A Transnational Approach,* 54.

[4] Ronan McGreevy, "Pioneering Study Charts Population Fall Since Famine," *The Irish Times,* August 3, 2011, accessed May 9, 2021, https://www.irishtimes.com/news/pioneering-study-charts-population-fall-since-famine/.

[5] Ronan McGreevy, "Pioneering Study Charts Population Fall Since Famine," *The Irish Times.*

[6] Maxwell, *Everyday Life in 19th Century Ireland,* 171, 173.

[7] Kinealy, Contributor, "Roscommon Part III: The Hungry Years," *Irish America.*

[8] Woodham-Smith, *The Great Hunger,* 202.

[9] Woodham-Smith, *The Great Hunger,* 204.

[10] Bartoletti, *Black Potatoes,* 90.

[11] Kinealy, Contributor, "Roscommon Part III: The Hungry Years," *The Irish Times.*

[12] Kinealy, Contributor, "Roscommon Part III: The Hungry Years," *The Irish Times.*

[13] Patrick Timon, "History of Fairymount/Tibohine," *Timon History, Genealogy, Publications and Film,* Extracts from a talk given by Patrick Timone to the Lough Gara Historical Society, Fairymount 1969, published in the *Roscommon Archeological and Historical Society Journal,* 1986, Vol. 1, accessed June 22, 2021, https://www.timon.ie/2017/gaelic/history-of-tibohine/.

[14] Patrick Timon, "Famine Times in Tibohine," Story told by Luke Callaghan, 80 years. Tibohine, December 1921, *Timon History, Genealogy, Publications and Film*, accessed May 31, 2021, http://www.timon.ie/2019/general/famine-times-in-tibohine/.

[15] Woodham-Smith, *The Great Hunger,* 206.

[16] Woodham-Smith, *The Great Hunger,* 212.

[17] Miller, *Emigrants and Exiles,* 292.

[18] Woodham-Smith, *The Great Hunger,* 224.

[19] Bartoletti, *Black Potatoes,* 132.

[20] Woodham-Smith, *The Great Hunger,* 206.

[21] Bartoletti, *Black Potatoes,* 120.

[22] "The Great Irish Potato Famine," *History Cooperative.*

[23] Thomas Cahill, "Why the Famine Came to Ireland," *Irish Central*, 2010, accessed May 19, 2020, https://www.irishcentral.com/roots/why-famine-came-to-ireland-93283629-237694481/.

[24] Woodham-Smith, *The Great Hunger,* 147.

[25] Coogan, *The Famine Plot,* 115.

[26] "The Great Irish Potato Famine," *History Cooperative.*

[27] "The Great Irish Potato Famine," *History Cooperative.*

[28] Woodham-Smith, *The Great Hunger,* 297.

[29] Miller, *Emigrants and Exiles,* 285.

[30] Admin, "The Great Famine 1845-1849," *Irish Country Life History.*

[31] Coogan, *The Famine Plot,* 90.

[32] Clarendon to Lord John Russell, October 23, 1847, *Clarendon Papers, Out Letter Books,* Vol.1. Lord John Russell to Clarendon, October 21, 1847, *Clarendon Papers, 1 A*, cited in Woodham-Smith, *The Great Hunger,* 317.

[33] Woodham-Smith, *The Great Hunger,* 300.

[34] Woodham-Smith, *The Great Hunger,* 300.

[35] Richard Cavendish, "Daniel O'Connell, Irish Nationalist, Dies in Genoa," *History Today,* accessed May 10, 2021, https://www.historytoday.com/archive/daniel-oconnell-irish-nationalist-dies-genoa/.

[36] Woodham-Smith, *The Great Hunger,* 300.

[37] "The Irish Potato Famine,1847," *Eyewitness to History.com,* accessed May 31, 2021, http://www.eyewitnesstohistory.com/irishfamine.htm/.

38 Thomas Cahill, "Why Famine came to Ireland," *Irish Central*, May 1, 2010, accessed June 1, 2020, https://www.irishcentral.com/roots/why-famine-came-to-ireland-93283629-237694481/.
39 Thomas Cahill, "Why Famine came to Ireland." *Irish Central.*
40 "The Great Irish Potato Famine," *History Cooperative.*
41 Woodham-Smith, *The Great Hunger,* 221.
42 Woodham-Smith, *The Great Hunger,* 195.
43 Christine Kinealy, "'The Bad Times': Visualizing the Famine in a Graphic Novel," *The Irish Times,* April 12, 2018, accessed May 31, 2021, https://www.irishtimes.com/life-and-style/abroad/the-bad-times-visualising-the-famine-in-a-graphic-novel-1.3458428/.
44 Bartoletti, *Black Potatoes,* 69.
45 "The Irish Potato Famine,1847," *Eyewitness to History.com,* (2006), accessed May 22, 2020, www.eyewitnesstohistory.com/irishfamine.htm/.
46 "The Irish Potato Famine,1847," *Eyewitness to History.com.*
47 Bartoletti, *Black Potatoes,* 68.
48 Bartoletti, *Black Potatoes,* 158.
49 "The Great Irish Potato Famine," *History Cooperative.*
50 Bartoletti, *Black Potatoes,* 73.
51 Bartoletti, *Black Potatoes,* 33.
52 Bartoletti, *Black Potatoes,* 155.
53 Miller, *Emigrants and Exiles,* 290.
54 Coogan, *The Famine Plot,* 104.
55 Coogan, *The Famine Plot,* 184-7.
56 Coogan, *The Famine Plot,* 184-7.

## Chapter 10

1 Niall O'Dowd, "Was it Genocide? What the British Ruling Class Really Said about the Irish Famine," *Irish Central,* June 16, 2019, accessed June 22. 2021, https://www.irishcentral.com/roots/genocide-what-british-ruling-class-said-irish-famine/.
2 Coogan, *The Famine Plot,* 214.
3 Coogan, *The Famine Plot,* 169.
4 Coogan, *The Famine Plot,* 214.
5 *The Times,* February 10, 1849, cited in Tim Pat Coogan, *The Famine Plot,* (New York: Palgrave Macmillan, 2012,) 226.
6 Coogan, *The Famine Plot,* 227.
7 O'Dowd, "Was it Genocide? What the British Ruling Class Really Said about the Irish Famine," *Irish Central.*

[8] *The Times,* July 26, 1848, cited in Tim Pat Coogan, *The Famine Plot,* (New York: Palgrave Macmillan, 2012,) 213.

[9] Coogan, *The Famine Plot,* 218.

[10] L. Perry Curtis, *Anglo-Saxon and Celts: A Study of Anti-Irish Prejudice in Victorian England,* (New York: New York University, 1968), cited in Tim Pat Coogan, *The Famine Plot,* (New York: Palgrave Macmillan, 2012,) 219.

[11] Coogan, *The Famine Plot,* 217-20.

[12] Coogan, *The Famine Plot,* 225.

[13] Coogan, *The Famine Plot,* 230.

[14] Woodham-Smith, *The Great Hunger,* 377, 407.

[15] "Timeline of the Irish Famine," *Irish Historian*, June 1848, accessed May 10, 2021, https://www.irishhistorian.com/IrishFamineTimeline.html#1848/.

[16] Bartoletti, *Black Potatoes,* 102-3.

[17] Bartoletti, *Black Potatoes,* 95.

[18] Woodham-Smith, *The Great Hunger,* 367, 370.

[19] Woodham-Smith, *The Great Hunger,* 367.

[20] Woodham-Smith, *The Great Hunger, 375.*

[21] "Timeline of the Irish Famine," *Irish Historian*, September, 1848.

[22] Coogan, *The Famine Plot,* 166.

[23] Woodham-Smith, *The Great Hunger,* 366.

[24] Woodham-Smith, *The Great Hunger,* 371.

[25] "Timeline of the Irish Famine," *Irish Historian,* June, 1849. accessed May 31, 2021, http://www.irishhistorian.com/IrishFamineTimeline.html#1849/.

[26] "The Doolough Famine Tragedy," *Ireland's Own*, accessed May 10. 2021, https://www.irelandsown.ie/the-doolough-famine-tragedy/.

[27] Bartoletti, *Black Potatoes,* 158-166.

[28] Bartoletti, *Black Potatoes,* 158-166.

[29] Woodham-Smith, *The Great Hunger,* 406.

[30] Coogan, *The Famine Plot,* 168.

[31] "Timeline of the Irish Famine," *Irish Historian,* January, 1849.

[32] "Clarendon to Lord John Russell, March 12, 1849," *Clarendon Papers,* Out Letter Books, Vol. IV, cited in Cecil Woodham-Smith, *The Great Hunger,* (New York: Old Town Books, 1962), 380.

[33] Woodham-Smith, *The Great Hunger,* 380.

[34] "Timeline of the Irish Famine," *Irish Historian,* March, 1849.

[35] Brian, "Encouraging Bible Verses for the Dark Times of Life," January 11, 2021, accessed May 31, 2021, https://luke1428.com/encouraging-bible-verses-for-the-dark-times-of-life/.

[36] "Timeline of the Irish Famine," *Irish Historian,* December, 1846, accessed May 31, 2021, http://www.irishhistorian.com/IrishFamineTimeline.html#1846/.

[37] "Timeline of the Irish Famine," *Irish Historian,* October, 1846.

[38] John Canon O'Rourke, *The Great Irish Famine,* (Dublin: Veritage Publications, abridged, 1874), 248-50, cited in O'Boyle, Phd., Mayo Research Institute, *Classical Economics and the Great Irish Famine: A Study in Limits* 17.

[39] Woodham-Smith, *The Great Hunger,* 86-7.

[40] Thomas Cahill, "Why Famine came to Ireland," *Irish Central.*

[41] O'Boyle, Phd., Mayo Research Institute, *Classical Economics and the Great Irish Famine: A Study in Limits,* 33.

[42] O'Boyle, Phd. Mayo Research Institute, *Classical Economics and the Great Irish Famine: A Study in Limits,* 11.

[43] O'Boyle, Phd. Mayo Research Institute, *Classical Economics and the Great Irish Famine: A Study in Limits,* 6.

[44] John Stuart Mill, *Autobiography and Literary Essays, Part of the Collected Works of John Stuart Mill,* 1981, edited by John M. Robson and Jack Stillinger, (Toronto, University of Toronto Press, 1981) Vol. 1, cited in O'Boyle, Phd. Mayo Research Institute, *Classical Economics and the Great Irish Famine: A Study in Limits,* 12.

[45] John Stuart Mill, *Autobiography and Literary Essays,* part of the *Collected Works of John Stuart Mill,* edited by John M. Robson and Jack Stillinger, (Toronto: University of Toronto Press, 1981), Vol.1., cited in O'Boyle, Phd., Mayo Research Institute, *Classical Economics and the Great Irish Famine: A Study in Limits,* 32.

[46] Joseph O'Connor, *Star of the Sea,* (Orlando: Harcourt, 2002), cited in "Charles Trevelyan," *Star of the Sea: A Postcolonial/Postmodern Voyage into the Irish Famine,* accessed on May 10, 2021, https://scalar.usc.edu/works/star-of-the-sea-a-postcoonialpostmodern-voyage-into-the -irish-famine/index/.

[47] Max Channon, "Son of a Cornish Clergyman called Trevelyan Hinders Brexit from Beyond the Grave," *Cornwall Live,* accessed May 10, 2021, https://www.cornwalllive.com/news/uk-world-news/som-clergyman-called-trevelyan-2581469.

[48] Coogan, *The Famine Plot,* 34.

[49] Ruan O'Donnell, *A Short History of Ireland's Famine,* (Dublin: O'Brien Press, Ltd., 2013.)

[50] Bartoletti, *Black Potatoes,* 15.

[51] Maxwell, *Everyday Life in 19th Century Ireland,* 134.

[52] Ian N. Gregory and Niall A. Cunningham, "The Judgment of God on an Indolent and Unself-reliant People: The Impact of the Great Irish Famine on Ireland's Religious Demography," *Journal of Historical Geography,* Volume 51, January 2016, 76-87, accessed May 10, 2021, https://www.sciencedirect.com/science/article/pii/S0305748815001012/.

[53] Coogan, *The Famine Plot,* 152.

[54] "Alexis de Tocqueville visits Ireland," *Ireland xo Reaching Out*, accessed June 26, 2020, https://irelandxo.com/ireland-xo/history-and-genealogy/timeline/alexis-de-tocqueville-visits-ireland#.

[55] Stanley W. Jevons, *The Theory of Political Economy, (*New York: Kelly and Millman,1957) Vol. 2, 277, cited in O'Boyle, Phd., Mayo Research Institute, *Classical Economics and the Great Irish Famine: A Study in Limits,* 27.

[56] Bartoletti, *Black Potatoes,* 78-9.

[57] Bartoletti, *Black Potatoes,* 75-9.

[58] "Was this the Most Wicked Man in Irish History?" *Independent.ie,* September 30, 2006, accessed June 1, 2021, https://www.independent.ie/opinion/analysis/was-this-the-most-wicked-man-in-irish-history-26367449.html/.

[59] Coogan, *The Famine Plot, 63.*

[60] "The Great Irish Potato Famine," *History Cooperative*, October 31, 2009, accessed June 26, 2020, https://historycooperative.org/the-irish-famine/.

[61] John Dorney, "The Great Irish Famine 1845-1851-A Brief Overview," *The Irish Story*, accessed May 19, 2020, https://www.theirishhistory.com/2016/10/16/the-great-irish-famine-1845-1851/.

[62] "The Irish Potato Famine, 1846-1850," *DoChara, Insider Guide to Ireland, 2008,* Updated March 31, 2017, accessed May 19, 2020, https://www.dochara.comtheirish/food-history/the-irish-potato-famine-1845-1850.

## CHAPTER 11

[1] "Sculpture in Ireland Honors Choctaw Nation," *East Texas Radio.com*, July 4, 2017, accessed February 17, 2021, https://easttexasradio.com/sculpture-in-ireland-honors-choctaw-nation.

[2] Christine Kinealy, Contributor, "International Relief Efforts During the Famine," *Irish America,* August/September, 2009, accessed May 10, 2021,

https://irishamerica.com/2009/08/international-relief-efforts-during-the-famine/.

[3] Christine Kinealy, Contributor, "International Relief Efforts During the Famine," *Irish America.*

[4] Christine Kinealy, Contributor, "International Relief Efforts During the Famine," *Irish America.*

[5] Christine Kinealy, Contributor, "International Relief Efforts During the Famine," *Irish America.*

[6] Coogan, *The Famine Plot,* 175.

[7] Woodham-Smith, *The Great Hunger: Ireland, 1845-1849.* (New York: Old Town Books, 1962), cited in Tim Pat Coogan, *The Famine Plot,* (New York: Palgrave Macmillan, 2012), 175.

[8] Christine Kinealy, Contributor, "International Relief Efforts During the Famine," *Irish America.*

[9] Mark Thornton, "What Caused the Irish Potato Famine?" *The Free Market*, April, 1998, Volume 16, Number 4, cited in *Mises Daily Articles*, March 17, 2017, accessed on May 10, 2021, https://mises.org/library/what-caused-irish-potato-famine/.

[10] Christine Kinealy, Contributor, "International Relief Efforts During the Famine," *Irish America.*

[11] Christine Kinealy, Contributor, "International Relief Efforts During the Famine," *Irish America.*

[12] Bartoletti, *Black Potatoes,* 85.

[13] Christine Kinealy, Contributor, "International Relief Efforts During the Famine," *Irish America.*

[14] Bartoletti, *Black Potatoes,* 80-1.

[15] Bartoletti, *Black Potatoes,* 167-8.

[16] John Dorney, "The Great Irish Famine 1845-1851 – A Brief Overview," *The Irish Story.*

[17] Christine Kinealy, Contributor, "International Relief Efforts During the Famine," *Irish America.*

[18] Central Relief Committee of the Society of Friends, *Transactions of the Central Relief Committee of the Society of Friends during the Famine in Ireland, in 1846 and 1847,* cited in Tim Pat Coogan, *The Famine Plot,* (New York: Palgrave Macmillan, 2012), 143.

[19] Christine Kinealy, Contributor, "International Relief Efforts During the Famine," *Irish America.*

## CHAPTER 12

1 "100 Irish Quotes and Sayings, *Inspirational Words of Wisdom*, accessed April 4, 2021, wow4u.com/irishquotesayings/.

2 Jim Donnelly, "The Irish Famine," *BBC,* last updated February 17, 2011, accessed June 1, 2021, http://www.bbc.co.uk/history/british/victorians/famine_01.shtml/.

3 "Food Exports from Ireland 1846-1847," *History Ireland*, published in *$18^{th}$-$19^{th}$-Century History, Features*, Issue 1, Spring 1997, "The Famine," Volume 5, accessed July 21, 2020, https://www.historyireland.com/$18^{th}$-$19^{th}$-century-history/food-exports-from-ireland-1846-47/.

4 Jim Donnelly, "The Irish Famine," *BBC*.

5 Christine Kinealy,"Food Exports from Ireland 1846-1847," *History Ireland,* cited in O'Boyle, Phd. *Classical Economics and the Great Irish Famine" A Study in Limits*, 9.

6 Donnelly, "The Irish Famine," *BBC*.

7 Thomas Cahill, "Why Famine came to Ireland," *Irish Central,* May 1, 2010.

8 Donnelly, "The Irish Famine," *BBC*.

9 Donnelly, "The Irish Famine," *BBC*.

10 Donnelly, "The Irish Famine," *BBC*.

11 Miller, *Emigrants and Exiles,* 287.

12 Donnelly, "The Irish Famine," *BBC*.

13 Thomas Cahill, "Why Famine came to Ireland," *Irish Central,* May 1, 2010.

14 Noel Kissane, *The Irish Famine,* (Dublin: National Library of Ireland, 1995), cited in O'Boyle, Phd. Mayo Research Institute, *Classical Economics and the Great Irish Famine: A Study in Limits,* 9.

15 "U.S. Cities with Population over 100,000," *Infoplease,* accessed May 11, 2021, https://www.infoplease.com/us/cities/us-cities-population-over-100000/.

16 Dennis Walsh, "Ireland, The Famine Years, % of Population," *Ireland's History in Maps,* accessed May 11, 2021, http://sites.rootsweb.com/~irlkik/ihm/ire1841.htm/.

17 Timothy W. Guinnane, "The Vanishing Irish: Ireland's Population from the Great Famine to the Great War," *History, Ireland,* Issue 2 Summer 1997, "The Famine," Volume 5, accessed May 11, 2021, https://www.historyireland.com/$20^{th}$-century-contemporary-history/the-vanishing-irish-irelands-population-from-the-great-famine-to-the-great-war/.

[18] Ambassador Daniel Mulhall, "Black '47: Ireland's Great Famine and its after-effects," *Embassy of Ireland USA,* December 3, 2018, accessed on May 11, 2021, https://www.dfa.ie/irish-embassy/usa/about-us/ambassador/ambassadors-blog/black47irelandsgreatfamineanditsafter-effects/.

[19] Walsh, "Ireland, The Famine Years," *Ireland's History in Maps.*

[20] Bartoletti, *Black Potatoes,* 168.

[21] "Timeline of the Irish Famine," *Irish Famine Timeline,* 1850, Irish Historian.

[22] Maxwell, *Everyday Life in 19th Century Ireland,* 186.

[23] "The Great Irish Potato Famine," *History Cooperative.*

[24] Timothy W. Guinnane, "The Vanishing Irish: Ireland's Population from the Great Famine to the Great War," *History, Ireland.*

[25] R.F. Foster, *Modern Ireland 1600-1972,* (Penguin Group, 1988,) 234, cited in "What was the impact of the Irish Famine on Ireland and the World?" accessed May 11, 2021, https://dailyhistory.org/What_was_the_impact_of_the_Irish_Famine_on_Ireland_and_the_world%3F/.

[26] Thomas Gallagher, *Paddy's Lament, Ireland 1846-1847, Prelude to Hatred,* (Houghton Mifflin Harcourt, 1987) 7.

[27] Guinnane, "The Vanishing Irish: Ireland's Population from the Great Famine to the Great War," *History, Ireland.*

[28] Cormac Ograda, "The population of Ireland 1700-1900: a survey," *Persee,* accessed July 17, 2020, https://www.persee.fr/doc/adh_0066-2062_1979_num_1979_1_1425/.

[29] "The Great Irish Potato Famine," *History Cooperative.*

[30] Guinnane, "The Vanishing Irish: Ireland's Population from the Great Famine to the Great War," *History, Ireland.*

[31] Miller, *Emigrants and Exiles,* 355.

[32] Miller, *Emigrants and Exiles,* 360, 363.

[33] Miller, *Emigrants and Exiles,* 359.

[34] "What was the impact of the Irish Famine on Ireland and the World?" *Daily History,org,* accessed on July 17, 2020, https://dailyhistory.org/What_was_the_impact_of_the_Irish_Famine_on_Ireland_and_the_world%3F/.

[35] Thomas Gallagher, *Paddy's Lament, Ireland 1846-1847, Prelude to Hatred,* (Houghton Mifflin Harcourt, 1987) 7, as cited in "What was the impact of the Irish Famine on Ireland and the World?" *Daily History,org.*

[36] Dennis Walsh, "Ireland's History in Maps," Map Collection, 1840's, Years of the Great Famine, *Rootsweb,* accessed July, 2,2020, https://sites.rootsweb.com/-irlkik/ire1841.htm/.

37 Wesley Johnston, "Effects of the Famine 1: Agriculture," 2001, accessed May 12, 2001, https://www.wesleyjohnston.com/users/ireland/past/famine/agriculture_post.html/.

38 "Encumbered Estates Act," *The History of Ireland,* accessed May 12, 2021, http://www.irishevents4u.com/Ireland/history/encumbered-est.htm/.

## CHAPTER 13

1 "Irish Quotes," *Goodreads,* accessed May 12, 2021, https://www.goodreads.com/quotes/tag/irish/.

2 Coogan, *The Famine Plot,* 230-1.

3 Coogan, *The Famine Plot,* Appendix 4.

4 "Rome Statute of the International Criminal Court," July 17,1998, accessed June 30, 2021, https://legal.un.org/icc/statute/99_corr/cstatute.htm/.

5 "Rome Statute of the International Criminal Court," July 17,1998.

6 "Rome Statute of the International Criminal Court," July 17, 1998.

7 Coogan, *The Famine Plot,* 190-1.

8 "Timeline of the Irish Famine," *Irish Famine Timeline,* September, 1848.

9 "Food Depots Close to Teach Irish a Lesson," *The Irish Times,* accessed on May 12, 2021, https://www.irishtimes.com/news/food-depots-close-to-teach-irish-a-lesson-1.79616/.

10 John Canon O'Rourke, *The Great Irish Famine,* (Veritas Publications, 1874, abridged, (248-250,) cited in O'Boyle, Phd, *Classical Economics and the Great Irish Famine: A Study in Limits,* 17.

11 Coogan, *The Famine Plot,* 175.

12 Aidan Lonergan, "Wexford Martyrs: 7 Facts about the Irish Catholics Hanged, Drawn and Quartered by Elizabeth I for Treason in 1581," *Irish Post,* July 5, 2019, accessed on May 12, 2021, https://www.irishpost.com/life-style/wexford-martyrs-7-facts-irish-catholics-hanged-drawn-quartered-elizabeth-treason-1581-168733/.

13 "Second World War and its Aftermath," *Ask About Ireland,* accessed on June 22, 2021, http://www.askaboutireland.ie/learning-zone/secondary-students/history/history-of-ireland-overview/the-second-world-war-and-/.

14 Edward M. Kennedy, "Address at the Public Memorial Service for Robert F. Kennedy," *American Rhetoric Top 100 Speeches,* 2001, accessed May 12, 2021, https://www.americanrhetoric.com/speeches/ekennedytributetorfk.htmlamericanrhetoric/speeches/ekennedytributeorfk.html/.

15 Colum Lynch, "Evidence to Prove Genocide in China," *Foreign Policy,* February 19, 2021, https://foreignpolicy.com/2021/02/19/china-uighurs-genocide-us-pompeo-blinken/.

16 "Intent," *The Free Dictionary by Farlex* accessed on May 12, 2021, https://legal-dictionary.thefreedictionary.com/intent/.

17 "Man Behind the Famine," *Irish Daily Mail,* September 28, 2018, accessed, May 12, 2021, https://www.pressreader.com/ireland/irish-daily-mail/20180925/282432760077444/.

18 "Sir Charles Trevelyan, 1st Baronet," *World Heritage Encyclopedia*, (Project Gutenberg-Self-Publishing Press nd,) accessed May 12, 2021, http://www.self.gutenberg.org/articles/Sir_Charles_Trevelyan,_1st_Baronet/.

19 "Sir Charles Trevelyan, 1st Baronet," *World Heritage Encyclopedia.*

20 John Simkin, "Lord John Russell," *Spartacus Educational,* accessed May 12, 2021, https://spartacus-educational.com/PRrussell.htm/.

21 John Andrew Hamilton, "Sir Charles Wood, First Viscount Halifax, 1800-1885," 1900, *A Web of English History*, accessed June 22, 2021, http://www.historyhome.co.uk/people/halifax.htm.

22 Frances Mulraney, "The Real Story of Queen Victoria and the Irish Famine," *Irish Central*, April 26, 2020, accessed May 12, 2021, https://www.irishcentral.com/roots/history/queen-victoria-irish-famine/.

23 Dinyar Patel, "Viewpoint: How British Let One Million Indians Die in Famine," *BBC News.* (June 10, 2016), accessed May 12, 2021, https://www.bbc.com/news/world-asia-india-36339524/.

## Chapter 14

1 "Patrick Pearse Quotes," *AZ Quotes,* accessed May 12, 2021. https://www.azquotes.com/author/44563-Patrick_Pearse/.

2 "Atlas of the Irish Revolution, Resources for Schools," Unit 1: The Land Movement, 1879-1882, Senior Cycle Worksheets, *UCC, College of Arts, Celtic Studies and Social Sciences,* accessed on May 12, 2021, https://www.rte.ie/documents/history/2021/01/u1.-lc-worksheets-the-land-movement.pdf/.

3 "Atlas of the Irish Revolution, Resources for Schools," Unit 1: The Land Movement, 1879-1882, 4,6, *UCC, College of Arts, Celtic Studies and Social Sciences.*

4 Miller, *Emigrants and Exiles*, 471.

5 "Atlas of the Irish Revolution, Resources for Schools," Unit 1: The Land Movement, 1879-1882, Descriptions and Quotations, 5-6, *UCC, College of Arts, Celtic Studies and Social Sciences.*

[6] Miller, *Emigrants and Exiles*, 437-40, 39.
[7] Miller, *Emigrants and Exiles*, 389.
[8] Miller, *Emigrants and Exiles*, 388.
[9] "Atlas of the Irish Revolution, Resources for Schools," Unit 1: The Land Movement, 1879-1882, Descriptions and Quotations, 24, *UCC, College of Arts, Celtic Studies and Social Sciences.*
[10] Miller, *Emigrants and Exiles*, 389.
[11] "Atlas of the Irish Revolution, Resources for Schools," Unit 1: The Land Movement, 1879-1882, 4,6,24. *UCC, College of Arts, Celtic Studies and Social Sciences.*
[12] Miller, *Emigrants and Exiles*, 540.
[13] "Atlas of the Irish Revolution, Resources for Schools," Unit 1: The Land Movement, 1879-1882, Descriptions and Quotations, *UCC, College of Arts, Celtic Studies and Social Sciences.*
[14] Miller, *Emigrants and Exiles*, 389.
[15] "Atlas of the Irish Revolution, Resources for Schools," Unit 1: The Land Movement, 1879-1882, Descriptions and Quotations, *UCC, College of Arts, Celtic Studies and Social Sciences.*
[16] "Atlas of the Irish Revolution, Resources for Schools," Unit 1: The Land Movement, 1879-1882, 24. *UCC, College of Arts, Celtic Studies and Social Sciences.*
[17] "Atlas of the Irish Revolution, Resources for Schools," *UCC, College of Arts, Celtic Studies and Social Sciences,* Unit 1: The Land Movement, 1879-1882, 21.24, 27.
[18] "Atlas of the Irish Revolution, Resources for Schools," Unit 1: The Land Movement, 1879-1882, Description, *UCC, College of Arts, Celtic Studies and Social Sciences.*
[19] Miller, *Emigrants and Exiles*, 389.
[20] Miller, *Emigrants and Exiles*, 472, 482.

## CHAPTER 15

[1] "The Immigrant Journey," *Oh Ranger.com*, accessed February 14, 2021, https://www.ohranger.com/ellis-island/immigration-journey/.
[2] Frank O'Donovan, "Estimated Population of Ireland in the 19th Century," *Irish Genealogy Toolkit,* August, 2017, accessed June 22, 2021, https://bmdnotices.com/Estimated-Population-in-Ireland-19th-Century.pdf/.
[3] Miller, Emigrants and Exiles,198.

4 "Ireland Emigration and Immigration," Family Search, edited June 2, 2020, accessed May 12, 2021, https://www.familysearch.org/wiki/en/Ireland_Emigration_and_Immigration/.

5 Miller, *Emigrants and Exiles*, 105.

6 Patrick Weston Joyce, "The Plantation of Ulster, 1605-1625," *Library Ireland*, accessed May 12, 2021, https://www.libraryireland.com/JoyceHistory/Ulster.php/.

7 Catherine O'Donovan, "The Cromwellian Settlement," accessed on May 12, 2021. https://www.clarelibrary.ie/eolas/coclare/history/cromwell_settlement.htm/.

8 Miller, *Emigrants and Exiles*, 52, 53, 198.

9 Miller, *Emigrants and Exiles*, 41,42,53.

10 Miller, *Emigrants and Exiles*, 53.

11 Miller, *Emigrants and Exiles*, 42.

12 Dr. Marjorie Bloy, "The Age of George III, Land Holding in Ireland," *A Web of English History*, last modified January 12, 2016, accessed May 12, 2021, http://www.historyhome.co.uk/c-eight/ireland/ire-land.htm/.

13 Miller, *Emigrants and Exiles* 33.

14 Miller, *Emigrants and Exiles* 287.

15 Edward Laxton, *The Famine Ships: The Irish Exodus to America*, (New York: Henry Holt Co.,1996), 74.

16 Miller, *Emigrants and Exiles*, 53.

17 Laxton, *Famine Ships*, 70-75.

18 Laxton, *Famine Ships*, 70,75-6.

19 Miller, *Emigrants and Exiles,* 193.

20 Miller, *Emigrants and Exiles*, 202-4.

21 Miller, *Emigrants and Exiles*, 209.

22 Miller, *Emigrants and Exiles,* 205, 211, 213.

23 Miller, *Emigrants and Exiles,* 207, 208.

24 Miller, *Emigrants and Exiles,* 9.

25 James S. Donnelly, Jr., "The Irish Agricultural Depression of 1859-64-Irish Economic and Social History," *Sage Journals*, June 1, 1976, accessed March 23, 2021, https://journals.sagepub.com/doi/abs/10.1177/033248937600300103?journalCode=iesa/.

26 Miller, *Emigrants and Exiles* 360.

27 Miller, *Emigrants and Exiles*, 194, 196, 207.

28 Miller, *Emigrants and Exiles*, 197-8.

29 Miller, *Emigrants and Exiles,* 198.

30 Miller, *Emigrants and Exiles,* 194-9, 202.

31 Miller, *Emigrants and Exiles,* 201, 204.

[32] Miller, *Emigrants and Exiles*, 394.
[33] Laxton, *Famine Ships*, 170-181.
[34] Miller, *Emigrants and Exiles*, 134, 138, 363, 405, 59, 408, 483, 105, 492.
[35] Laxton, *Famine Ships*, 170.

## CHAPTER 16

[1] "Irish Quotes," *Goodreads,* accessed April 5, 2021, https://www.goodreads.com/quotes/tag/irish?page=1/.
[2] Miller, *Emigrants and Exiles*, 566.
[3] Miller, *Emigrants and Exiles*, 566, 253.
[4] "Irish Emigration to America – The Journey," *National Museum of Ireland,* accessed June 22, 2021, https://www.museum.ie/en-IE/Collections-Research/Folklife-Collections/Folklife-Collections-List-(1)/Other/Emigration/Irish-Emigration-to-America-The-Journey/.
[5] Maxwell, *Everyday Life in 19th-Century Ireland,* 173, 177, 168, 172, 174-5, 170.
[6] "Irish Emigration to America – The Journey," *National Museum of Ireland.*
[7] Miller, *Emigrants and Exiles*, 253-4.
[8] Miller, *Emigrants and Exiles,* 353.
[9] Denise Rose Del Gaudio, "I Have Not Told the Worst of it by any Means. It Could Not Be Put in Print. The Transatlantic Voyage of Euro-Immigrants to the United States, 1841-1900," 2010, *Dickinson College Honors Theses*, Paper 83. accessed June 22, 2021, https://scholar.dickinson.edu/cgi/viewcontent.cgi?article=1082&context=student_honors/.
[10] Miller, *Emigrants and Exiles*, 254.
[11] Miller, *Emigrants and Exiles*, 271.
[12] Maldwyn, A. Jones, *American Immigration*, 105, cited in "Transatlantic Crossing -Cost," *Central Michigan University–Clarke Historical Library,* accessed May 12, 2021, https://www.cmich.edu/library/clarke/ResearchResources/Michigan_Material_Local/Beaver_Island_Helen_Collar_Papers/Subject_Cards/EmigrationandImmigrantLife/Pages/Transatlantic-Crossing.aspx/.
[13] Miller, *Emigrants and Exiles*, 271,237.
[14] Marcus Hansen, *The Atlantic Migration*, 244-51, cited in "Transatlantic Crossing-Cost," *Central Michigan University-Clarke Historical Library.*
[15] Miller, *Emigrants and Exiles*, 216, 197.
[16] Oscar Handlin, *The Uprooted*, Chapter11, cited in "Transatlantic Crossing-Cost," *Central Michigan University-Clarke Historical Library.*

[17] "Irish Ports of Emigration," *Emerald Heritage,* accessed on May 12, 2021, https://emerald-heritage.com/blog/2017/irish-ports-of-emigration/.

[18] Patton, *To the Golden Door,* 154-5, as cited in "Transatlantic Crossing-Cost," *Central Michigan University-Clarke Historical Library.*

[19] B. Dupont, D. Keeling, and T. Weiss, *Passenger Fares for Overseas Travel in the 19th and 20th Centuries*, 36, Figure 5, August 15, 2012, accessed March 25, 2021, https://www.eh.net/eha/wp-content/uploads/2013/11/Weissetal.pdf/.

[20] "The Immigrant Journey," *Oh Ranger.com*, accessed October 28, 2020, ohranger.com/ellis-island/immigration-journey/.

[21] Laxton, *Famine Ships,* 194-197.

[22] Patton, *To the Golden Door,* 154-5, cited in "Transatlantic Crossing-Cost," *Central Michigan University-Clarke Historical Library.*

[23] Patton, *To the Golden Door,* 154-5, cited in "Transatlantic Crossing-Cost," *Central Michigan University-Clarke Historical Library.*

[24] Patton, *To the Golden Door,* 154-5, cited in "Transatlantic Crossing-Cost," *Central Michigan University-Clarke Historical Library.*

[25] "Journey to America," *Spartacus Educational.com*, accessed May 12, 2021, https://spartacus-educational.com/USAEjourney.htm/.

[26] Raymond L. Cohn, "The Transition from Sail to Steam in Immigration to the United States," *The Journal of Economic History, Research Gate,* Download Full Text PDF, Table 4, accessed on May, 12, 2021, https://www.researchgate.net/publication/4772287_The_Transition_from_Sail_to_Steam_in_Immigration_to_the_United_States287_The_Transition_from_Sail_to_Steam_in_Immigration_to_the_United_States/.

[27] John Killick, "Transatlantic Steerage Fares, British and Irish Migration, and Return Migration, 1815-1860," *Economic History Review,* 67, 1 2014, 170-191, JSTOR, accessed March 26, 2021, https://www.jstor.org/stable/42921701/.

[28] Cohn, "The Transition from Sail to Steam in Immigration to the United States," *The Journal of Economic History, Research Gate.*

[29] Cohn"The Transition from Sail to Steam in Immigration to the United States," *The Journal of Economic History, Research Gate.*

[30] Cohn, "The Transition from Sail to Steam in Immigration to the United States," *The Journal of Economic History, Research Gate.*

[31] "The Immigrant Journey," *OhRanger.com.*

[32] Drew Keeling, "Shipping Companies and Transatlantic Migration Costs: The Case of Cunard, 1880-1914," Appendix 1: "Steerage Fares and

Passengers and Key U.S. Recessions, Cunard Lines, Liverpool-New York Route, 1883-1914," 20, August, 2008, accessed March 26, 2021, https://ebha.org/ebha2008/papers/Keeling_ebha_2008.pdf/.

33 Drew Keeling, "Shipping Companies and Transatlantic Migration Costs: The Case of Cunard, 1880-1914," 20.

34 Lawrence H. Officer and Samuel H. Williamson, "Computing 'Real Value Over Time with a Conversion between U.K. Pounds and U.S. Dollars, 1791 to Present," *Measuring Worth*, 2021, accessed May 12, 2021, https://www.measuringworth.com/calculators/exchange/result_exchange.php/.

35 Cohn, "The Transition from Sail to Steam in Immigration to the United States."31, Table 1. *The Journal of Economic History, Research Gate.*

36 Guillet, *The Great Migration*, 236-9, cited in "Transatlantic Crossing," *Central Michigan University–Clarke Historical Library.*

37 Guillet, *The Great Migration*, 50, cited in "Transatlantic Crossing, Length of Voyage" *Central Michigan University–Clarke Historical Library.*

38 Cohn, "The Transition from Sail to Steam in Immigration to the United States." 31, Table 1.

39 Miller, *Emigrants and Exiles*, 428.

40 Cohn, "The Transition from Sail to Steam in Immigration to the United States," 31, Table 1, *The Journal of Economic History, Research Gate.*

41 Officer and Williamson, "Computing 'Real Value' Over Time with a Conversion between U.K. Pounds and U.S. Dollars, 1791 to Present".

42 "The Inflation Calculator," accessed March 26, 2021, https://westegg.com/inflation/infl.cgi?money-84&first=1862&final=2020/.

43 Miller, *Emigrants and Exiles*, 237.

44 Lawrence H. Officer and Samuel H. Williamson,"Computing Real Value Over Time with a Conversion Between U.K. Pounds and U.S. Dollars, 1791 to Present," *Measuring Worth*, 2021, https://www.measuringworth.com/exchange/.

45 Cohn, "The Transition from Sail to Steam in Immigration to the United States," 31, Table 4, *The Journal of Economic History, Research Gate.*

## CHAPTER 17

1 "Enterprise on the Water," *On the Water, Maritime Nation 1800-1850*, accessed May 12, 2021, https://www.americanhistory.si.edu/onthewater/exhibition/2_3.html/.

[2] *Free Map Tools*, accessed on March 26, 2021, https://www.freemaptools.com/how-far-is-it-between-new-york-city-usa-and-liverpool_-england.htm/.

[3] Mark Staniforth, *Shipwrecks: Images and Perceptions of the Nineteenth Century,* 51-2, accessed May 12, 2021, https://core.ac.uk/download/pdf/229433464.pdf/.

[4] "Australia Emigration and Immigration," *Family Search*, accessed March 26, 2021, https://www.familysearch.org/wiki/en/Australia_Emigration_and_Immigration/.

[5] Mark Staniforth, *Shipwrecks: Images and Perceptions of the Nineteenth Century*, 51-2.

[6] "Journey to America," *Spartacus Educational.com,* accessed February 17, 2021, Spartacus-educational.com/USAEjourney.htm/.

[7] Laxton, Famine Ships, 137-140.

[8] Woodham-Smith, The Great Hunger, 212.

[9] Laxton, *Famine Ships*, 49.

[10] "Chronicles Insight – Ships and Steerage," 21, *Ireland Reaching Out*, December 9, 2019, accessed May 12, 2021, https://irelandxo.com/ireland-xo/news/chronicles-insight-ships-and-steerage/.

[11] Woodham-Smith, *The Great Hunger*, 216.

[12] "Irish Emigration to America – The Journey," *National Museum of Ireland*, accessed June 22, 2021, www.museum.ie/en-ie/en-IE/Collections-Research/Folklife-Collections/Folklife-Collections-List-(1)/Other/Emigration/Irish-Emigration-to-America-The-Journey/.

[13] Laxton, *Famine Ships*, 126-9.

[14] Laxton, *Famine Ships,* 130-2.

[15] "Journey to America," *Spartacus Educational.com,* accessed February 17, 2021, https://spartacus-educational.com/USAEjourney.htm/.

[16] Guillet, *The Great Migration* 67-68, cited in "Transatlantic Crossing," *Central Michigan University–Clarke Historical Library.*

[17] Laxton, *Famine Ships,* 193.

[18] Guillet, *The Great Migration,* 11, 67-8, cited in "Transatlantic Crossing," *Central Michigan University–Clarke Historical Library.*

[19] C. Dickens, *All the Year Round*, Vol. VII, March to September, 1862, 113, cited in Albert D. Biderman, Margot Louria, Joan Bacchus, "Historical incidents of Extreme Overcrowding," B5-6, Bureau of Social Science Research, Washington D.C., accessed April 3, 2021, https://apps.dtic.mil/dtic/tr/fulltext/u2/609752.pdf/.

[20] "Transatlantic Crossing," *Central Michigan University–Clarke Historical Library.*

21 Guillet, *The Great Migration* 11, 67-8, cited in "Transatlantic Crossing," *Central Michigan University–Clarke Historical Library.*

22 Albert D. Biderman, Margot Louria, Joan Bacchus, "Historical Incidents of Extreme Overcrowding," B11, Bureau of Social Science Research, Washington D.C., accessed May 12, 2021, https://apps.dtic.mil/dtic/tr/fulltext/u2/609752.pdf/.

23 United States Senate, "Reports of the Immigration Commission, 61st Congress, 3rd Session," Doc No. 753, (Washington, D.C.: Government Printing Office, 1911), 13-23. cited in Biderman, Louria, Bacchus, "Historical Incidents of Extreme Overcrowding," B11.

24 "Transatlantic Crossing- Overcrowding," *Central Michigan University–Clarke Historical Library.*

25 Del Gaudio, "I Have Not Told the Worst by any Means, It Could Not Be Put in Print: The Transatlantic Voyage of Euro-Immigrants to the United States," 28, 64.

26 Biderman, Louria, Bacchus, "Historical Incidents of Extreme Overcrowding," B4.

27 Del Gaudio, "I Have Not Told the Worst by any Means, It Could Not Be Put in Print: The Transatlantic Voyage of Euro-Immigrants to the United States," 27.

28 Del Gaudio, "I Have Not Told the Worst by any Means, It Could Not Be Put in Print: The Transatlantic Voyage of Euro-Immigrants to the United States," 46.

29 Franklin D. Scott, ed, *World Migration in Modern Times*, 34-9, cited in "Transatlantic Crossing- Overcrowding."

30 Del Gaudio, "I Have Not Told the Worst by any Means, It Could Not Be Put in Print: The Transatlantic Voyage of Euro-Immigrants to the United States," 27.

31 F. J. Haskin, *The Immigrant*, (New York: Fleming H. Revell Co., 1913), cited in Biderman, Louria, Bacchus, "Historical Incidents of Extreme Overcrowding," B10.

32 Guillet, The Great Migration 11, 36, cited in "Transatlantic Crossing," *Central Michigan University–Clarke.*

33 Del Gaudio, "I Have Not Told the Worst by any Means, It Could Not Be Put in Print: The Transatlantic Voyage of Euro-Immigrants to the United States," 39.

34 Woodham-Smith, *The Great Hunger*, 211.

35 "Journey to America," *Spartacus Educational*, accessed February 17, 2021, https://spartacus-educational.com/USAEjourney.htm.

[36] Steiner, *From Alien to Citizen*, 38, cited in Del Gaudio, "I Have Not Told the Worst by any Means, It Could Not Be Put in Print: The Transatlantic Voyage of Euro-Immigrants to the United States," 40.

[37] Del Gaudio, "I Have Not Told the Worst by any Means, It Could Not Be Put in Print: The Transatlantic Voyage of Euro-Immigrants to the United States," 42-3.

[38] Brandenburg, *Imported Americans,* 190, cited in Del Guadio, "I Have Not Told the Worst by any Means, It Could Not Be Put in Print: The Transatlantic Voyage of Euro-Immigrants to the United States, 42.

[39] *"Journey to America,"* *Spartacus Educational*, accessed February 17, 2021, https://spartacus-educational.com/USAEjourney.htm/.

[40] Patton, *To the Golden Door*, 150, cited in "Transatlantic Crossing-Cost," *Central Michigan University-Clarke Historical Library.*

[41] Laxton, *Famine Ships*, 200.

[42] Laxton, *Famine Ships*, 193, 197.

[43] Bruce M. Stave, John F. Sutherland, and Aldo Salerno, *From the Old Country: An Oral History of European Migration to America, 32 (*New York: Twayne, 1994), cited in Del Gaudio, *"I Have Not Told the Worst by any Means, It Could Not Be Put in Print: The Transatlantic Voyage of Euro-Immigrants to the United States,"* 51.

[44] U.S. Congress, "*Reports of the Immigration Commission*, Investigation 3," 37, 61[st] Congress, 3d sess., 1911, cited in Del Gaudio, "I Have Not Told the Worst by any Means, It Could Not Be Put in Print: The Transatlantic Voyage of Euro-Immigrants to the United States," 51.

[45] Laxton, Famine Ships, 12.

[46] Guillet, *The Great Migration* 11, 96-7, cited in "Transatlantic Crossing," *Central Michigan University–Clarke Historical Library.*

[47] Laxton, Famine Ships, 197.

[48] "Journey to America," *Spartacus Educational.com.*

[49] Laurence Geary, "Epidemic Diseases of the Great Famine," *History Ireland,* Issue 1, Spring 1996, "The Famine," Volume 4, accessed on March 28, 2021, https://www.historyireland.com/18th-19th-century-history/epidemic-diseases-of-the-great-famine/.

[50] Geary, "Epidemic Diseases of the Great Famine," *History Ireland.*

[51] Geary, "Epidemic Diseases of the Great Famine," *History Ireland.*

[52] "Journey to America," *Spartacus Educational.*

[53] "Journey to America," *Spartacus Educational.*

## CHAPTER 18

1 "Quotes by Thomas Francis Meagher," *What Should I Read Next?* accessed May 15, 2021, https://www.whatshouldireadnext.com/quotes/Thomas-francis-meagher-the-glory-of-the-old/.

2 Woodham-Smith, *The Great Hunger,* 215-6.

3 Woodham-Smith, *The Great Hunger,* 215-6, 220,228-9.

4 "Transatlantic Crossing," *Central Michigan University–Clarke Historical Library.*

5 Woodham-Smith, *The Great Hunger,* 213.

6 "Transatlantic Crossing, Overcrowding," *Central Michigan University–Clarke Historical Library.*

7 Woodham-Smith, *The Great Hunger,* 217-22.

8 Woodham-Smith, *The Great Hunger,* 222-4.

9 Woodham-Smith, *The Great Hunger,* 225-6.

10 Guillet, *The Great Migration,* 96-97, cited in "Transatlantic Crossing," *Central Michigan University–Clarke Historical Library.*

11 Woodham-Smith, *The Great Hunger,* 225.

12 Woodham-Smith, *The Great Hunger,* 228-30.

13 Woodham-Smith, *The Great Hunger,* 231.

14 Woodham-Smith, *The Great Hunger,* 232-5.

15 Woodham-Smith, *The Great Hunger,* 235.

16 Woodham-Smith, *The Great Hunger,* 238.

17 Woodham-Smith, *The Great Hunger,* 237.

18 Woodham-Smith, *The Great Hunger,* 212.

19 Woodham-Smith, *The Great Hunger,* 211.

20 Scott, ed., *World Migration in Modern Times,* 34-39, cited in "Transatlantic Crossing, Overcrowding," *Central Michigan University–Clarke Historical Library.*

21 Marcus Hansen, *The Atlantic Migration,* 102, 255, cited in "Transatlantic Crossing, Overcrowding and Regulation," *Central Michigan University–Clarke Historical Library.*

22 "Shipping in the 19th Century," *Britannica,* accessed March 29, 2021, https://www.britannica.com/technology/ship/Shipping-in-the-19th-century/.

23 *Documents of the Board of Aldermen of the City of New York,* From No. 1 to No. 90, inclusive-from May 1837, to May 1838. Vol. IV. (New York: Printed by Order of the Common Council, 1838), Document No. 10, pp. 61-75 and Document No. 12, pp. 81-4, cited in Sveida, "Castle Garden as an Immigrant Depot," 22, Division of History, Office of Archeology and

Historic Preservation, National Park Service, U.S. Department of the Interior, December 2, 1968, accessed May 16, 2021, http://www.npshistory.com/publications/cacl/castle_garden.pdf/.

24 Guillet, *The Great Migration,* 11, 67-8, cited in "Transatlantic Crossing," *Central Michigan University–Clarke Historical Library.*

## Chapter 19

1 "Immigration Quotes," *Goodreads,* accessed May 15, 2021, https://goodreads.com/quotes/tag/immigration/.

2 "Major U. S. Immigration Ports," *Ancestry.com,* accessed May 15, 2021, http://www.pittsburgcogenealogical.org/C%20Educ/20%20Immigration%20routes/social%20research%20us%20ports.pdf/.

3 Svejda, "Castle Garden as an Immigrant Depot," 41, 43.

4 Harper's Weekly, Vol. 11, No. 78, June 26, 1858, p. 405, cited in Svejda "Castle Garden as an Immigrant Depot," 51.

5 Don H. Smith, *Castle Garden, the Emigrant Receiving Station in New York Harbor,*" 42, December 2, 1968, accessed on May 16, 2021, https://ensignpeakfoundation.org/wp-content/uploads/2013/05/NJ10.1_Smith.pdf/.

6 Svejda, "Castle Garden as an Immigrant Depot," iii.

7 "Major U. S. Immigration Ports." accessed on June 1, 2021, https://balibrary.librarycalendar.com/sites/default/files/2021-02/social%20research%20us%20ports.pdf/

8 Smith, *Castle Garden, the Emigrant Receiving Station in New York Harbor,* 41, 42.

9 *New York Daily Times*, May 24, 1855, p.4, as cited in Dr. George J. Svejda, "Castle Garden as an Immigrant Depot 1855-1890, 37, accessed June 22, 2021, http://npshistory.com/publications/cacl/castle_garden.pdf/.

10 Svejda, "Castle Garden as an Immigrant Depot 1855-1890, 44.

11 Smith, *Castle Garden, the Emigrant Receiving Station in New York Harbor,*" 41, 44, 46.

12 Smith, *Castle Garden, the Emigrant Receiving Station in New York Harbor 44, 46.*

13 Svejda, "Castle Garden as an Immigrant Depot 1855-1890, 44-7, 50-9.

14 State of New York, "Messages from the Governors Comprising Executive Communications to the Legislature and Other Papers Related to Legislation from the Organization of the First Colonial Assembly to 1683 to and including the year 1906. With Notes." Edited by Charles Z. Lincoln. Published by Authority of the State. Vol. IV. (Albany: J. B. Lyon

Company, State Printers, 1909), pp. 851-852, Hereinafter cited as Messages from the Governor, cited in Svejda, "Castle Garden as an Immigrant Depot 1855-1890, 48.

15 Svejda, *"Castle Garden as an Immigrant Depot 1855-1890*, 47.

16 Smith, *Castle Garden, the Emigrant Receiving Station in New York Harbor,* 42, accessed June 1, 2021 https://ensignpeakfoundation.org/wp-content/uploads/2013/05/NJ10.1_Smith.pdf/.

17 "Castle Garden: America's First Immigration Center," *The Battery*, accessed on May16, 2021, http://www.castlegarden.org/.

18 Smith, *Castle Garden, the Emigrant Receiving Station in New York Harbor,* 51.

19 Smith, *Castle Garden, the Emigrant Receiving Station in New York Harbor, 42,* 51.

20 Laxton, Famine Ships, 24-25.

21 "U.S.History: Ellis Island," *Ducksters*, accessed on May 16, 2021, https://www.ducksters.com/history/us_1800s/ellis_island.php/.

22 *Ellisisland.se,* "Application Process-To Arrive," accessed May 16, 2021, http://www.ellisisland.se/english/ellisisland_immigration4.asp/.

23 "Ellis Island, The Immigrant Journey," *Oh Ranger.com*, accessed on May 16, 2021, http://www.ohranger.com/ellis-island/immigration-journey/.

24 Devlin Family, "What Happened on Ellis Island?" *Devlin Family Online,* accessed on May 16, 2021, http://www.devlin-family.com/EllisHappened.htm/.

25 *Ellisisland.se,* "Application Process at Ellis Island-Interrogation, " accessed on June 1, 2021, http://www.ellisisland.se/english/ellisisland_immigration1.asp/.

26 Devlin Family, "What Happened on Ellis Island?"

27 Rachel Feinmark, "Part 1: The Story of Ellis Island…As a Museum," *Tenement Museum,* accessed May 16, 2021, https://www.tenement.org/blog/part-i-the-story-of-ellis-island-as-a-museum/.

28 "Ellis Island, The Immigrant Journey," *Oh Ranger.com.*

## Chapter 20

1 "100 Irish Quotes and Sayings," *Inspirational Words of Wisdom.*

2 Woodham-Smith, *The Great Hunger*, 262.

3 Miller, *Emigrants and Exiles*, 319.

4 Woodham-Smith, *The Great Hunger*, 205, 253, 265-6.

5 Miller, *Emigrants and Exiles,* 267, 274, 322.

6 Woodham-Smith, *The Great Hunger*, 240.

7 Miller, *Emigrants and Exiles*, 318, 320, 323, 326, 505-6.

8 Miller, *Emigrants and Exiles*, 332. 428, 510, 517, 519, 552.

9 "St. Patrick's Cathedral," *NY FACTS*, accessed May 16, 2021, https://nyfacts.com/st-patricks-cathedral/.

10 Miller, *Emigrants and Exiles*,340, 526-7,531-2, 535.

11 Miller, *Emigrants and Exiles*, 341, 511.

12 Miller, *Emigrants and Exiles*, 327, 360-1.

13 Miller, *Emigrants and Exiles*, 360.

14 "President John F. Kennedy, Dublin Ireland," June 28, 1963, Address Before the Irish Parliament," accessed February 5, 2021, https://www.jfklibrary.org/archives/other-resources/John-f-kennedy-speeches/irish-parliament-19630628/.

15 "President John F. Kennedy, Dublin Ireland," June 28, 1963, Address Before the Irish Parliament.

16 "An American Tragedy at Fredericksburg: Clash of the Irish Brigades," *History Arch,* accessed July 2, 2021, http://historyarch.com/2017/12/12/an-american-tragedy-at-fredericksburg-clash-of-the-irish-brigades/.

17 "President John F. Kennedy, Dublin Ireland," June 28, 1963, Address Before the Irish Parliament.

18 Miller, *Emigrants and Exiles*, 497.

19 "Irish immigration to America from 1846 to the Early 20th Century," accessed May 16, 2021, https://www.irish-genealogy-toolkit.com/Irish-immigration-to-America.html#topofpagelink/.

20 "Irish Immigration to America: 1846 to the early 20th century," *Irish Genealogy Toolkit.*

21 Miller, *Emigrants and Exiles*, 493, 495.

22 Claddagh Design, "The Irish in New York," *History, Ireland,* August 17, 2020, accessed on May 16, 2021, https://www.claddaghdesign.com/history/irish-new-york/.

23 Modesto M.J. Donna, *The Braidwood Story*, 76-81.

24 Miller, *Emigrants and Exiles*, 511.

# BIBLIOGRAPHY


Admin. "The Great Famine, 1845-1849." *Irish Country Life History.* November 12, 2012. http://countrylifehistory.ie/index.php/2012/11/the-great-famine-1845-1849/.

Ancestry.com. "Major U.S. Immigration Ports." Accessed June 24, 2021. http://www.pittsburgcogenealogical.org/C%20Educ/20%20Immigration%20routes/social%20research%20us%20ports.pdf/.

Ask About Ireland. "Second World War and its Aftermath." Accessed June 24, 2021. http://www.askaboutireland.ie/learning-zone/secondary-students/history/history-of-ireland-overview/the-second-world-war-and-/.

Aykroyd, W.R. "The Conquest of Famine." *The Effects of Lack of Food.* Chapter 2, Summarized by: Josef Skoldeberg. Accessed June 24, 2021. http://la.utexas.edu/users/hcleaver/357L/357Lsum_s4_Aykroyd_Ch2.html/.

AZ Quotes. "Patrick Pearse Quotes." Accessed June 24, 2021. https://www.azquotes.com/author/44563-Patrick_Pearse/.

Background on the Irish Famine You Won't Find Elsewhere. "Execution of Landlord Denis Mahon."Accessed June 24, 2021. https://theninthwavenovel.wordpress.com/2011/02/16/the-execution-of-denis-mahon/.

Bartoletti, Susan Campbell. *Black Potatoes: The Story of the Great Famine, 1845-1850.* (Boston, Massachusetts: Houghton Mifflin Company, 2001.)

*Black '47: Justice Comes Home.* Directed by Lance Daly. Produced by Fastnet Films and Sansa Film. Performed by Weaving, Hugo and James Frecheville. 2017.

Bloy, Marjorie, Ph. D., Senior Research Fellow. "Britain, Ireland and the Disastrous 1801 Act of Union." The Victorian Web. Last added January 14, 2002. https://victorianweb.org/history/ireland1.html/.

Brandenburg. *Imported Americans.* as cited in Del Gaudio, "I Have Not Told the Worst by any Means, It Could Not Be Put in Print: The Transatlantic Voyage of Euro-Immigrants to the United States," 42. May 23, 2010. https://scholar.dickinson.edu/student_honors/83/.

Brian. "Encouraging Bible Verses for the Dark Times of Life." *Luke 1428.* January 11, 2021. https://luke1428.com/encouraging-bible-verses-for-the-dark-times-of-life/.

*Britannica.* "Shipping in the 19th Century." Accessed June 25, 2021. https://www.britannica.com/technology/ship/Shipping-in-the-19th-century/.

Brody, Hugh. *Inishkillane: Change and Decline in the West of Ireland.* Middlesex, England and Victoria, Australia: Penguin Books, 1974.

Cahill, Thomas. "Why Famine Came to Ireland." *Irish Central.* 2010. https://www.irishcentral.com/roots/why-famine-came-to-ireland-93283629-237694481/.

Cardinale, Vogel. O;Brien, Batzer. "Sliding Coffin Cross Display Will Mark 1845-1850 Irish Famine." *The Buffalo News.* September 29, 1996. https://buffalonews.com/news/sliding-coffin-cross-display-will-mark-1845-50-irish-famine/article_554d9943-5e28-5e06-99a1-92b755a46234.html/.

Castle Garden. "Castle Garden: America's First Immigration Center." Accessed June 24, 2021. http://www.castlegarden.org/.

Cavendish, Richard. "Daniel O'Connor, Irish Nationalist Dies in Genoa." *History Today.* Vol. 47, May 1997, 5. https://www.historytoday.com/archive/daniel-oconnell-irish-nationalist-dies-genoa/.

Central Relief Committee of the Society of Friends. *Transactions of the Central Relief Committee of the Society of Friends during the Famine in Ireland, in 1846 and 1847.* Cited in Tim Pat Coogan, *The Famine Plot,* New York: Palgrave Macmillan, 2012, 143.

Channon, Max. "Son of a Cornish Clergyman Called Trevelyan Hinders Brexit from Beyond the Grave." *Cornwall Live.* Accessed June 24, 2021. https://www.cornwalllive.com/news/uk-world-news/son-cornish-clergyman-called-trevelyan-2581469/.

Climate-Data-Org. "Roscommon Climate." Accessed June 25, 2021. https://en.climate-data.org/europe/ireland/roscommon/roscommon-11861/.

Clare County Library. "Guide to Ennistymon Union 1839-185, Disease." Accessed June 24, 2021. https://www.clarelibrary.ie/eolas/coclare/history/workdisease.htm/.

Clarendon Papers. 1A. *Lord John Russell to Clarendon.* 1847. Cited in Cecil Woodham-Smith, The Great Hunger New York: Old Town Books, 1962.317.

*Clarendon Papers,* Out Letter Books, Vol. 1. "*Clarendon to Lord John Russell.*" 1847. Cited in Cecil Woodham-Smith, *The Great Hunger.* New York: Old Town Books, 1962. 317.

Cohn, Raymond L. *Journal of Economic History.* "The Transition From Sail to Steam In Immigration To The United States. Research Gate. June, 2005. https://www.researchgate.net/publication/4772287_The_Transition_from_Sail_to_Steam_in_Immigration_to_the_United_States/.

Coogan, Tim Pat. *The Famine Plot: England's Role in Ireland's Greatest Tragedy.* New York: Palgrave Macmillan, 2012.

*Cromwell to Lenthal in Abbot.* 14, October, 1649. "Writings of Oliver Cromwell." *vol. 2, 140-43.* Cited in Michael Sochru. *God's Executioner: Oliver Cromwell and the Conquest of Ireland.* London: Faber and Faber, 2008. 97.

Curtis, L. Perry. *Anglo-Saxon and Celts: A Study of the Anti-Irish Prejudice in Victorian England.* New York: New York University, 1968. Cited in New York: Palgrave Macmillan, 2012, 219.

Del Gaudio, Denise Rose. "I Have Not Told the Worst by any Means. It Could Not be Put in Print: The Transatlantic Voyage of Euro-Immigrants To The United States, 1841-1900." Dickinson College, Dickinson Scholar Honors Thesis Paper *83.* May 23, 2010. https://scholar.dickinson.edu/cgi/viewcontent.cgi?article=1082&context=student_honors/.

Devlin Family. "What Happened on Ellis Island?" *The Devlin Family Online.* Accessed June 24, 2021. http://devlin-family.com/EllisHappened.htm/.

Dickens, C. *All the Year Round,* Vol. VII, March 15 to September, 1862, 113. Cited in Albert D. Biderman, Margot Louria, Joan Bacchus, "Historical Incidents of Extreme Overcrowding," B5-6, Bureau of Social Sciences Research, Washington D.C. March, 1963. https://apps.dtic.mil/dtic/tr/fulltext/u2/609752.pdf/.

Dochara. "The Irish Potato Famine 1846-1850." *Dochara, Insider Guide to Ireland, 2008.* Updated March 31, 2017. https://www.dochara.comtheirish/food-history/the-history/the-irish-potato-famine-1845-1850/.

*Documents of the Board of Aldermen of the City of New York.* From No. 1 to No. 90, inclusive - from May 1837, to May 1838. Vol. IV. New York: Printed by Order of the Common Council,

1838. Document No. 10, pp. 61-75 and Document No. 12, pp. 81-84. Cited in "Castle Garden as an Immigrant Depot," 22. Division of History, Office of Archealogy and Historic Preservation, U.S. Department of the Interior, December 2, 1968. http://www.npshistory.com/publications/cacl/castle_garden.pdf/.

Donnelly, James S. "The Irish Agricultural Depression of 1859-64, Economic and Social History." *Sage Journals.* June 1, 1976. https://journals.sagepub.com/doi/abs/10.1177/033248937600300103?journalCode=iesa/.

Donnelly, Jim. "History, The Irish Famine." *BBC.* Updated February 17, 2017. http://www.bbc.co.uk/history/british/victorians/famine_01.shtml/.

Dooley, Terence A.M. "Estate Ownership and Management in Nineteenth and early Twentieth Century Ireland." aughty.org. Accessed June 24, 2021. http://www.aughty.org/pdf/estate_own_manage.pdf/.

Dorney, John. "The Great Irish Famine 1845-1851: A Brief Overview." The Irish Story. October 18, 2016. https://www.theirishhistory.com/2016/10/18/the-great-irish-famine-1845-1851/.

Duckster's. "U.S. History: Ellis Island." Accessed June 24, 2021. https://www.ducksters.com/history/us_1800s/ellis_island.php/.

Dupont, Brandon, Drew Keeling, Thomas Weiss. "Passenger Fares for Overseas Travel in the 19th and 20th Centuries" Figure 5, *36.* August 15, 2012. https://www.eh.net/eha/wp-content/uploads/2013/11/Weissetal.pdf/.

East Texas Radio. "Sculpture in Ireland Honors Choctaw Nation." East Texas Radio.com. July 4, 2017. https://easttexasradio.com/sculpture-in-ireland-honors-choctaw-nation/.

Editors of Encyclopedia Britannica, Updated by Amy Tikkanen. "Roscommon County, Ireland." *Britannica.* Accessed June 24, 2021. https://www.libraryireland.com/Thom1862/Roscommon.php/.

Editors, Encyclopaedia Britannica. "Irish Rebellion, Irish History, 1798." *Britannica.* Accessed June 24, 2021. https://www.britannica.com/event/Irish-Rebellion-Irish-history-1798/.

Ellisislandse. "Application Process-To Arrive." Accessed June 24, 2021. http://www.ellisisland.se/english/ellisisland_immigration4.asp/.

Elmer, Mary and Gordon. "Balfe History." SCR. Accessed June 24, 2021. https://scribd.com/doc/106952600/Balfe-History/.

Emerald Heritage. "Irish Ports of Immigration." Accessed June 24, 2021 https://emerald-heritage.com/blog/2017/irish-ports-of-emigration/.

*Encyclopedia.com.* "John Mitchel." Updated August 13, 2018. https://www.encyclopedia.com/people/history/british-and-irish-history-biographies/john-mitchel/.

*Encyclopedia.com.* "Poor Law Amendment Act of 1847 and the Gregory Clause." Accessed June 25, 2021. https://www.encyclopedia.com/international/encyclopedias-almanacs-transcripts-and-maps/poor-law-amendment-act-1847-and-gregory-clause/.

Eye Witness to History.com. "Irish Potato Famine," 1847. 2006. http://www.eyewitnesstohistory.com/irishfamine.htm/.

*Family Search.* "Australia Emigration and Immigration." Accessed June 24, 2021. https://www.familysearch.org/wiki/en/Australia_Emigration_and_Immigration/.

*Family Seaerch.* "Ireland Emigration and Immigration.". Last Edited June 2, 2020. https://www.familysearch.org/wiki/en/Ireland_Emigration_and_Immigration/.

Famine. "Background on the Irish Famine You Won't Find Elsewhere." Wordpress.com. Accessed June 24, 2021. https://theninthwavenovel.wordpress.com/the-famine/.

Feinmark, Rachel. "Part 1: The Story of Ellis Island...As a Museum." *Tenement Museum.* Accessed June 25, 2021. https://www.tenement.org/blog/part-i-the-story-of-ellis-island-as-a-museum/.

Foster, R. F. *Modern Ireland 1600-1972.* Penguin Books, Ltd., 1988, https://dailyhistory.org/What_was_the_impact_of_the_Irish_Famine_on_Ireland_and_the_world%3F/.

Fraser, Antonia. *The King and the Catholics: England, Ireland, and the Fight for Religious Freedom, 1780-1829.* London: Orion Publishing Group, Ltd., 2018.

*The Free Dictionary by Farlex.* "Intent.".Accessed June 25, 2021. https://legal-dictionary.thefreedictionary.com/intent.

Free Map Tools. "How Far is it Between New york City, USA and Liverpool, England." https://www.freemaptools.com/how-far-is-it-between-new-york-city_-usa-and-liverpool_-england.htm.

*The Gael: Land Issues.* "Evictions." August 1901. http://www.maggieblanck.com/Mayopages/Eviction.html/.

GaelicMatters.Com, The Home of Gaelic and Irish Culture "The Biggest Traditional Irish Sports." Accessed June 24, 2021. https://www.gaelicmatters.com/traditional-irish-sports.html/.

Gallagher, Thomas. *Paddy's Lament, Ireland 1846-1847, Prelude to Hatred.* Boston: Houghton Mifflin Harcourt, 1987. Cited in "What was the Impact of the Irish Famine on Ireland and the

World?) https://dailyhistory.org/What_was_the_impact_of_the_Irish_Famine_on_Ireland_and_the_world%3F/.

Geary, Laurence. "Epidemic Diseases of the Great Famine." History Ireland. Published in *18th-19th-Century* History. Features, Issue 1 Spring 1996, "The Famine," Volume 4. https://www.history-ireland.com/18th-19th-century-history/epidemic-diseases-of-the-great-famine/.

Goodreads. "Immigration Quotes." Accessed June 24, 2021. https://www.goodreads.com/quotes/tag/immigration/.

*Goodreads* "Irish Quotes.". June 25, 2021. https://www.goodreads.com/quotes/tag/irish/.

Gordon, Capt. Report No. 9, 1846. Enclosed, Geo. Pincher, Sub-Inspector Police to Inspector-General; Copy of Evidence Drs. Daniel Donovan and Patrick Due. B of W Corr. I, 219-20. November 2, 1846. Cited in Cecil Woodham-Smith, *The Great Hunger, Ireland 1845-1849.* New York: Old Town Books, 1962. 141.

Graham, Brendan. "Historical Notes: God and England Made the Irish Famine ." Independent. December 3, 1998., https://www.independent.co.uk/arts-entertainment/historical-notes-god-and-england-made-the-irish-famine-1188828.html/.

Gray, Peter. *Famine Land and Politics: British Government and Irish Society 1843-1850.* Dublin: Irish Academic Press, 1999. Cited in Tim Pat Coogan, *The Famine Plot.* New York: Palgrave Macmillan, 2012.

*The Great Calamity: The Irish Famine 1845-1852.* Boulder: Roberts Rinehart Publishers. 1995. First Published in Ireland by Gil and Macmillan, Ltd. 1994.

Green, Michael. "A Biography of Wolfe Tone." *Wolfe Tone.* Accessed June 24, 2021. https://www.ireland-information.com/articles/wolfetone.htm/.

Gregory, Ian N. and Niall A. Cunningham. "The Judgement of God on an Indolent and Unself-reliant people: The Impact of the Great Irish Famine on Ireland's Religious Demography." *Journal of Historic Geography.* Volume 51, January, 2016, 76-87. https://www.sciencedirect.com/science/article/pii/S0305748815001012/.

Guest Contribution. "The Great Irish Potato Famine." History Cooperative. October 31, 2009. https://historycooperative.org/the-irish-famine/.

Guillet. "The Great Migration." *Central Michigan University-Clarke Historical Library.* Cited in Transatlantic Crossing. https://www.cmich.edu/library/clarke/ResearchResources/Michigan_Material_Local/Beaver_Island_Helen_Collar_Papers/Subject_Cards/EmigrationandImmigrantLife/Pages/Transatlantic-Crossing.aspx/.

Guinnane, Timothy W. "The Great Irish Famine and Population: The Long View." AEA Papers and Proceedings. Vol. *84, No.2, 303-08* . 1994. https://www.mayoresearch.org/files/GREATFAMINE.pdf/.

Hamilton, John Andrew. "Sir Charles Wood, First Viscount Halifax, 1800-1885." A Web of English History. 1900. http://www.historyhome.co.uk/people/halifax.htm/.

Handlin, Oscar. *The Uprooted.* Chapter 11, Cited in Transatlantic Crossing-Cost," Central Michigan University-Clarke Historical Library. https://www.cmich.edu/library/clarke/ResearchResources/Michigan_Material_Local/Beaver_Island_Helen_Collar_Papers/Subject_Cards/Emigrationand ImmigrantLife/Pages/TransatlanticCrossing.aspx/.

Hansen, Marcus,. *The Atlantic Migration, 244-51.* Cited in Central Michigan University-Clarke Historical Library. "Beaver Island History - Helen Collar Papers." Accessed June 25,

2021 https://www.cmich.edu/library/clarke/ResearchResources/Michigan_Material_Local/Beaver_Island_Helen_Collar_Papers/Pages/default.aspx/.

*Harper's Weekly.* Vol. 11, No. 78. June 26, 1858, 405. Cited in "Castle Garden as an Immigrant Depot," 22, Division of History, Office of Archeology and Historic Preservation, National Park Service, U.S. Department of the Interior, December 2, 1968. http://www.npshistory.com/publications/cacl/castle_garden.pdf/.

Haskin, F.J. *The Immigrant.* Cited in Albert D. Biderman, Margot Louria, Joan Bacchus, "Historical incidents of Extreme Overcrowding." B5-6, Bureau of Social Science Research, Washington D.C. Accessed April 3, 2021. https://apps.dtic.mil/dtic/tr/fulltext/u2/609752.pdf/.

History Ireland. "The Vanishing Irish: Ireland's Population from the Great Famine to the Great War." Issue 2, Summer 1997. The Famine, Volume 5. https://www.historyireland.com/20th-century-contemporary-history/the-vanishing-irish-irelands-population-from-the-great-famine-to-the-great-war/.

History Ireland, Ireland's History Magazine. "Food Exports from Ireland 1846-47." Published in 18th-19th Century History, Features Issue 1. Spring 1997. "The Famine." Volume 5. Accessed June 24, 2021. https://www.historyireland.com/18th-19th-century-history/food-export/.

History Cooperative. "The Great Irish Potato Famine." October 31, 2009. https://historycooperative.org/the-irish-famine/.

The History of Ireland. "Encumbered Estates Act." Accessed June 24, 2021. http://www.irishevents4u.com/Ireland/history/encumbered-est.htm/.

*The History Place.* "Irish Potato Famine-Before the Famine." https://www.historyplace.com/worldhistory/famine/before.htm/.

Independent.ie. "Was this the Most Wicked Man in Irish History?" September 30, 2006. https://www.independent.ie/opinion/analysis/was-this-the-most-wicked-man-in-irish-history-26367449.html/.

Infoplease. "U. S. Cities with Population over 100,000." Accessed June 24, 2021.https://www.infoplease.com/us/cities/us-cities-population-over-100000/.

Inspirational Words of Wisdom. "100 Irish Quotes and Sayings." Accessed June 24, 2021. https://www.wow4u.com/irishquotessayings/.

Inspiringquotes.us. Wolfe Tone Quotes and Sayings-Page 1. Accessed June 26,2021. https://www.inspiringquotes.us/author/5451-wolfe-tone/.

Ireland's Great Famine 1845-1849."Famine 3, Peel's Relief Programme to July, 1846." Last Updated 2001. https://www.wesleyjohnston.com/users/ireland/past/famine/tory_july_1846.html/.

Ireland's Great Famine 1845-1849. "Famine 4, The Winter of 1846-1847." Last Updated 2001. https://www.wesleyjohnston.com/users/ireland/past/famine/tory_july_1846.html/.

*Ireland xo, Reaching Out.* "Chronicles Insight - Ships and Steerage." December 9, 2019. https://irelandxo.com/ireland-xo/news/chronicles-insight-ships-and-steerage/.

*Ireland xo, Reaching Out* St. Baoithin's Catholic Church. Accessed June 25, 2021. https://irelandxo.com/ireland-xo/visiting/st-baoithins-roman-catholic-church/.

*Ireland xo, Reaching Out.* "Timeline: Alexis de Tocqueville visits Ireland." Accessed June 25, 2021. https://irelandxo.com/ireland-xo/history-and-genealogy/timeline/alexis-de-tocqueville-visits-ireland#/.

Ireland's Own. "The Doolough Famine Tragedy." Accessed June 25 2021. https://www.irelandsown.ie/the-doolough-famine-tragedy/.

Irish Central Staff. "Daniel O'Connell - Quotes from Ireland's 'Liberator." Irish Central. May 15, 2020. https://www.irish-central.com/roots/history/Daniel-oconnell-quotes/.

*Irish America.* December/January 2018. "Roscommon Part III: The Hungry Years." https://irishamerica.com/2017/12/roscommon-part-iii-the-hungry-years/.

*Irish Central.* "Ireland's Great Hunger-What Really Happened to the Food in Ireland." February 1, 2019. https://www.irish-central.com/roots/history/facts-great-hunger-irish-famine-food-ireland-dates/.

*Irish Daily Mail.* "Man Behind the Famine." June 25, 2021. https://www.pressreader.com/ireland/irish-daily-mail/20180925/282432760077444/.

Irish Genealogy Toolkit. "Irish Immigration to America: 1846 to the early 20th Century." June 25, 2021. https://www.irish-genealogy-toolkit.com/Irish-immigration-to-America.html/.

Irish Historian. "Timeline of the Irish Famine." Accessed June 25, 2021. https://www.irishhistorian.com/IrishFamine Timeline.html#1848/.

*The Irish News.* "*'tithe war' in North United Catholic and Dissenter.*" July 2, 2013. http://www.irishnews.com/opinion/2013/07/02/news/-tithe-war-in-north-united-catholic-and-dissenter-63852/.

*The Irish Times.* "The Bad Times: Visualizing the Famine in a Graphic Novel." April 12, 2018. https://www.irishtimes.com/life-and-style/abroad/the-bad-times-visualising-the-fami ne-in-a-graphic-novel-1.3458428/.

*The Irish Times.* "Death of Wolfe Tone."Accessed June 24, 2021. https://www.irishtimes.com/opinion/letters/the-death-of-wolfe-tone-1.904217/.

*The Irish Times.*"Food Depots Close to Teach Irish a Lesson." 2018. https://www.irishtimes.com/news/food-depots-close-to-teach-irish-a-lesson-1.79616/.

Jevons, Stanley W. *The Theory of Political Economy.* 277. New York: Kelly and Millman, 1957. Vol.2 Cited in O'Boyle, Phd. "Classical Economics and the Great Irish Famine: A Study in Limits." 27. https://www.researchgate.net/publication/227589638_Classical_Economics_and_the_Great_Irish_Famine_A_Study_in_Limits/.

Johnson, Ben. "Henry VIII." Historic UK, The History and Heritage Accomodation Guide. Accessed June 24, 2021. https://www.historic-uk.com/HistoryUK/HistoryofEngland/Henry-VIII/.

Johnston, Wesley. "Effects of the Famine 1: Agriculture." Ireland's Great Famine, 1845-1849. Last Updated 2001. https://www.wesleyjohnston.com/users/ireland/past/famine/agriculture_post.html/.

Jones, Maldwyn A. *American Immigration,* 105. Cited in "Transatlantic Crossing (Cost)," Central Michigan University-Clarke Historical Library. Accessed June 25, 2021. https://www.cmich.edu/library/clarke/ResearchResources/Michigan_Material_Local/Beaver_Island_Helen_Collar_Papers/Subject_Cards/EmigrationandImmigrantLife/Pages/Transatlantic-Crossing.aspx/.

Joyce, Patrick Weston. "The Plantation of Ulster, 1605-1625." Library Ireland. Accessed June 25, 2021. https://www.libraryireland.com/JoyceHistory/Ulster.php/.

Keeling, Drew, Department of History, University of Zurich. "ebha.org." "Shipping Companies and Transatlantic Migration Costs: The Case of Cunard, 1880-1914." August 2008. https://ebha.org/ebha2008/papers/Keeling_ebha_2008.pdf/.

Keneally, Thomas. *The Great Shame.* New York: Nan A. Talese, Doubleday imprint. 1999.

Kennedy, Edward M. "Address at the Public Memorial Service for Robert F. Kennedy." American Rhetoric:Top 100 Speeches. 2001. https://www.americanrhetoric.com/speeches/ekennedytributetorfk.html/.

Kennedy, President John F. "Address Before the Irish Parliament, Dublin, Ireland." June 28, 1963. https://www.jfklibrary.org/archives/other-resources/John-f-kennedy-speeches/irish-parliament-19630628/.

Killick, John. "Transatlantic Steerage Fares, British and Irish Migration, and Return Migration, 1815-1860." The Economic History Review/Volume 67/Issue 1. 170-91. July 12, 2013. https://onlinelibrary.wiley.com/doi/pdf/10.1111/1468-0289.12014/.

Kinealy, Christine. *A Death Dealing Famine, The Great Hunger in Ireland.* Chicago, Illinois: Pluto Press, 1997.

Kinealy, Dr. Christine. "Food Exports from Ireland 1846-47." History Ireland: 18th-19th Century History, Features, Issue 1. Spring, 1997, "The Famine," Volume 5. Accessed June 25, 2021. https://www.historyireland.com/18th-19th-century-history/food-exports-from-ireland-1846-47/.

Kinealy, Dr. Christine, Contributor. "International Relief Efforts During the Famine." Irish America. August/September 2009. https://irishamerica.com/2009/08/international-relief-efforts-during-the-famine/.

Kissane, Noel. "The Irish Famine." National Library of Ireland. Dublin, 1995. Cited in O'Boyle, Phd. Classical Economics and the Great Irish Famine" A Study in Limits, 9.

Laxton, Edward. *The Famine Ships: The Irish Exodus to America.* New York: Henry Holt Co., 1996.

Library Ireland. "Roscommon County Directory, 1862."Accessed June 25, 2021. https://www.libraryireland.com/Thom1862/Roscommon.php/.

Lonergan, Aiden. "Wexford Martyrs: 7 facts about the Irish Catholics hanged, drawn and quartered by Elizabeth I for treason in 1581." Irish Post. July 5, 2019. https://www.irishpost.com/life-style/wexford-martyrs-7-facts-irish-catholics-hanged-drawn-quartered-elizabeth-treason-1581-168733/.

Lynch, Colum. "Evidence to Prove Genocide in China." *Foreign Press.* February 19, 2021. https://foreignpolicy.com/2021/02/19/china-uighurs-genocide-us-pompeo-blinken/.

Lynch, Paul. "Victoria, Famine Queen, and the Silence of the Survivors." The Irish Times. October 6, 2017. irishtimes.com/culture/books/Victoria.famine-queen-and-the-silence-of-survivors-1.3246729.

Maxwell, Ian. *Everyday Life in 19th-Century Ireland.* Dublin: The History Press Ireland, 2012.

Mayo Clergy. "Evidence given to the Devon Commission 1843-45, quoted by Liam Swords." *The Famine in North Connacht.* Columba Press. 1999. Cited in Tim Pat Coogan. *The Famine Plot. New York:* Palgrave and Macmillan. 2012.

McGreevy, Ronan. "Pioneering Study Charts Population Fall Since Famine." The Irish Times. August 3, 2011. https://www.irishtimes.com/news/pioneering-study-charts-population-fall-since-famine-1.588108/.

Mill, John Stuart. "Autobiography and Literary Essays, part of the Collected Works of John Stuart Mill." Edited by John M. Robson and Jack Stillinger, Vol. 1 John. Toronto: University of Toronto Press n.d. Cited in O'Boyle, Phd., "Classical Economics and the Great Irish Famine: A Study in Limits." 32.

Mill, John Stuart on Ireland. 1979. "Editorials from the Morning Chronical." Philadelphia: Institute of Human Issues. Cited in Edward J. O'Boyle Phd., Mayo Research Institute. "Classical Economics and the Great Irish Famine: A Study in Limits. Accessed June 25, 2021. https://www.mayoresearch.org/files/GREATFAMINE.pdf/.

Miller, D. W. "Catholic." Hynes; Connell, 113-161; G. Birmingham, *Irishmen All* London 1914. 184; S. O'Faolain, *The Irish: A Character Study* NY, 1949. 129-146. Cited in Kerby A. Miller, *Emigrants and Exiles.* New York: Oxford University Press. 1985. 126.

Miller Kerby A. *Emigrants and Exiles: Ireland and the Irish Exodus to North America.* New York: Oxford University Press, 1985.

Mitchel, John. *An Apology for the British Government in Ireland.* Dublin: O'Donoghue and Company, 1905. https://www.encyclopedia.com/people/history/british-and-irish-history-biographies/john-mitchel/.

Mulhall, Ambassador Daniel. "Blog by Ambassador Mulhall on Black 47: Ireland's Great Famine and its after-effects." Embassy of Ireland, USA. December 3, 2018. https://www.dfa.ie/irish-embassy/usa/about-us/ambassador/ambassadors-blog/black47irelandsgreatfamineanditsafter-effects/.

Mulraney, Frances. "The Real Story of Queen Victoria and the Irish Famine." Irish Central. April 26, 2020. https://www.irishcentral.com/roots/history/queen-victoria-irish-famine/.

Murphy, Barry. "Connacht." July 4, 2013. https://barrysguided-tours.com/connacht/.

*National Geographic.* "Peat, The Forgotten Fossil Fuel." Accessed June 25, 2021. https://www.nationalgeographic.org/media/peat-forgotten-fuel/.

National Irish Freedom Committee. "Famous Quotations." Accessed June 24. 2021. https://irishfreedom.net/Famous%20Qoutations/Famous%20Quotations.htm/.

National Museum of Ireland. "Irish Emigration to America - The Jouney." Accessed June 25, 2021. https://www.museum.ie/en-IE/Collections-Research/Folklife-Collections/Folklife-Collections-List-(1)/Other/Emigration/Irish-Emigration-to-America-The-Journey/.

Nee, Dennis F. Irving O'Shea Robinson and D.J. Reardon. "The Irish Famine: Complicity In Murder." Washington Post, September 27, 1997: https://www.washingtonpost.com/archive/opinions/1997/09/27/the-irish-famine-complicity-in-murder/5a155118-3620-4145-951e-0dc46933b84a/.

*New York Daily Times.* May 24, 1955, p. 4. "Castle Garden as an Immigrant Depot 1855-1890." Accessed June 25, 2021. http://npshistory.com/publications/cacl/castle_garden.pdf/.

NY FACTS. "St. Patrick's Cathedral." Accessed June 25, 2021. https://nyfacts.com/st-patricks-cathedral.

O'Brien, R. Barry. "The Rebellion of 1641." Library of Ireland. The Irish Ecclesiastical Record, 4th Series, Vol. XVII, No.449 May, 1905. https://www.libraryireland.com/articles/rebellion1641/index.php/.

O'Connor, Joseph. "Star of the Sea: A Postcolonial/Postmodern Voyage into the Irish Famine." Scalar.USC.edu. Accessed June 25,20021. https://scalar.usc.edu/works/star-of-the-sea-a-postcolonialpostmodern-voyage-into-the-irish-famine/index/.

O'Donnell, Ruan. *A Short History of Ireland's Famine. Dublin:* O'Brien's Press Ltd. 2013..

O'Donovan, Catherine. "The Cromwellian Settlement." Clare County Library. Accessed June 25, 2021. https://www.clarelibrary.ie/eolas/coclare/history/cromwell_settlement.htm/.

O'Donovan, Frank. "Estimated Population of Ireland in the 19th Century." Irish Genealogy Toolkit. August 2017. https://bmdnotices.com/Estimated-Population-in-Ireland-19th-Century.pdf/.

O'Dowd, Niall. "Was it Genocide? What the British Ruling Class Really Said about the Irish Famine." Irish Central. June 16, 2019. https://www.irishcentral.com/roots/genocide-what-british-ruling-class-said-irish-famine/.

O'Ferrell, Richard and Robert O'Connell. "Commentarius Rinuccinianus de Sedis Apostolicae Legatione ad Foederatos Hiberniae Catholicos per Annos 1645-9." Vol. 4. Dublin 1932-49. 295. Cited in Michael O. Siochru, *God's Executioner.* London: Faber and Faber. 2008. 95.

O'Ferrell, Richard and Robert O'connell. "Commentarius Rinuccinianus, 'Petition of the Surviving inhabitants of Wexford." Vol.4, 296-7." National Library of Ireland, MS 9696, ff. 30-3. Vols. Cited in Michael O. Siochru. *God's Executioner.* London: Faber and Faber. 2008. 97.

Officer, Lawrence H. and Samuel H. Williamson. "Computing 'Real Value' Over Time with a Conversion Between U.K. Pounds and U.S. Dollars, 1791 to Present." *Measuring Worth, 2021.* Accessed June 25, 2021. https://www.measuringworth.com/calculators/exchange/result_exchange.php/.

O'Grada, Cormac. "The Population of Ireland, 1700-1900, A Survey." Persee. 1979. https://www.persee.fr/doc/adh_0066-2062_1979_num_1979_1_1425/.

Oh Ranger.com. "Ellis Island National Monument, The Immigrant Journey." Accessed June 25, 2021. http://www.ohranger.com/ellis-island/immigration-journey/.

O'Keeffe, Helen. "Atlas of the Irish Revolution, Resources for Schools, Unit 1: The Land Movement, 1879-1882." Accessed June 25, 2021. https://www.rte.ie/documents/history/2021/01/u1.-lc-worksheets-the-land-movement.pdf/.

Old Filibuster - Curmudgeonly Musings. "The Workhouse-an Unworkable Solution to Irish Poverty." Accessed June 25, 2021. http://www.oldfilibuster.com/the-workhouse-ndash-an-unworkable-solution-to-irish-poverty.html/.

On the Water. "Enterprise on the Water." On the Water, Maritime Nation 1800-1850. Accessed June 25, 2021. https://americanhistory.si.edu/onthewater/exhibition/2_3.html/.

O'Raifeartaigh, Tarlach. "St. Patrick, Bishop and Patron Saint of Ireland." Britannica. Accessed June 25, 2021. https://www.britannica.com/biography/Saint-Patrick/.

O'Rourke, John Canon. *The Great Irish Famine.* 248-250. Dublin: Veritage Publications, 1902. Abridged, 248-50. 1874. Cited in O'Boyle Phd., "Classical Economics and the Great Irish Famine: A Study in Limits." Accessed June 25, 2021. https://www.researchgate.net/publication/227589638_Classical_Economics_and_the_Great_Irish_Famine_A_Study_in_Limits/. 17.

Patel, Dinvar. "Viewpoint: How British Let One Million Indians Die in Famine." BBC News. June 11, 2016. https://www.bbc.com/news/world-asia-india-36339524/.

Patton. *To The Golden Door. 154-155.* Cited in "Transatlantic Crossing-Cost," Central Michigan University-Clarke Historical Library. Accessed June 25, 2021. https://www.cmich.edu/library/clarke/ResearchResources/

Michigan_Material_Local/Beaver_Island_Helen_Collar_Papers/Subject_Cards/EmigrationandImmigrantLife/Pages/Transatlantic-Crossing.aspx/.

Powderly, M.D., William G. "How Infections Shaped History: Lessons from the Irish Famine." Transactions of the Clinical and Climatological Association, PMC. 2019. Accessed June 25, 2021. https://www.ncbi.nlm.nih.gov/pmc/articles/PMC6735970.

Rea, Tony and John Wright. *Ireland: A Divided Island.* Oxford, New York: Oxford University Press, 1998. 6. https://books.google.com/books?id=wL5Nup6gIKUC&printsec=copyright#v=onepage&q&f=false/.

Reed, Derek. "The Workhouse." Irish Famine Exhibition. December 21, 2019. https://www.theirishpotatofamine.com/blogs/blog-1/the-workhouse/.

"Rome Statute of the International Criminal Court." July 17,1998. Accessed June 30, 2021, https://legal.un.org/icc/statute/99_corr/cstatute.htm/.

Ross, David. "The Corn Laws." Britain Express. Accessed June 25, 2021. https://www.britainexpress.com/History/victorian/corn-laws.htm/.

Scally, 1995:274. Cited in Stephen A. Brighton. *Historical Archealogy of the Irish Diaspora: A Transnational Approach.* 54. Knoxville, Tennessee: The University of Tennessee Press, 2009. Google Books. https://books.google.com/books?id=4p07hjxezAcC&pg=PA1&source=gbs_toc_r&cad=2#v=onepage&q&f=false/.

Scott, ed. Framklin D. *World Migration in Modern Times.* Cited in "Transatlantic Crossing-Overcrowding, Central Michigan University, Clarke Historical Library. https://www.cmich.edu/library/clarke/ResearchResources/Michigan_Material_Local/Beaver_Island_Helen_Collar_Papers/Subject_

Cards/EmigrationandImmigrantLife/Pages/Transatlantic-Crossing.aspx/.

Simkin, John. "Lord John Russell." Spartacus Educational. Last Updated January, 2020. https://spartacus-educational.com/PRrussell.htm/.

Siochru, Michael O. *God's Executioner: Oliver Cromwell and the Conquest of Ireland.* London, England: Faber and Faber, Ltd., 2008.

Smith, Cynthia E. "The Land-Tenure System in Ireland: A Fatal Regime." Marquette Law Review. Volume 76, Issue 2, Winter, 1993. 2006. https://scholarship.law.marquette.edu/cgi/viewcontent.cgi?/.

Smith, Don H. "Castle Garden, the Emigrant Receiving Station in New York Harbor." 42. https://ensignpeakfoundation.org/wp-content/uploads/2013/05/NJ10.1_Smith.pdf/.

Spartacus Educational.com "Journey to America." Accessed June 25, 2021. https://spartacus-educational.com/USAEjourney.htm/.

Staniforth, Mark. "Shipwrecks Images and Perceptions of the Nineteenth Century Maritime Disasters." Sydney Studies in Society and Culture. Accessed June 25, 2021. https://core.ac.uk/download/pdf/229433464.pdf/.

State of New York. *Messages from the Governors Comprising Executive Communications to the Legislature and Other Papers Related to Legislation from the Organization of the First Colonial Assembly to 1683 to and including the year 1906. With Notes.*" Edited by Charles Z. Lincoln, Published by the Authority of the State, Vol. IV. Albany: J.B. Lyon Company, State Printers, 1909. 851-852. Hereinafter cited as Messages from the Governor. Cited in Sveida, "Castle Garden as an Immigration Depot 1855-1890." 48. Accessed June 25, 2021. http://www.npshistory.com/publications/cacl/castle_garden.pdf/.

Stave, Bruce M., John F. Sutherland, and Aldo Salerno. *From the Old Country: An Oral History of European Migration to America* New York: Twayne, 1994. 32. Cited in Del Gaudio. "I Have Not Told the Worst by any Means, It Could Not Be Put in Print: The Transatlantic Voyage of Euro-Immigrants to the United States. Acessed June 25, 2021. https://scholar.dickinson.edu/cgi/viewcontent.cgi?article=1082&context=student_honors/.

Steiner. *From Alien to Citizen.* Cited in Denise Rose Del Gaudio, "I Have Not Told the Worst by any Means, It Could Not Be Put in Print: The Transatlantic Voyage of Euro-Immigrants to the United States." 40. Accessed June 25, 2021. https://scholar.dickinson.edu/cgi/viewcontent.cgi?article=1082&context=student_honors/.

The Times. London, July 26,1848. cited in Tim Pat Coogan, *The Famine Plot.* New York: Palgrave Macmillan, 2012. 226.

Thornton, Mark. "What Caused the Irish Potato Famine?" The Free Market. Vol. 16, No. 4, April, 1998. Cited in Mises Daily Articles. Mises Institute. March 17, 2017. https://mises.org/library/what-caused-irish-potato-famine/.

Timon, Patrick. *Famine Times in Tibohine.* 2019. https://www..timon.ie/2019/general/famine-times-in-tibohine/.

UK Parliament. "Constitutional Differences." Accessed June 29, 2021. https://www.parliament.uk/about/living-heritage/evolutionofparliament/legislativescrutiny/parliamentandireland/overview/constitutional-differences/.

U. S. Congress. 61st Congress. 3d sess., 1911. "Senate Immigration Commission. {Investigation 3}. Reports of the Immigration Commission." 37. Cited in Denise Rose Del Gaudio. "I Have Not Told the Worst by any Means, It Could Not Be Put in Print: The Transatlantic Voyage of Euro-Immigrants to the

United States." https://scholar.dickinson.edu/cgi/viewcontent.cgi?article=1082&context=student_honors/.

Ulster Historical Foundation, Telling the Story of the People of Ulster. "Movement of British Settlers into Ulster during the 17th Century." Accessed June 25, 2021. https://www.ancestryireland.com/understanding-plantation/movement-of-british-settlers-into-ulster-during-the-17th-century/.

Ulster Historical Foundation, Telling the Story of the People of Ulster. "Religion, The Penal Laws." Accessed June 25, 2021. https://www.ancestryireland.com/history-of-the-irish-parliament/background-to-the-statutes/religion/.

United Nations. Convention on the Prevention and Punishment of the Crime of Genocide. December 9, 1948. https://www.un.org/en/genocideprevention/documents/atrocity-crimes/Doc.1_Convention%20on%20the%20Prevention%20and%20Punishment%20of%20the%20Crime%20of%20Genocide.pdf/.

United Nations Office of Legal Affairs. "Rome Statute of the International Criminal Court." July 17, 1998. https://legal.un.org/icc/statute/99_corr/cstatute.htm/.

United States Senate. Reports of the Immigration Commission. 61st Congress, 3rd Session, Doc. No. 753, Washington D.C.: Government Printing Office, 1911, 13-23. Cited in Biderman, Louria and Bachus, "Historical Incidents of Extreme Overcrowding," B11. Accessed June 25, 2021. https://apps.dtic.mil/dtic/tr/fulltext/u2/609752.pdf/.

Walsh, Dennis. "Ireland the Famine Years, % of Population." Ireland's History in Maps. 1996-2009. http://sites.rootsweb.com/~irlkik/ihm/ire1841.htm.

*WDC Insights Blog.* "Census 2016: Looking Back 175 Years-Changes in the Western Region Population." May 22, 2017.

https://wdcinsights.wordpress.com/2017/05/22/census-2016-looking-back-175-years-changes-in-the-western-region-population/.

Weld, Isaac. "Survey of the County of Roscommon-Extent-Boundaries." *Statistical Survey of the County of Roscommon.* Printed by R. Graisberry, 1832. https://archive.org/details/statisticalsurv00socigoog/page/n6/mode/2up/.

What Should I Read Next? Quotes by Thomas Francis Meagher. Accessed June 25, 2021. https://www.whatshouldireadnext.com/quotes/Thomas-francis-meagher-the-glory-of-the-old/.

Williams, Leslie A. "Daniel O'Connell, The British Press and the Irish Famine: Killing Remarks." *Google Books.* Roscommon Morning Chronicle, December, 1845. 8.(4.) Accessed June 25, 2021 https://books.google.com/books?id=zn1BDgAAQBAJ&pg=PT118&lpg=PT118&dq=nicholas+balfe+forgave+one+ha+one+lf+his+tenants'+rent+in+1845&source=bl&ots=SgJOW4L4ty&sig=ACfU3U2lC6Op-IlzZEpz5DkGi8MaR9VeIw&hl=en&sa=X&ved=2ahUKEwjZyPT0qbbwAhWQW80KHS_3DIAQ6AEwA3oECAU/.

Winstanley, Michael. "Ireland and the Land Question, 1800-1922." Lancaster Pamphlets, 2007. Cited in Dr. Marjorie Bloy. The Age of George III, Land Holding in Ireland. A Web of English History. Last modified January 12, 2016. http://www.historyhome.co.uk/c-eight/ireland/ire-land.htm/.

Woodham-Smith, Cecil. *The Great Hunger, Ireland 1845-1849.* New York: Old Town Books, 1962.

World Heritage Encyclopedia. "Sir Charles Trevelyan, 1st Baronet." Project Gutenberg Self-Publishing Press. http://www.self.gutenberg.org/articles/Sir_Charles_Trevelyan,_1st_Baronet/.

Your Dictionary. "Ireland Quotes." Accessed June 25, 2021. https://quotes.yourdictionary.com/Ireland.

Your Dictionary. "Famine Quotes." Accessed June 25, 2021. https://quotes.yourdictionary.com/famine.

Made in the USA
Columbia, SC
21 September 2021

45286677R00157